THE TREASURE CHEST

BLAKE

Published by Blake Publishing Ltd,
98–100 Great North Road, London N2 0NL, England

First published in Great Britain in 1993

ISBN 185782 0460

British Library Cataloguing-in-Publication Data: A catalogue record for this book is available from the British Library.

Typeset by MFK Typesetting Ltd., Hitchin, Herts

Printed and bound in Great Britain by Cox and Wyman, Reading, Berkshire

1 3 5 7 9 10 8 6 4 2

This book is dedicated to my children Karl and Kandy, and to my husband Charlie whose devotion has made this book possible. I love you all.

1

IN THE BEGINNING THERE WAS KARL AND KANDY . . .

My darlings Karl and Kandy,

By the time you read this, you will already know about the box of treasures I have left for you, and, by now, you will also know why.

When I look back, I realise that I only discovered what living was all about when I had you two babies. Through the letters I have left for you in your treasure chest, you will learn that for ages, I wasn't able to have children. I went to see several doctors, had some medical treatment, and then, against all the odds, you two were born. True to Murphy's Law, however, if anything can go wrong, it will. I had spent a lifetime searching for real happiness and, then, when I found it, I learnt that I had also developed cancer. I was only 33. You Karl, were only two years old, and Kandy was one.

My first thought was, what would happen to my babies? Who would look after you while you grew up; who would advise you after I had gone? And do it in the way that only a mother can?

You mean so much to me and I know I mean so much to you, but, as I write this, I can't escape the fact that you are so young. By the time you become teenagers, I may be just a hazy memory. You might spend your lives wondering what your mother was really like. Was I good? bad? kind? fair? Was I decadent or well principled? What were my beliefs? Did I have any at all? You would want to know all about your roots, all the things a simple photograph can't tell you.

I spent many sleepless nights worrying about the things you'll need to know and the guidance you'll require throughout your lives. Then the answer came to me. It was so simple and obvious. I would look after you long after I had gone. I would tell you absolutely everything about yourselves and me and wouldn't leave a thing out, not even the things most people spend a lifetime trying to hide.

Someday a teacher may ask what your mummy does for a living. You might reply that I passed away when you were very small. The teacher might say: 'Oh, I'm sorry. Then you didn't know your mummy at all.' But you will be able to say: 'Oh, yes, Miss. I *know* her very well.'

Once I knew what I had to do, I set to thinking how to go about it and that's when I hit on the idea of the treasure chest.

It is filled with photographs and video tapes of Mummy and yourselves. There are Dictaphone tapes of Mummy's advice to you, a Dictaphone so that you have no excuse *not* to listen to them, memories, letters and the perfume I wear every day, so that you can remember what Mummy smelled like. There are legal documents and the names of, and contact number for, people who knew me during my life. I have even included a cotton hanky for each of you – for life won't always be easy and you'll need something to wipe away your tears. The Dictaphone tape will be given to you at certain stages during your growing lives, because there are certain things that you may not be able to understand at too young an age.

Life is a never-ending series of falls and recoveries. You will make countless mistakes along the way but that is all a part of growing up. Most caring parents would do anything to stop their children from making the same mistakes that they did, but, in my experience, although you can advise children not to do certain things, they will anyway. Even if I were alive, there is no guarantee you would heed my warnings. I wouldn't dream of dictating to you how to lead your lives.

However, I can tell you what has happened in my life. You will learn that I had a lot of fun through the years – and more than my fair share of disasters. I did as many silly, foolish things as I did good. I'm sure some pennies will drop as you read the letters and listen to the tapes, for, by that time, you may have encountered similar incidents. You must reach your own decisions about how to deal with life's hurdles. I can only let you know how I dealt with mine and perhaps that will help you to help yourself. I hope that you will come to the best conclusions possible and make the right choices.

Most of all, by my leaving this treasure chest, you will know how much Mummy really, truly loved you. If it is possible still to feel love after one has gone, then, certainly, I will love you for all eternity, for you are the treasures in my life and I shall cherish you for all time.

All Love,
Mummy xx

2

EXPECT THE UNEXPECTED . . .

In life unpredictable things happen that can completely alter the future. They can dash any hopes, dreams or ambitions one may have. In my case, just when I thought I had my whole life in front of me with you two darlings and Daddy, I fell ill with cancer. I always thought we would have tomorrow, but now I'm not so sure.

Only a short time ago I assumed I would watch you through every stage of life, attend your weddings and babysit your children. We would laugh together, cry together, have differences and resolve them. I would see you through your growing pains, first loves and choice of career or badger you relentlessly if you had no direction. I would help to guide you to being whatever you wanted to be. I would be there when you needed me, and, in old age, I would simply wish you needed me again. Quite naturally, like most people, I took all these things for granted. What I never foresaw was the possibility that my two babies would grow up without me.

I remember the day my dreams died. Karl, you were two years old and Kandy was one. We had been house-hunting. One day, Charlie (Daddy to you), surprised us by announcing that we were all going to move to a house we adored. In the excitement of planning our new life, I began to feel off-colour and very weak. At first I thought I was just coming down with a bug and decided that there was nothing to worry about. However, I never really shook it off and I didn't have proper flu symptoms. I became concerned about my constant tiredness and the fact that I had more of a monthly cycle than normal. I assumed I was losing a lot of iron and thought that maybe I had become anaemic. I could not understand it because I had always been so energetic.

We planned to move in three months' time, so I thought I should see a doctor and get myself into peak condition for the event. I thought he would simply recommend some vitamins. He examined me and did a smear test, which is an ordinary test most women have done every couple of years to check for cervical cancer. I was due for one around that time, so it was just routine.

Ten days later a letter dropped through the door. It was from the surgery, requesting that I see my doctor immediately. It didn't tell me anything else. I became very worried. I contacted my GP who immediately referred me to a specialist at Newham General Hospital. Once there, I was seen by Mr Naftalin who was a consultant in gynaecology. I underwent a thorough examination. Mr Naftalin recommended that I have a biopsy done straight away. (That means taking segments of tissue from an inflamed or affected area.) In my case, it was from the cervical area. I was frantic with worry and instantly asked if I had cancer. Mr Naftalin replied: 'I can't answer your question until the results of your biopsy come back from the laboratory.' I wanted to know how long it would take. Seven to ten days was the reply.

Mr Naftalin had a caring nature and it was easy to trust him, but it didn't ease my worry. I knew that waiting for the test results would be the longest ten days of my life. Four days after the biopsy was taken, I developed severe stomach pains. I thought I might have developed an infection from the biopsy test, so I phoned Mr Naftalin. He suggested that I go to Casualty straight away and said he would discuss my case with a registrar, who would be waiting for my arrival.

After an examination, it was agreed that I should be admitted. I was put on a course of antibiotics and, during the following hours, I continued to worry about my biopsy results. I asked the registrar if he knew anything about it. He looked through my folder and said there was no record of test results.

Waiting is the worse thing ever. The test results were always at the back of my mind and no matter how hard I tried to bury them, worry about my results kept surfacing. I couldn't concentrate on anything else. In order to help myself to relax I thought I would amuse myself by making the most of my stay in hospital. I decided to treat it like a bit of a holiday. It was strange not to be chasing you two around the house. Daddy was looking after you now, so I took advantage of the break by putting my feet up and watching lots of TV. It was a real luxury to watch a show uninterrupted. Being a complete chatterbox, I also talked for hours on end with other patients. I even took their visitors hostage and had the ward ringing with laughter.

On the fourth day, however, a Friday, the party was over. Mr Naftalin sent a message that he would pop in on the following Monday to discuss the results of my biopsy. I came to the conclusion that he already knew the results. Deep inside, I had my own, strong, suspicions about what he would say to me. I was frantic with worry. I couldn't wait three days to find out what was happening inside me, so I tried to persuade Mr Naftalin's registrar to give me the results of the biopsy. However, he told me that he had to abide by the rules and that only Mr Naftalin, as my consultant, had the authority to discuss that matter with me. I insisted that Mr Naftalin be contacted straight away. The registrar was sympathetic and understood how I felt. He left my bedside and came back ten minutes later with a nurse. Even before he opened his mouth, I knew that he was the bearer of bad news.

He asked the nurse to pull the curtains around my bed to afford us some privacy. Then he sat at the foot of the bed and looked me straight in the eyes. At that moment I pitied him, for he looked quite desolate. He didn't know where to begin. I said, 'It's okay. I know. I've got cancer.' The word 'cancer' made me shiver from the hair on my head to the end of my toes. I had heard of so many people dying of that disease and suddenly I, too, had joined death row.

All I could think about was you two. I thought I had experienced fear in the past but I didn't know the real meaning of the word until that day. Tears rolled down my cheeks. I tried to be brave but the more I tried the more impossible it became. I felt as if a bomb had been placed on my lap and was about to explode.

The registrar tried to reassure me, saying they felt sure they had caught the disease in time. They were sending me home that afternoon, but a date was fixed for me to return to the hospital. I asked if I could remain an extra day as I felt I needed time to pull myself together.

One of the other patients in the ward thought it necessary

to contact Daddy straight away. She asked me for my home phone number and I must have given it to her, although I don't remember doing so, because Daddy arrived shortly afterwards.

Daddy was six feet away from the bed before I spotted him. I just blurted it out. He was stunned and tried desperately to comfort me but no words of compassion could ease the horror of what was happening to me and I asked Daddy to leave within 30 minutes of his arrival. I just needed to be alone.

I spent the next 24 hours trying to prepare myself to come home and lead a normal life. At this stage, I couldn't bring myself to tell you two how sick Mummy was because, at that point, I didn't really know myself. All I knew was that I had cancer. The doctors said they would learn more from an operation which they planned to carry out on me two weeks later. They booked me in for 8 April 1991, to have a hysterectomy, which involves the total removal of all reproductive organs plus a few extra bits. It could be that everything would turn out just fine. Anyway, that's what I hoped.

One week before my operation, I had to have a series of tests done on my heart, lungs and kidneys to ensure that I was strong enough to undergo such surgery. My tests results were good, making me the perfect candidate for an operation. I was at the end of my tether. It seemed that I was healthy enough for an operation but maybe not healthy enough to live. I wondered where the justice was in that.

I was so fortunate to have Daddy to rely on. I would have gone to pieces had it not been for him. He always seemed to do the right thing at the right time. He always knew what to say and what not to say. In the beginning, Daddy never brought up the topic of cancer. Somehow, he instinctively knew not to broach the subject. I was having untold difficulty in trying to come to terms with it in my own mind; I would have had a nervous breakdown if someone had tried to discuss it with me. I wasn't ready to talk about it. I was like a time bomb waiting to go off.

During the week leading up to the operation, Daddy tried to keep me occupied. I confess to having been useless as a mother to both of you at that point because I had fallen apart through my fears and anxieties. Daddy was an absolute champion and just got on with things.

There are many fortunate people who will never have to face a situation like this but also a large number who will. To those who have done so in the past or will in the future, my heart goes out.

Well, darlings, the evening came before I was due to go into hospital. You two were to be looked after by a neighbour. As I stood in my bedroom, packing my suitcase, I became very afraid. I suddenly and inexplicably feared that I wouldn't come out of the operating theatre alive. The most unreasonable imaginings entered my mind. I tried to calm myself but couldn't stop the crazy thoughts from flowing. I attempted to console myself with the fact that at least I was fortunate enough to have had children before my reproductive organs were removed. Then I suddenly broke down and begged Daddy not to let them do it. At the same time, I knew the operation had to be done, despite my fear.

Daddy sensed that I was losing control, and he did the most remarkable thing. He said he was nipping out for a packet of cigarettes but, instead, he drove to the hospital and told the ward sister that if he didn't bring me immediately, there was no way they would get me in there at all. He actually felt that I might run away and he was quite right. I was so scared that I was on the brink of doing just that. I was going to run as far away as I could, hoping it would make everything better.

I waited nearly an hour, wondering where Daddy was. Then intuition told me to ring the hospital. I asked to be put through to the ward that I was booked into. I asked for Charlie and was stunned to discover that he was there. I slammed down the phone without speaking to Daddy and drove to the hospital in a fury to see what he was playing at. I marched up to the ward in a rage and was greeted by a nurse. It appeared that she was expecting me. She invited me to join Daddy and the ward sister in an office. The sister was very nice. She looked at me and said: 'You're early, Mrs Reid! Oh, well, you're here now. There's no point in you going all the way home just to come back tomorrow.' I was fuming. I knew Daddy and the sister had conspired to get me there but by now I was exhausted by all the anxiety and mixed emotions, so I threw in the towel and surrendered.

They had got me there and I knew the elaborate ploy was for my own good. I settled in while Daddy went home and collected my bags. The sister gave me a single room for privacy. She was very diplomatic and seemed to know what was needed without asking. I just wanted to be left on my own. I sat alone and wondered what I had done to deserve the disease. I felt guilty knowing that it would affect your lives. I could see that it already had. Even now you were being shuffled from one babysitter to another. Because of my hospital visits, I kept disappearing without explanation. You would ask where I was going and if you could come too but I couldn't tell you what was going on and you used to look at me as though I was abandoning you.

It was affecting Daddy too. He was trying desperately to see to my needs but there was no one there to see to his. I'm not suggesting that you two could have looked after Daddy – you were far too young to understand.

On 8 April 1991, at 6.45 a.m., I was prepared for the theatre. I put on a white cotton gown that tied at the back. White surgical stockings were pulled on to my legs to prevent blood clots from forming. My hair was swept back under a cap. They were all rather unsightly items but they had a sensible purpose.

I was lying down and Daddy was seated on a chair next to my bed. I looked at him and thought what a good man he was. I wondered, with amusement, if he thought I looked fetching in my pre-op garments. It was the first light-hearted thought I had had in weeks. I was just about to tell Daddy when a nurse entered the room with a small tray in her hand. She said it was time for me to go to sleep. She had come to give me some injections which make you drowsy before you go to an operating theatre. I didn't want them at that moment because there were still things I wanted to say to Daddy about you and himself. The nurse was skilled, however, and wasn't prepared to wait a second longer. I had only reached the third word of my pleas for just a few more moments with Charlie before a needle pricked me in the bottom.

As the nurse left the room, Daddy held my hand so tight. He knew I was desperately frightened and tried to reassure me in every way possible but, really, what could be said to a person whose life was in question?

I remember drifting and trying desperately to keep my eyes open. My mouth was going dry and I was drifting further and further away. I remember thinking: '. . . not now . . . there's so much I've got to say to Charlie . . .' But it was too late; I was gone.

The porters arrived to take me to the theatre. They lifted me from my bed on to the trolley. I was not awake but I could hear Daddy's voice saying that everything was going to be fine and I felt as if I was floating when my body was moved. Daddy walked with me as I was pushed along to the theatre doors. I remember hearing his voice saying: 'See you when you come out.'

I couldn't speak so I thought: 'Yes, Charlie . . . in my coffin.' It was a horrible way to respond to a person who meant and did so much for me. It was the fear that made such a monster rise in me at times and I felt very bad about it, so at least I still knew the difference between right and wrong. That is what fear does to people.

For the next 48 hours I had little recollection of events. I was in intensive care and I vaguely remember coming to and that Daddy was there. I wanted to talk to him but it was difficult with tubes and drips and things coming out of every part of my body. I had an oxygen mask on and Charlie bent nearer to try to hear what I was saying but it was too difficult to get words out. He explained where I was and that I would be there for some time. I remember feeling stabs of horrific pain and then the nursing staff would top up my painkiller and I would drift back into a deep, welcome sleep. Poor Daddy's torment must have been just as bad as mine but he never showed it. I later learned that, during my operation, he just paced back and forth waiting for a progress report. God knows what he must have been going through.

The ward sister was a saint. She was a great comfort to Charlie at that time and spent ages talking to him and reassuring him. She made him 22 cups of tea in all. I had no inkling of what was happening to me but, looking back, I know it was just as hard on him. As I write this, I can say to you that I love Charlie so much that it hurts at times. We are very much like one person.

I recall waking up at one point to find him sitting by my bed holding on tightly to my hand. My fingers were so numb that I thought they would drop off. I kept trying to say things to him and he was struggling to decipher my words. It was frustrating for both of us. I tried desperately to communicate but couldn't. I looked into his pale blue eyes and I saw teardrops fall. He took a deep breath. I think he was embarrassed that I saw his tears. He told me to go back to sleep as I needed all the rest I could get. I was glad to see him before anyone else as he was always a source of great strength. I kept dozing off unexpectedly. I remember feeling grateful that I had woken up from the operation itself. That was a lot more than I had originally expected.

Daddy sat at my bedside 24 hours a day for four solid days, waiting for me to wake up properly and make sense of the world again. I wondered at the time if I had what it would take to do the same for him.

Four days after my operation, I woke up with a vengeance. I regained full control of my faculties, I could communicate and I knew what was going on around me. I no longer fell asleep every few minutes. Daddy was standing right by the bed and we talked and talked. He had put your photos by the bed so that every time I woke up I would see them but I must admit that I hadn't registered seeing them until that day.

Shortly afterwards, Mr Naftalin came to see me. He said the operation seemed to have been a success. I would leave intensive care and return to the ward where he would visit me later that day. I was relieved. I felt well and the severe pain was under control. As I was wheeled into my little room, I could smell the scent of flowers. My room was overflowing. They had come mostly from close friends, plus a few bouquets from people I barely knew. The sisters insisted that the flowers be removed because they were using up the oxygen in my room. To my dismay, the visitors waiting for my arrival from intensive care were asked to leave as well. Only Daddy was allowed by my bedside.

I hadn't seen you two for days, but you were always in my thoughts when I was awake. I knew it would be a while before you would see me and I didn't want you to see me in the poorly state I was in. I wanted you to see me as you knew me, happy, funny Mummy. You mustn't think that at any time I intentionally neglected you. I always made my decisions with your best interests at heart.

During the days that followed, I felt better and stronger each day. I returned home to find you as calm as newborn kittens as opposed to your normal boisterous selves. It made me wonder if you had had lobotomies in my absence, then I discovered that Daddy had explained that you mustn't jump all over Mummy because I wasn't strong enough to handle it straight away.

Unknown to you two, there was a fear in the back of my mind that plagued me for a long time. Because cancer is associated with death, I feared that one day I would no longer be around to love, feed and protect you. I tried to get things back to normal as quickly as possible, even though I felt wrenched apart by my anxieties and I was worried that you might sense it. I kept telling myself that you needed to know the truth at some point; you had to understand what was going on. I didn't want you to see me ill for a long time, then, all of a sudden, to disappear from your lives for ever without any explanation. I thought it was your right to know. I just didn't know at that point when it would be appropriate and how I would go about it.

The time came for me to start radiation treatment at the London Hospital. I had to have it for four weeks but I didn't have to stay in hospital. I was able to travel there and back on a daily basis. The actual treatment only took a couple of minutes each day. I decided it was important for Karl to come with me but not Kandy as you were still a bit too young. I had to let you, Karl, see where Mummy kept disappearing to. You needed to understand some of it. I thought that if you truly understood that Mummy wasn't well, you wouldn't blame me for leaving you alone. You had to understand that it was not my fault.

At the hospital, you sat by Mummy. I had a lump in my throat from holding back the tears so that you wouldn't see how frightened I was. Although you didn't say much, I could see you were absorbing things going on around you.

The room where I had my treatment was radioactive, so you sat with a nurse when it was my turn to go in there. Over a period of time, you learned from the nurses about the type of cancer Mummy had. Soon, you were rattling off facts just like a little doctor.

Eventually, when I thought you had a rough idea about how ill I was, I decided to explain to you about people who die and why they die. You were nearly four years old. I started by explaining about angels and how good they are. I told you that, when people died, angels came to take their spirits away because their bodies no longer worked. The sick person's body would be left behind. I remember you replying quickly that I wouldn't be going away with the angels yet. Your soft brown eyes were filled with so much hope that I couldn't bring myself to pursue the subject. I realised you weren't ready to face that possibility. I just wanted to throw my arms around you, Karl, and squeeze and hold you tight, but I felt that, if I did, you would sense my fear and know the truth. I didn't want that to happen at that time and avoided it. I knew the time would come when you would learn to accept what was happening to me. Then you wouldn't be so shocked or angry with me when it was my time to join the angels.

As we got nearer to our house, you asked me if Kandy knew that the angels might take Mummy away. Softly I answered no. I realised I had underestimated you. I knew, at that moment, that you completely understood what was happening to me – just that you were going to absorb the knowledge in your own way and in your own time. After that, I often wondered exactly how much Kandy knew as well.

I had been treading carefully in order to protect you and, at the same time, I was trying to help you to understand what the future held. I was racing against time to help you, at such a young age, to come to terms with the inevitable. But, Karl, you were as clever as Charlie. You lifted me out of my misery, by taking it upon yourself to let me know that you were, in fact, aware of everything.

As soon as we got indoors, you ran to tell Daddy what the nurse at the hospital had taught you. I was relieved that you understood about my illness and about dying. I had hoped you would, but, for some reason, I then lapsed into a deep depression. I went right down to the bottom of the pit. Daddy was quick on the uptake. Kettle on, tea made – he knew something was bothering me. He told you two to go upstairs and play. I knew what was coming – the inquisition that always helped me to get things off my chest.

I told him I was just suffering the after effects of the radiation treatment, which literally burns some areas of the body black. I said I had started feeling weak from the burns and sores. But Charlie knew it went deeper than that and so, in a flood of tears, I blurted out about our conversation in the car. Once again Charlie's familiar, warm arms wrapped me in comfort. He said I had done the right thing by endeavouring to make you, Karl, understand, but it didn't stop the pain and anguish inside.

Charlie was great at getting me to stop dwelling on certain things. He quickly piped up: 'Did you put the special cream on your burns?' Of course, I had totally forgotten. The burns were so sore that I had difficulty in walking and looked like a cowboy who has just got off his horse. I was burned from my navel around to the base of my spine. I couldn't even soak the wounds in a cold bath because if water touched the affected area, the skin would peel off like a stripped banana. I knew I had to endure this for four weeks as it was my only hope of living a bit longer. Meanwhile, my whole world was collapsing around me. I wondered what would happen if the treatment didn't buy me the extra time I had hoped for – a few more years, a few more months, a few more anything. What would happen to you both? What about Daddy? There were no answers.

Only five weeks had passed since I had been diagnosed and the mental torture was as agonising as the physical side. I still hadn't come to terms with having cancer and there were no guarantees as to the outcome. I was still disturbed by the fear of what would happen to my children if I died, especially while you were still so young. It was a fear that was to haunt me, relentlessly, for some time to come. However, often out of bad comes good. My mad state brought a lot of things in my life into proportion. My values changed. For example I had always been very houseproud. Now it suddenly seemed unimportant. My time would be better spent enjoying my babies rather than dusting the furniture twice a day. I also decided I would live what was left of my life doing exactly what I wanted to do and wouldn't do anything I really didn't want to do any longer.

I often thought it was impossible for anyone to understand what goes on in the mind of a person who knows their days are numbered. It was impossible to express my fears and anxieties to the point where other people could feel or sense what I was really going through. Cancer is frightening and some people, even if they could put themselves in a cancer victim's shoes, would choose not to. After what I went through, I couldn't really blame them.

On my final day of treatment, it was decided that I needed a further twenty hours of radiation, only this time internally. If it weren't for you two, I would have jumped off a building rather than go through that. I thought about the pain of the external burns and imagined what that would be like inside my body. I told Charlie I was about to snap and I couldn't take any more.

Charlie came with me on the morning of the twenty-hour treatment. When we entered the hospital corridors, we had to find our way to a ward I hadn't been to before. It was like a scene from a terrifying horror film. This was my first real encounter with the other cancer patients. I remember the sense of death as I neared the ward. My first sensation was that the ward had no atmosphere. It was a dead zone. There was a row of beds on either side. I don't remember how many. I saw emaciated people receiving blood transfusions, with no hair on their heads or faces. They were clearly all very sick. The air smelled of disinfectant but it didn't succeed in covering the smell of bodies rotting away. I thought, 'I'm going to end up this way . . .' Tears fell from my eyes. Charlie froze. I could feel every nerve in my body shaking. I was so worked up that I began hyperventilating.

It is hard writing about this even now. Of all the things that happened to Mummy, this is still my most horrid memory – seeing people dying of something I have too.

The reality of it all was too much. I panicked and ran out of the ward. Charlie came after me. He, too, was in a state and, when he looked at me, I saw in his eyes that I wasn't Anne Reid any longer, I was a cancer patient, one of them . . .

The nurses caught me and firmly, but kindly, ushered me back to the ward. They escorted me to my room which was at the end of the ward. I had to pass patients aged from 16 to 65. Daddy was ashen and stuck to me like glue. As we approached the room, it looked like any other room. The only difference was that the door was so thick that dynamite couldn't penetrate it. There was a six-inch-square window, made of glass at least eight inches thick.

The nurse left Daddy and me alone and then returned and handed me a pump, known as a Ventolin inhaler, to help me to regulate my breathing. I looked at her. She was calm and organised but had the glow of an angel. She had seen it all before.

I tried to pull myself together but Daddy and I were scared to death. We were offered a cup of tea. I don't know what it is about the British but a cup of tea always gets whipped up when anything goes wrong. My cup was tap dancing in the saucer because my hands were shaking so much. Daddy took my cup of tea and sat it on the locker. I started pacing up and down the room. As the day wore on, I had blood tests, X-rays and whatever else was needed to ensure that I could undergo the treatment next morning. Again, I was a good candidate for treatment. I asked Daddy to find out if he could stay the night in my little room. I just couldn't bear to be left alone. I was pleased when the nurse informed us that close relatives could stay and would be accommodated with a fold-up bed.

I lay in a big, fluffy, comfortable bed and Daddy lay in a

tiny camp bed close to the floor. Just because Daddy was there, I managed to doze off. My sleep was broken a few times, but it was strange: as soon as I woke, Daddy's eyes popped open too. We seemed to be in the same bodies although on separate beds.

At 6.30 a.m. the nurse came in with tea. I needed to go to the loo but I couldn't face walking through that ward again. Daddy said I had to go and pushed me along just the way I used to do with you. I was scheduled to go to the theatre at 2 p.m. It was an eight-hour wait. Daddy went out to buy a new set of Scrabble. It was our favourite game. I am sure you will remember all the times you asked if you could play with us.

Daddy and I played non-stop Scrabble. There wasn't much conversation. We were both trying to hide our fears, scared that if we opened our mouths we would put our feet in them and upset each other. It is difficult to see someone so sick and even harder when you love them. It doesn't take much to end up in tears.

At 1.30 p.m. the nurse appeared. It was like history repeating itself. I changed into the familiar white surgical gown and cap. Daddy walked alongside as I went to the theatre, once again assuring me all would be fine. I could remember thinking, 'How much more can my body take?' I began to think that the mental strain was causing far greater agony than the physical pain.

I was put to sleep to have this particular treatment done. Daddy had stopped smoking cigarettes by now but I could tell by the tortured look on his face that he had picked a bad time to quit. When I went into the theatre, they said it would take half an hour to put the radiation mechanism into my body. It took three hours, during which Daddy found himself once again at the mercy of cigarettes.

The radiation applicator was placed internally through my vagina. The radiation travels through the applicator to the inside of the body. The radiation machine, which would be attached to the applicator, was waiting for me in my room.

Once back in my room, everybody asked me how I was feeling but I just wanted to get it over and done with. Before being fitted to the waiting machine, I had to have an intricate X-ray to ensure that everything was in its correct place and hadn't shifted while I was being transported. The technicians were satisfied with the X-ray. I saw it and it looked extraordinary. At this point I became fascinated as opposed to frightened. I wondered what would happen next. I knew that once I was attached to the machine, the only time my door would be opened was in an absolute emergency or during meal times. This was important as the more it was opened, the longer I would have to remain in there. I was interested to learn that this type of treatment had to be mathematically calculated according to the size and weight of the patient, in order to assess the amount of radiation to be given. I chatted to the technician who told me I would feel no pain but maybe only a slight discomfort caused by the pressure of the applicator. He was absolutely right.

I asked the nurse what would happen if I needed to go to the toilet. She told me that a catheter had been fitted to my bladder, which meant that I didn't have to use the loo as the tube did it all. I was also given drugs to slow my bowel right down so that I wouldn't need to have a movement. Isn't it fascinating what doctors can do to the human body?

At this point, Daddy was still with me, but not for much longer, for the treatment was soon to start. Everyone had to evacuate the room because it would become radioactive. As I heard the big door close I could see Daddy's face through the tiny window. Then, all of a sudden I felt a click and I knew that the radiation sources were now actively being dispersed inside me.

There was a telephone by my bed, through which I could contact the outside world. You must remember how much time Mummy spent on the phone. I liked the phone as much as I like jewellery. Wouldn't you believe it, that phone was out of order. It was funny watching Daddy trying to do sign language through the little window. It was difficult to communicate as we couldn't hear each other.

I had a remote-controlled TV in my room. The control was by my bedside but it was impossible for me to move because I was tied to the bed with a corset to ensure that the applicator stayed in place. I didn't need the control anyway because only one channel worked. Daddy had packed stacks of my favourite tapes to listen to, mainly Patsy Kline. Twenty hours locked in a room without company or a telephone nearly drove me crackers. I just stared at the clock, hoping and praying for mealtimes, not because I wanted to eat but because, as soon as the door opened, I managed a quick hello to Daddy and a smile.

Daddy really amazed me. Although we had no contact

while I was being treated, he still waited outside my room the entire time. If there were a loyalty and support award, it would have to go to Daddy.

I didn't sleep very well that night because I was still hooked up to the machine. To ask someone to stay on their back for that amount of time, especially a hyper person like your Mummy, is like asking birds not to fly. I woke up numerous times hoping and praying that the hours would pass quickly. I was also thinking about poor old Daddy, sitting outside, and of course, about what was happening to you both.

There was only a couple of hours left before daybreak, which meant that the door would be opened for my breakfast delivery. Of course, once again, Daddy was there to say: 'Hi, how are you?' I had another full day to go. I had only been hooked up for sixteen hours, but then the machine broke down, which meant I had to stay on longer than expected. I was hooked up until 5 p.m., and I spent the time listening to music.

At one point, I had a reaction to the anaesthetic or the drugs or perhaps the hospital food, and vomited. Had it not been for ever-loyal Daddy looking through that tiny window, I would have choked to death on my own vomit. He saw it happen and alerted the nurses who cleared my breathing passage.

I shall never forget that day. At 5 p.m., bang on time, not a minute before or after, I heard the machine automatically switch off. My door flew open and I was bombarded by nurses, doctors, technicians and, among the crowd, ever-loving Charlie. Everyone was fussing round me. To my horror, I was told that the applicator would be removed without an anaesthetic. I was a little frightened but then thought, 'What the hell, it's trivial compared to some other things in life. It can't be much more difficult than giving birth.'

A nurse undid the corset while the machine was unhooked. They asked if I was in good shape. Yes, yes, yes, anything, yes! I just wanted to get out of there. The most difficult part was when the applicator had to be removed. I had to use what is called the bearing-down position. That's what women do when they give birth. I couldn't believe it. I was about to give birth to a radiation applicator. I was hit by a small panic attack but the worry was for nothing, I was still waiting for it to happen when, in actual fact, it had already come out. I didn't feel a thing. I can't express how relieved I was. I was told I would have to stay in for one more night for observation to make sure my blood pressure etc. was in order. Everything had to be satisfactory before they would allow me to go home.

The following morning, Daddy arrived to pick me up at nine o'clock sharp. I was packed and pacing and waiting. I was bursting with the excitement of going home again, only this time it was far more pleasant. I wasn't fragile or in pain. You kids could have jumped on me like a trampoline and I would have been quite happy. During the drive home I remember suddenly feeling optimistic and saying: 'Will this be it? Is it possible the radiation killed all the cancer?' Daddy wisely said that only time would tell. Suddenly my optimism faded. I don't know why but I had a strong intuition that there was more to come. I learned later to be realistic and positive, and not to live on false hopes.

Daddy thought it would be better if we moved to another

house to try to start afresh. A new beginning might help me to put the recent events behind me. I was inclined to agree. It would take my mind off my illness.

The next month seemed to be very hectic. We were house-hunting, packing and preparing to go. I wasn't fit enough to lift heavy items, which annoyed me because I was always independent and didn't like to rely on other people doing things for me.

We moved to a huge house. The living room was a good 35 feet long. It had four bedrooms, a large kitchen and a bathroom with a big, round jacuzzi bath. It was grand. We had lots of fun in there for a while. There was a separate shower room but you two never used it because you were always having jacuzzi bubble baths. Every time I checked on you, I was always met by a circular wall of bubbles. I guess we originally thought the comfort would be nice but, in reality, it turned out to be a lot of work. As much as I liked it, I couldn't cope with it and we moved again within half a year.

Packing and unpacking again was a major hassle but you kids regarded it as great fun. As quickly as I put something in a box, and turned my back to do something else, you would have it all unpacked again.

When we arrived at the new house, you explored it like inquisitive kittens. You knew every square inch of the house ages before I did. It was leading up to Christmas and we settled in very quickly. We liked the house and, as I write this, it is where we still live.

Karl had the big double room and Kandy had the smallest, but that all seemed somewhat irrelevant as you both somehow managed to work your way into Mummy and

Daddy's room and once you were in there, we couldn't get rid of you. We might as well have lived in a one-bedroom flat as the other bedrooms never seemed to get used.

I'll never forget our first Christmas there. That was when you, Karl, decided to burn the house down. You will be reminded of that on one of the tapes and in a letter I have left in the treasure chest, entitled 'Kandy and Karl's Lives Together as a Team'.

I kept popping back to the hospital during the months that followed, for a few tests. Nothing major was happening to my body. I felt and looked better than I had in ages. Once again, I started thinking brightly about our futures. I believed I had that dreaded disease licked until, one awful day, four months after Christmas, one year since the nightmare began, I discovered a lump in my lower regions.

3

DOUBLE TAKE . . .

It took months to recover from what we dubbed 'The Great Christmas Fire'. I remember wondering what you two would get up to next. It struck me how nice it was to have thoughts like that. The torment of my cancer had become a thing of the past and I had reached the point where it rarely entered my thoughts. When I did think about it, it was usually with the view that I had been one of the lucky ones. Then, just when everything looked bright, I discovered a lump in my vaginal area. I cannot find words to explain the horror. I knew what it meant and I ran down the stairs screaming hysterically. I really thought I was in the clear, but I guess it's never the end when you have this type of illness; not until the lights finally go out.

Without any hesitation, I phoned Allen Naftalin, Mummy's consultant. He told me to come to his clinic that very afternoon. He looked at the lump and arranged for me to have it removed in hospital the following Monday. I was in hospital for only 24 hours. After the operation I was told not to worry. I would have the results, as to whether it was malignant or not, soon enough. A couple of days passed. I was in a state of nerves so I phoned Mr Naftalin because, once again, I couldn't bear the wait. He was very understanding and promised to call me at home as soon as he had the results.

A few days passed before I found a message from him

on my answerphone. I could tell by the tone of his voice on the tape that the information I was about to receive was not good. I dialled his number, already knowing what he would say. I didn't want to hear it. Before he had a chance to say a word, I said: 'It's spreading. It's malignant.'

He told me how sorry he was and asked me to come into hospital in two weeks' time for an operation called a wide incision. The tissue surrounding the tumour was to be cut away and examined under a microscope for cancer cells. My stay in hospital would be about five days.

I arrived at the hospital early one Monday morning in May 1992 and settled in with ever-loyal Daddy at my side. I was going to the theatre the following morning but I wasn't very concerned because I knew it was a minor operation.

What I didn't expect was for it to turn into something of a fiasco. It was pre-op time once again and I was becoming an old pro at the routine. I waited for the anaesthetist to find a vein in which to insert the needle. The hunt was on but the poor guy couldn't find a suitable area to inject the sleeping drug. On a couple of occasions, I saw Mr Naftalin peer anxiously through the window and give the anaesthetist a look which said, 'Isn't she ready yet?' I had to laugh at Mr Naftalin – all dressed up in his operating greens and nowhere to go!

The first needle had gone straight through my vein and that little mistake rendered that vein unsuitable. However, the anaesthetist was persistent and had a go once again in another vein. No joy, Mummy was still wide awake. Mr Naftalin was pacing back and forth like an expectant father. I shouted to him that it was a women's prerogative to be late. He should have been used to it. It wasn't the first time I had kept him waiting to go to the theatre. The irony was that Mummy, Mr Naftalin and the anaesthetist were all Scottish. We had a laugh about how the Scots stick together.

By 3 p.m. I was wide awake again. It had been only a mild anaesthetic and recovery was swift. Mr Naftalin visited before he went home, to inform me that he would give me the test results as soon as they arrived.

It was lunchtime, three days after the operation, when Mr Naftalin appeared in the ward. I heard him ask the sister as to my whereabouts. I was standing behind the lunch trolley pinching an extra pudding.

He had rolls of paper in his hand. They were my test report. He turned and saw me. There was a happy look in his eyes. My report said there were no cancer cells in the tissue. No cancer! No cancer! No cancer! Everybody, the nurses, other patients, myself and Mr Naftalin shrieked over the good news. Everyone was congratulating me. Tears poured down my face. Unbelievably, it was the only time Daddy wasn't present. After all he had been through Daddy really deserved to be around for the good news.

Mr Naftalin told the sister to give me a sherry and I was grateful as it helped to calm me down. If the truth be known, I could have done with something a lot stronger. I adored Mr Naftalin but couldn't wait to see the back of him so that I could phone Daddy and share the good news. Within twenty minutes, Daddy was at my side. He must have broken all the speed limits that day. As soon as he spotted me, he burst into tears. We both trotted off for a cigarette. I decided that I could have one. After all, I was going to live!

The following morning I was released from Newham General Hospital. I felt as if I had been released from a prison sentence. I said my farewells to all the staff and patients. As much as I adored them, I meant it when I said it was nice to have known them and I sincerely hoped never to see any of them again. Little did I know that those faces were to return like bad pennies.

Meantime, Daddy and I decided there was a lot of catching up to do. We were going to make up for lost time. We started off by making plans to do what we really enjoyed most, taking you two to the seaside. We spent the next month and a half just having fun.

One summer night in July, Daddy decided to cook a romantic meal for Mummy while we pondered on what we would do with the remainder of the summer. That evening, the wine flowed and we were caught up in the euphoria of having a life together and making plans. Daddy served prawns, followed by a tender steak with salad and courgettes. When we had finished our meal, Daddy and I began to play like two love-struck teenagers. You may wrinkle your nose at this now but, believe me, you won't in the years to come. Anyway, one thing led to another. Daddy and I started kissing and cuddling. It had been a long time since we had been intimate. Grown-ups do like to kiss and cuddle and we had missed out on that for many, many months because of Mummy's illness.

Then, while we enjoyed our first union in a long time, Daddy discovered a lump in Mummy which altogether shattered our magic. Intimacy with Daddy was never to happen again.

I picked up the phone, screaming for Mr Naftalin. He was as disappointed as I was at the news. It was just as if Mummy always seemed to climb to the top of a ladder and then fall off. Needless to say, I was soon back in Newham General Hospital to have another tumour removed. It was malignant and it was spreading. After that discovery, Mr Naftalin said that I should be referred to St Bartholomews, where there was a specialist department for cancers. He himself had done everything he could for me and I was very grateful. He explained it would take some weeks before my first appointment at Barts.

Daddy and I decided to continue with our summer plans but this time it was with a different attitude. We weren't doing it because I was going to live, but because of the very real possibility that it might be our last chance to do this sort of thing together. I might not have had great knowledge in the medical field but I was no fool. I knew those tumours were coming fast and furious. In my eyes, so many things became unimportant again. Money became unimportant. Bills were suddenly unimportant. Even my rekindled interest in the house became unimportant. Material things didn't matter any more. All that mattered was my babies, Charlie, my health and what was left of my life.

The next couple of months proved to be happy. We went on a beach crawl and visited every seaside resort possible. We all loved the water and I had to be near it. We would always stay overnight at whatever waterfront we found. Both of you enjoyed yourselves so much that you couldn't help but make us feel very guilty at having to return to London. It was nearing the time for my visit to Barts, which is what we called St Bartholomews Hospital. Daddy decided on a slow drive to London. It had been a long summer. Once we had settled you two in bed, Daddy and I spoke about how watching you play brought back memories of our own childhoods.

Mummy was soon back in hospital. I spent weeks having chemotherapy. This is a slow drip, which, if it works, helps to shrink tumours. It also makes a person feel quite off-colour. Some people lose their hair. I did. I lost all the hair on my head including my eyebrows and eyelashes. One day I was running a brush through my thick, brown hair and Daddy went rigid. He hugged me from behind and said: 'Anne, please don't get upset or frightened. All the hair from the back of your head is lying on the floor.' He just held me as I wept and wept.

I lay in the bath that night, after taking a long, depressing look at myself. Only two years before I had been a beautiful woman, with a size-10 figure, long, thick hair and a very pretty china-doll face. Now, my once-attractive body was bloated from the chemotherapy. Starting from my stomach area, mounds of blubber hung over my hips and thighs. My chin was so large that, when I lay on my side, I could see it spread in front of me like a puffy sack. My stomach looked like a road map after all my operations. I had thick, unsightly scars everywhere. I bore no resemblance whatsoever to the woman I had been a short time ago. I cried and cried. Daddy came into the bathroom to ask me why I was sobbing.

I just looked at him and said: 'Oh, Charlie, how can you

sleep in the same bed with me? How can you sleep with a person who looks like this? I don't even resemble a woman any more. I look like a fat, old, ugly, bald man.'

He said he would make me a cup of tea and we would talk about it. A long time passed and I wondered what was keeping him. Then he appeared at the bathroom door dressed in the pretty undergarments Mummy use to wear. He had on stockings, suspenders, a lacy pair of knickers and a bra. He had make-up on and one of the wigs he had bought me that day because I had lost my hair. In his hand was a silver tea tray. He was a sight. I laughed so hard that it hurt. I couldn't stop laughing for ages. He served me the tea as if everything was normal. When I recovered from my fit of laughter, I asked him what he was playing at. Your Daddy is a dream. He just looked at me and the sweetest words came from his made-up lips. He said: 'Well, Anne, my darling. If you are a man, then surely I must be a woman!' I grabbed him and hugged him, nearly pulling him into the bath. We didn't need to discuss my insecurity about my rapidly changing looks. No matter what I looked like, I was still enough of a woman for Charlie and, in his eyes, very beautiful.

At Christmas 1992, Mummy and Daddy arranged for Father Christmas to deliver your toys. This Christmas was going to be very special. I had just finished chemotherapy and was grateful, at least, that I would be able to spend Christmas at home.

At seven on Christmas morning, the doorbell rang. As soon as you heard it you raced from your rooms and literally fell down the last four stairs. You were so excited because you had spotted Father Christmas from a bedroom window. When I opened the front door, Father Christmas stood there with two enormous sacks, one for each of you. Karl couldn't get him into the house quickly enough. Kandy, you were on the stairs, frozen stiff with shock. Daddy had to pull you away and carry you into the front room to explain who Father Christmas was.

You were unbelievable. You started chatting and didn't stop. Father Christmas introduced himself as St Nicholas and told you all about the little elves who were busy working for him in the toy factory. I was wildly impressed. You were both intrigued by his tales. Daddy and I stood in the background while Father Christmas helped you to unwrap all your toys. I must say I was choked with emotion. I couldn't watch the scene any longer. I feared it might be the last time I saw you open Christmas presents.

Kandy, you looked at me cheekily and asked me to make Father Christmas a cup of tea. As I went to get on with it, I could hear both of you telling Father Christmas that Mummy was sick. I knew Father Christmas was already aware of this. I was so proud of your concern. It was your day but you still found time to explain about Mummy. It was then that I realised you were growing up. I shuffled through a battlefield of toys to deliver the tea to Father Christmas. He was very dedicated and stayed for one and a half hours until every parcel had been opened. Then he left, explaining that he had to go to visit lots more children before the day was out. Once we were on our own, we played with the toys and games.

At that particular time, Mummy had been feeling very unwell. I don't know if you will remember that. Against medical advice I was determined not to return to hospital because I didn't want your Christmas to be ruined. I became tired very quickly. Daddy made room on the sofa for me to lie down. Then he begged me to let him phone the hospital. I was, in fact, very sick. I wondered if I was losing the battle. I lay on the sofa for a while while you played with your toys. I remember taking aspirin every few hours to keep the fever I had developed at bay. By the end of the evening, I was so weak that I couldn't get off the sofa to go to the loo.

By that time, Daddy wasn't having my objections any longer. I begged him not to call a doctor and tried in vain to convince him and myself that I would be all right. Then, as I rapidly went from bad to worse, I realised I needed medical assistance, and needed it soon.

By eight o'clock on Christmas night, you two were shattered. It had been a long day for you both. I was grateful when you went to bed because by now I needed the space to be ill without hiding it. I didn't take you up to bed that evening. I was no longer able to climb the stairs. Daddy did the honours. I felt guilty at being ill on Christmas Day as I had promised you both that I wouldn't have to go back to hospital. I was mistaken. My resistance was so low from the chemotherapy that I didn't realise how prone I was to infections. I had caught some bug or other.

Once you were both tucked up in bed, Daddy and I were able to sit and talk. It was difficult at the time to talk simply because I worried that you might overhear things. You seemed to pick up a lot more than we gave you credit for at the time but by the same token, I recognised and appreciated your quick wisdom.

I remembered telling Daddy that I was frightened to

phone the hospital because I didn't want to leave my babies again. I knew that if the hospital was contacted, I would be ordered straight in because my symptoms were cause for alarm. I had a high temperature and the shivers. My body was overheating and shivering is nature's way of attempting to cool down the system.

Daddy made a deal with me that he would let me stay at home that night if I let him call a doctor first thing in the morning. Reluctantly, I agreed. I knew it had to be done; I couldn't fool myself any longer. I was so weak that I never left the couch. I had to go to the loo during the night but couldn't make it; Daddy had to bring a potty to me. I guess that's one of the ugly, though not the worst, sides of being ill and weak.

The following morning Daddy called the cancer hospital rather than our GP. He had sat up all night, waiting for daybreak, just to ensure that he could phone at the earliest possible moment. As soon as he explained to the doctors about my fever, I was admitted straight away. I felt really frustrated and angry because I thought I was breaking my promise to you two. Once again, my little bag was packed. A babysitter arrived and Daddy drove me to hospital. I gave you both a big hug and kiss. It broke my heart more than ever before. I would have given anything at that point to read your thoughts. I got into the car and, as I looked back, you were standing by the doorway. I couldn't help but wonder if you knew how I felt.

So, on Boxing Day, 1992, Mummy was admitted to St Bartholomews with severe chest complaints. It was discovered that I had a rampant infection in my lungs. The doctors' main concern was that I shouldn't end up with double pneumonia or pleurisy. As soon as I was put to bed, a drip was put into my veins to feed antibiotics into my system. I needed two different types; the other one had to be taken orally. The doctors finished hooking me up to the intravenous drip and Daddy burst out crying.

I asked him what the problem was. He said he would give or do anything to trade places with me. As sweet as he was, I believed that if anyone knew how I really felt, they wouldn't willingly trade places with me and I wouldn't want that to happen to anyone, especially to someone I loved.

I think at this point it all became too much for him. I admit that I felt the same. I didn't want him to remain with me too much longer; I wanted him to get back to you. As far as I was concerned, Boxing Day was still part of Christmas and I didn't want it spoiled any more than it already was. He was reluctant to go but he understood. As soon as he had left, I delved into my own thoughts. Once again, I began to panic over the unknown. The cancer was more deeply rooted than I had imagined.

I pulled myself together and decided I simply had to become well enough to go home. The days that followed mainly consisted of resting and waiting to get better. I thought I might get home for Hogmanay, the Scottish New Year's Eve celebration. All Scots look forward to that particular evening but my New Year's Eve was to be spent in Barts as the doctors felt I was not ready to go home. I was very upset as I wanted to bring in the New Year of 1993 with my babies and Charlie.

Daddy stayed with me the whole day and evening of 31 December, 1992. You were at home with the babysitter, ever-loyal Linda, otherwise known as your godmother, Karl. At 8 p.m. the hospital staff changed shifts. As luck would have it, the nurses who came on duty that evening just happened to be my favourites. I decided that I had to pull myself out of the doldrums and accept that I would not, under any circumstances, make it home that evening. (I did, at one point, think of sneaking out!)

I made a resolution to adopt a new attitude about my situation, no matter how bad it might become. I promised myself that, from that moment on, I would always make the best of a bad situation. Daddy was with me and there was no time like the present to start.

There was a tray in the ward which had bottles of alcoholic beverages placed neatly on top. They had been donated to the hospital. The area above my right eye, which should have had an eyebrow on it but didn't because of the chemotherapy, lifted quizzically as I stared at the booty. I went up to a nurse called Katherine and talked to her about Hogmanay. One of her parents was Scots and she was fully aware of how we celebrated New Year. Following my new resolution, I decided that there was no reason in the world to change tradition, especially as I had a half-Scotswoman willing to be my partner in crime – I mean my partner in keeping up with tradition!

We rolled the entire ward, some twenty beds full of cancer patients, chemo-drips and all, into one line, side by side. While Charlie prepared countless pizzas and bowls of salad in the ward kitchen, I grabbed a notepad and pen and whizzed round all the patients taking drinks orders. Believe me, if they wanted it, it was on the trolley. I remember one old lady, 90 years of age, who asked for a whisky toddy. I nearly fell over at this order because I didn't know how to make it. However, I was a quick learner. She gave me a verbal rundown of the recipe and I took the bottle of whisky into the kitchen, heated some milk, added whisky and was pleased with the results. I took it back to the old lady but, to my absolute horror, she took her first sip and it nearly killed her. She gasped, wheezed and coughed. I had made it too strong. I ran back to the kitchen for more milk to thin out the whisky. When I returned she tasted it once more. I had got it right. She survived but, just as I left to tend to the other patients, she shouted out that she wanted a Babycham. By this time I was in hysterics.

Every time I got a drink for someone, I had sips myself. I was quite tipsy, merry, over the top, inebriated, or all of the above. When I think that I was a cancer patient in a cancer ward it wasn't bad going. Mummy was exceedingly merry and so were the rest of the patients. It was their last big party before their exit. I don't think anyone in the ward had expected a New Year like it.

One patient in particular, whom I will never forget, was called Paddy. He liked a bet on the horses and he liked a drink. Every time I passed his bed, I would give him another dram of brandy. At midnight, when the New Year began, we had the television on so that we could hear Big Ben's chimes. We were sitting with our pizza, all quite merry, wishing each other a happy New Year. All of a sudden, Paddy, who was being treated for a brain tumour, decided that he had to go to the loo. It was hilarious. He had his chemo-drip attached and he was trying to push the wheeled trolley along beside him. He had had far too much brandy and the nurse had her work cut out helping him back to bed. As soon as he hit the pillow he was out until the morning.

Katy, another patient, went to sit on a chair and it collapsed. She lay flat on the floor. I was worried but then she looked up and said: 'Don't worry lovely, I'm on my way out anyway!'

The patients pretended to be medical staff. We all had a life-threatening disease but laughed in the face of it. We went to each other's beds and checked each other's pulses and drips. For three hours we forgot our problems and didn't have a care in the world. We pinched stethoscopes and took turns listening to each other's hearts and our own. I had to listen to my own because the person who tried to listen to mine was deaf.

At 1.30 a.m., Daddy decided it was time to go. I was glad because I was exhausted. It wasn't the New Year I had hoped for but, in its own way, it was good. At least it made a lot of people happy when it was least expected.

I crawled into my bed. Some nurses from another ward discovered the empty bottles and went spare. They told me to stay put in my bed for everyone's good and said the ward seemed worse than St Trinians.

The few days that followed were satisfactory. The doctors were pleased that I was making progress but bewildered by the blood test results of all the patients. We kept our party a close secret!

I was excited because I knew I'd be coming home. I only had to wait for my blood count to return to normal. Two days later, I was allowed out. How glad I was to see you.

You told me off, Karl, for going back into hospital. I felt so ashamed and guilty but it was beyond my control. You both forgave me in the end or pretended to, anyway.

As the months passed, Mummy started to become stronger. Everyone could see a difference in me but I had stopped living in hope. I had to face facts; every time I got better, it was a sign that things would get worse. I didn't slip into a false sense of security this time round. I was tormented with the thought of what would happen to you two. I knew that I wouldn't be able to take too many more operations. I knew I had to be grateful for whatever time I had on remission. I admired a cherry blossom, its beautiful petals falling to cover the ground like confetti. I looked at the tree and thought, 'At least you will come back again next year, unlike myself.' I knew I had to do something for your futures. I had to find a way to guide and take care of you after I went. It was during that remission, when I was tortured by the thought of what would become of my babies, that I hit on the idea of the treasure chest.

I decided that I should start by telling you about my life so that you will truly understand all the things Mummy was made of, bad as well as good. If you understand your roots first, it may make it easier for you to understand yourselves and why you are so very important to me.

I haven't left any stone unturned. There is a reason for this. Should you ever venture into your parents' past, you may have to depend on other people helping you to form a picture of what your ancestors were like. If I tell you all there is to tell, no one will ever be able to misinform you. Everything in my letters and tapes is absolutely true.

I'm glad I made the treasure chest when I did. Since I

began it, I have never stopped adding to it. It is only five months since I last left hospital after being told I was in remission. It is now June 1993 and I'm back in hospital again. I had a sneaky look at my medical folder, which contains things they don't tell the patients. The bit that I read, the bit they didn't tell me, says, 'Anne's cancer is far more advanced than originally thought.' I have used my time wisely.

Now, I guess, the only place to start is at the beginning.

4

MUMMY – AGED 5

I can recall certain incidents in my life as far back as the age of two and a half. I clearly remember my father, mother, brother John and twin sisters Sheena and Annie. Apart from my immediate family, the Donaldsons, the earliest and most vivid memory imprinted on my mind is of a woman called Aunt Isobelle. She was the niece of my mother, Alexzina. Throughout my life, the memory of her was continually cropping up in my mind. Aunt Isobelle had a deep impact on me and was to prove a very important part of my future, although I didn't know that at the time.

I'll never forget when I first met her. I was taken to her home by my mother. We passed eerie gas lamps on a very long street leading to Aunt Isobelle's flat. It was like something out of an old Sherlock Holmes film.

We walked through a dark passageway and up a flight of stairs before entering Aunt Isobelle's flat. I even remember the colours of the rooms and the clothes she wore that particular day. The contents of her home were sparse. In retrospect, I suppose she had little money at the time. It must have been her first flat. The flat was open-plan and the toilet was outdoors. This was very common in those days in Scotland and England. There was no bath or shower indoors or out. Isobelle washed herself in a tin bathtub which was stored in her bedroom when not in use. There was no hot running water, only cold taps. When I innocently enquired how she bathed, she explained that she put the tin bath near the kitchen sink and heated water on the cooker. Using a saucepan, she would bail out the soiled water down the drain of the sink. Some years later, I marvelled at what she went through to clean herself as she always smelled so sweet and fresh.

I recollect studying the kitchen with great interest. There was a sink and a greyish-blue cooker below a window. To the left was a wooden kitchen surface which, when lifted, revealed a coal bunker. A large coal-fuelled fireplace, with a huge, black, cast-iron surround, provided enough heat to warm the entire sitting room and kitchen. Two armchairs were situated near the fireplace and I remember the bedroom being very cold as there was no form of heating beyond the sitting room.

This woman made a disturbing impression on me. From the moment I met her, I felt as if I belonged with her and I sensed that she shared those feelings without ever saying so. It was an unspoken communication between us.

Much to my delight, arrangements were made that day for me to visit Aunt Isobelle on a regular basis. In the months that followed, my twin sisters, would take me to Auntie's by bus and drop me off before going on to school. They would collect me again on their way home. Aunt Isobelle babysat me for the next eighteen months before I started attending preschool. On one occasion, when the twins came to collect me, they were greeted by the dirtiest little girl they had even seen. I had managed to make myself completely filthy. My sisters were so horrified that they washed me before taking me home, but not before giving me a good telling off. Isobelle jumped to my defence and said that I had the right to play and explore and collect as much grime as was necessary along the way.

I noticed how she always defended me. She had a peculiar understanding of the adventure in my soul and, more important, a willingness to indulge me. She seemed to gain as much, if not more, joy than I did from my little adventures. Aunt Isobelle took a very real pleasure in my company. She laughed with me the whole time. Nothing I did made her angry. When I was with Aunt Isobelle, I dreaded the moment of the twins' arrival. I never wanted to leave her and didn't know why. Even at that age, I questioned those feelings. I clearly remember little pains in my heart when I had to say goodbye every evening. Sometimes I could see past her parting smile, straight through to the desolation in her eyes as I was led away.

Isobelle also popped over to my house on numerous occasions and if it wasn't too late in the evening, I was allowed to stay awake and spend some time with her. Inevitably, however, I would be sent to bed so that Mum and Isobelle could talk privately.

I sorely missed Isobelle when I started preschool. I wished that I could just trot off and visit her on my own but that was impossible as I was so young. I seriously thought about it on many occasions, though, as I knew by then exactly how to get to her home. I swore that when I was a little older, I would go to Aunt Isobelle's every single day and not allow anyone to stop me.

I saw less of Isobelle in the summer months as the twins were out of school and there always seemed to be someone at home. I have a vivid memory of our huge back garden. I tore around the lawn, merrily tripping over my toys which liberally littered a large area of the dark green grass. By day, the garden resembled an untidy toy shop. By night, the grounds were tidy and bore no trace of my daytime activities. I always seemed to play on my own while Dad pottered around, weeding and planting seasonal vegetables. There was a rockery in the garden which, apart from me, was Dad's pride and joy. He was constantly doing things to improve it.

I have a vivid memory of the summertime leading up to my fourth birthday. This is the first time I can remember welcoming and appreciating the sunshine and warmth the summer months offered. I was fascinated at how the sun danced off my bare arms, setting my tanned skin aglow. I would pause in the middle of whatever game I was playing and take deep breaths, inhaling the perfume of the flowers in bloom. Always close by my side were my pram and two dolls, one black and one white. I played house and cradled the dolls lovingly in my arms as if they were my own real babies.

Our neighbours had an aviary filled with pretty, chirping birds. As an adult, I often wondered if that aviary aided my early memories. Animals tend to embed memories in children more than anything else. I would stand, clutching one doll under each arm, and endlessly bombard the neighbour with questions about the birds. In retrospect, it must have been torture for them to endure a whole summer of daft questions. I was such a chatterbox that they would plead with me to be quiet. If you have any early memories of me, among those would surely be the fact that I didn't change much in that department.

I dreaded when the sun moved and shaded the garden as

it was always a sign that it was time to go indoors. Day after day, the routine was the same and I would beg to stay out just a little bit longer. Something about the garden environment gave me a tremendous sense of freedom. Having the run of the garden and chatting with grown-up neighbours made me feel like a proper adult. However, all my pleading would fall on deaf ears for, when Daddy went indoors, so did I. That was the golden rule. Daddy said I was only safe as long as he could see me. It seemed so unfair at the time.

Daddy would carry all my toys indoors, including my precious three-wheeled bicycle which I had received the Christmas before. I knew that playtime was over. I would sulk in my room, looking out of the window and plotting that, when I grew up, I would stay in the garden as long as I wanted. Maybe even for days!

As an innocent child, I had no idea about danger. As an adult and mother, I look back and know my father did what was best, no matter how unreasonable it seemed to me at the time. It would be fair to describe myself as a daddy's girl. Most of the memories I retained up to the age of five are fondly filled with Daddy and little else. He called me Cuddles, a typical Scottish endearment for little girls. Even at such a tender age, however, it was apparent to me that I had a good relationship with my father and a practically non-existent one with the rest of the family. I knew I was a novelty and somewhat spoiled as my brother was twenty years my senior and my twin sisters fifteen years older than myself. The tremendous age gap between me and the others played a major part in giving me a delightful first five years of life.

I seemed to go everywhere with Dad. He would cycle off

to the betting shop with me propped up on the handlebars of his push bike. I used to grip on for dear life as he careered down the roads. It was like a funfair ride each and every time. He wasn't a sincere gambler but would enjoy a shilling (5p) bet on the horses every Saturday. Afterwards, he worked his way to the local pub to meet up with his neighbours and friends. I wasn't allowed in the pub so I played with all the other children who waited outside for their wayward fathers. The men prided themselves on managing to consume a few pints of beer away from their wives' prying eyes.

If Mum had known what Dad was getting up to, she would have had a fit. She detested drink and smoking almost as much as she detested a flutter on the horses. Dad loved all three.

Dad's little flutter and the meetings at the pub always remained our secret but he smoked openly in front of Mother, twenty cigarettes a day, and got told off by her about it right up to the months leading to his death, but she only did it because she cared. From what I remember, Mum and Dad got along very well but I always wondered how they could be so compatible when Mum deplored Dad's favourite little pleasures. He went to great extremes to hide his secret pints from Mum. She never could understand his unpredictable behaviour at the weekends. He was always a jovial man but was even more so after he had had a bit of Saturday beer. On one occasion, after we returned from the pub, Dad decided to cook while Mum was out. I was playing outdoors by the window, where Dad could keep an eye on me. He fell asleep and left a pot bubbling away on the stove. The next thing I knew, there was smoke pouring out of the window and front door. I ran to fetch a neighbour and Dad was rescued. I assure you he wasn't the most popular man in town when Mum returned home.

Dad had a few close shaves with death in this lifetime, including nearly getting knocked down by a bus. I always thought that God looked after him because he was such a sweet man. I don't know what I would have done without him.

I always covered up for Dad, keeping his secrets safe, and he always did the same for me. I remember another adventurous Saturday when Dad sat outdoors reading a paper while I cycled to the top of a steep hill on my shiny little bicycle. I turned the bike around and flew down, with great squeals of delight. I repeated the uphill-downhill trek over and over and, each time, shouted proudly for Dad to watch. On a final descent, however, which was at a breath-taking speed, I did something wrong and found myself catapulted over the handlebars of my bike.

It is remarkable what one can think of in a short space of time between leaving the seat of a bicycle at great speed and hitting the ground. I wondered if my bicycle would survive. I wondered if my mother would explode over me soiling my pretty blue cardigan, red skirt, white socks and new black pumps. I didn't worry about getting cut to ribbons; I only feared what my mother would do when she found me that way. Finally, at the tail end of that thought, my little body met the ground and skidded across the gravel.

I hobbled over to Dad with tears streaming down my grubby pink cheeks. My elbows and legs were badly grazed and blood trickled in little rivers to my socks. My bicycle lay in a heap at the bottom of the hill, in worse condition than I was. I looked at my father, who managed to remain calm even though stricken with horror. I blurted out that I was scared of what Mummy would say. I looked at him with pleading eyes and lips that quivered like a bowl of jelly. Dad told me to stop blubbing and got on with the job in hand. He cleaned me thoroughly and then set out to repair my bicycle. By the time he finished, it looked as if it had never touched the ground, unlike myself.

Daddy, bless his soul, mended me with less skill than he had applied to the bicycle and covered me in endless bandages and plasters. Mum came home, took one look at me and paused for a brief moment before bursting into laughter. I was greatly relieved.

I felt very secure and friendly with my father as I was very much included in his day-to-day activities. As the years passed, my closeness to him led to hostile feelings between my mother, sisters and myself.

Dad was a hard worker. He worked shifts as a spinner in a jute mill and his changing hours afforded us a lot of time together during the day. He had a lot of time for me and, with his witty, dry sense of humour and impulsive ways, was always bags of fun. I was fortunate that he was always there for me because I saw less and less of Aunt Isobelle and Dad's presence compensated a little for her absence.

During one of her visits, I learned that she had moved and made a new life for herself. She had given birth to a baby son but was not married, which confused me. At that age, I thought girls had babies *because* of the act of marriage. I couldn't understand how she had managed to have one without getting married first. I put that thought to the back of my mind to ponder on another day as I wanted to enjoy every minute of Isobelle's visits, which were becoming rare.

The season was changing and now Dad chose to stay bundled up in the sitting room rather than play with me outdoors in the cold. Happy memories moved with the seasons. There was no central heating 30 years ago in Dundee and the house was very cold indeed. The cold never bothered me, however, as Dad made up for it by carrying out an endearing, vigilant bedtime routine. He used to take my night clothes, sheets and blankets, and warm them in front of the coal fire. Mum would dress me in my heated nightie before Dad tucked me into the warm, snug bed he had made.

I remember the good-night games Dad and I played every bedtime. Mum washed my hands and face before running a toothbrush over my teeth, then I would run downstairs to where Dad was waiting and make any possible excuse to stay awake a little longer. Call it genetic if you will, but you two darlings try every trick in the book to stay awake as well.

My reasons for staying awake became more inventive with each passing day. Dad would play along by pretending to fall for my tricks. I was delighted when I thought my cunning had bought me extra time. Without fail, Dad would carry me upstairs and ask me if I had brushed my teeth and washed my hands and face, knowing full well Mum had already done so. He would tickle me and say, 'Let me see those tegs,' which is what the Scottish call teeth. I would giggle and arch backwards in his arms. I remember always seeing the stairs leading to my room from an upside-down view.

Once I was tucked into bed and Dad bade me goodnight, I would respond by asking for a slice of bread spread with treacle. He would object. I would plead, knowing full well that I would get my way. When I became a mother, I did the same with my children. Perhaps you can remember the night-time games I played with you.

I slept in a single bed surrounded by my dolls. When I was four and a half years old, I developed whooping cough, a viral infection which can kill children. It lasted for months and made me cough so violently that I would vomit and struggle for breath. Dad and Mum decided that I should be moved into their room where they could keep a better eye on me. They feared I might choke to death during a coughing fit. Mum would comfort me and guide me through the fear. Sometimes I coughed so violently that I turned blue. It was horrifying for my parents. They feared for my life but, as a typical child, I thought the worst part of whooping cough was not being able to play in the garden. The danger of coughing to death didn't concern me at all. I just wanted to go out. It must have been frustrating for my parents to see me with such a longing. I couldn't understand why I wasn't allowed outdoors and it was impossible, try as hard as they did, to explain it to me. Over the next few months, the whooping cough slowly went away. As a child, those months felt like years.

I was coming to school age. Soon after my fifth birthday, Mum took me shopping for a school uniform. I remember it clearly. I was so proud of my little navy pleated skirt, navy cardigan, white shirt, black and yellow tie, little blazer, white socks and black shoes.

I stood there on Monday morning, the first day of school, feeling wildly excited. I had admired myself in the mirror many times, drinking in the sight of the grown-up girl in the reflection. My mother snapped at me to stop being so vain and threatened to remove all the mirrors from the house.

As we left, I struggled to get one last look at my reflection in a window pane. Suddenly, I remembered that I had forgotten my packed snack of white bread and treacle. By this point, my mother was fairly fed up with me. I had an energy overload due to the excitement of my first day at school. It totally exhausted her. However, I was determined to have my sandwich and dragged Mum back to the house. I must admit I wasn't in her good books that morning but I didn't care as long as I got my sandwich.

As we worked our way back towards Balerno Primary School, we stopped off in the sweet shop. My mother clearly felt the need to bribe me. This episode will sound familiar as you are aware of the many times I found the need to bribe you with the odd sweet just so that I could have a peaceful life. My mother knew how to get her way just as well as I knew how to get mine. I never stopped her from bribing me, although half the time it wasn't even necessary.

Hand in hand, we progressed peacefully while I merrily munched my sweets. Then my excitement suddenly turned to fear when I saw the school and all the other pupils of assorted ages. I had second thoughts. I wanted to take my sandwiches and go back home. I started crying, kicking and screaming. My mother said I would be all right and would enjoy attending school. I never believed that was possible.

Mum tore my clutching little hand out of hers and left me screaming in the hands of my new teacher. With the other pupils, I was led to the cloakroom, where we hung our little blazers on designated hooks. I stood looking at all the other children, some crying and some laughing – a whole group of tiny strangers like myself. At this point I decided to eat my sandwich. I started to unwrap it and, to my horror, I was politely told to put it back in my satchel. I retorted nastily that I was going to eat it. The teacher reminded me that I wasn't at home and would do as I was told. Well, I was stunned. It became apparent that there was a very real possibility that I wouldn't get my way. I came to the conclusion that it was about time I left.

As I bolted for the door, the teacher pulled me back into the classroom and I threw the most astonishing fit of temper. Out of the blue, she smacked me on the back of the legs and I decided, right then, that I didn't like this woman at all. She was clearly a force to be reckoned with.

I sat at my little desk and began to sulk. From that moment on, I refused to have any form of communication with my teacher. I was desperate to go home. At 12.30 the bell rang for the lunch break and, I must admit, I was glad to see the back of my new teacher. I put my little blazer on to play in the recreation area and decided it was as good a time as any to head home. The janitor stopped me and asked where I was going. I answered, 'Home. Where are you going?' He asked my name and I proudly answered, 'Anne Donaldson.' He marched me back to the dining hall and explained the dangers of young children leaving school on their own. He said young children are much safer in the presence of an adult. He told me that children could sometimes be led away by strangers and that, if something like that occurred, I would never see my family again. I could get knocked down by a car. I could get lost. Lots of horrible things could happen.

We went back to class at 1.30 and I resumed my normal place at my little desk. My attitude had changed slightly. My early-morning grudge disappeared as I discovered that my first day at school was mainly play. I decided that school wasn't so bad after all. I could get used to playing all day. It was a bit like being at home except that there were lots of other children.

My teacher explained to me there were rules that must be obeyed. As it was my first day, she would allow for my tantrums. At that point the school bell went and she asked all the children to tidy up quietly. It was time to go home at last. I ran out of the classroom, pulled my little blazer off its hook and turned to be greeted by the most wonderful sight, my Dad. He was as excited as I was about my first day at school. I was full of news.

I told him I had tried to go home during the lunch break because the teacher had smacked me. He asked why I was smacked. I told him it was because of my sandwiches. He gave me a look that I knew all too well, as if to say, 'We know better, Cuddles.' As we strolled down the road, I asked if I had to go back to school tomorrow. He laughed and replied that I had to go five days a week, Monday to Friday.

As soon as we got home, I went straight to find my dolls.

I spoke to them as if they were little humans and told them about my eventful day at school. Dad always laughed to see me speak to my dolls but, in my little world, they were very real.

It was nearing six o'clock in the evening and my mother was due home from work. I couldn't wait to tell her about my first day at school. My sisters decided to take me to the bus stop to meet Mum. Rex, our family dog, came with us. Rex was a German Shepherd. He was incredibly intelligent and had the reasoning of a human being. My twin sisters had Rex very well trained. He would literally take my little hand in his mouth and hold me at the kerb until the road was clear. Once he was satisfied the road was safe, he would lead me across.

As Mum came off the bus, she could see my cheeky little face glowing with excitement. I desperately wanted to tell her about my first day at school. I began chattering non-stop. My sisters and mother stood on the pavement laughing and asking me to slow down. My mouth was going so fast that I didn't make sense. As we carried on walking home, Mum asked how much mischief I had got up to that day. I told her about the janitor. She laughed. She said, 'Typical wee Anne.'

That night, my life changed for ever. I learned I was to be put to bed, religiously, by 7.30 every evening. That was not what I was used to. I protested, but my parents explained that I had to get my rest so that I would be alert during lessons the following day. As I went to bed that night, I thought over and over about school. I could barely sleep because my mind was so active. I came to the conclusion that my first day at school had been a wild success, despite the difference I had had with the teacher, but I resented having to go to sleep so early for what I assumed was to be the rest of my life.

As the months wore on I settled down at school very well. I became popular as I developed into an extrovert and prankster who always had everyone laughing, except my teacher. I was always being pulled to one side and reminded that I was at school to be educated as a scholar, not a stand-up comedian. I distracted the other children from their lessons with my effervescent personality. I was always very hyper and full of beans and my abundance of energy meant that I couldn't stay still for very long and always lost my concentration. I became very much a leader and a thorn in my teacher's side. I imagine, in retrospect, that I was a monster, but not a horrible one; a fun one. They say that there is one in every class and in that class it was me. I enjoyed shocking and surprising my school chums. I loved it when I made them laugh. I loved being an entertainer.

My best partner in crime was a boy named Brian Bunter. He had one glass eye and I enticed him to play endless, merciless tricks on the other children with that eye. The straw that broke the camel's back, as far as the teacher was concerned, was when I persuaded glass-eye Brian to put his false eyeball in one of the other children's tapioca pudding. The way they served tapioca at school was with a lump of jam in the middle. In this case, the only thing in the middle of the tapioca was Brian's glass eye. Just picture it. A girl was about to tuck into her pudding when, staring her in the face, in the centre of her spoon, was an eyeball. The poor victim screamed and wet herself out of sheer horror.

Needless to say, what I had viewed as an amusing prank landed me in an amazing amount of trouble. Brian and I were questioned over the incident but the more I looked at Brian, the more I wanted to laugh. By now, the teacher's patience had worn thin. I was marched to the headmistress and punished with what was called 'three of the best'. In those days, teachers were allowed to hit children on the knuckles with a belt or wooden ruler. I got the belt. It hurt and I cried. Incredibly, Brian, who owned the glass eye, got off scot-free.

It got to the point where Brian and I would sit in absolute hysterics without even a clue as to what we were laughing at. Just looking at each other sent us into giggling fits. It became a major distraction from our schoolwork and I was always accused by the teacher of being the main instigator. At the time I felt that she always picked on me but, in reality, she was quite right.

My reputation spread through the school and I became a living legend even among children who were much older than me. It got so bad at one point that my parents were asked to come and see the headmistress. I thought I was just having fun and couldn't work out what all the fuss was about. I now realise that the teachers had the other pupils to think about and that I was a terrible distraction. It was in everybody's interest to get me under some form of control. The punishment dished out by my parents was as follows. I was sent to bed without playtime, the privilege of watching television and last, but not least, supper. I remember sitting in my room, crying constantly. I devised little ways of getting out of the room. I pretended I had to use the toilet the whole time and falsified fever and illness. I pretended I was dying of thirst but my parents had heard it all before. Nothing worked.

I must clarify one thing. It sounds as if I was a little horror, but I wasn't. I felt I was a normal fun-loving child. Sadly, my family started taking a different view. As far as they were concerned, their once cute little girl had become nothing but trouble. I didn't believe they were right. I was just an energetic extrovert who loved to make people laugh. I hated Mum's sudden resentment of me.

It was a turning point in my life and my relationship with my parents underwent a great change. As the months wore on, I got into endless trouble but it also seemed that I couldn't do anything right even when I tried. Mum was so annoyed with me that she couldn't see the efforts I made to make amends. If it wasn't my mother trying to correct me and snapping at me constantly over any little thing, it was my older sisters. Discontent set in as I neared my sixth birthday. I couldn't believe that, only a year before, I had been a little girl who was adored and pampered.

As I approached my sixth birthday, it was apparent that I was caught in a vicious circle. I was a child accustomed to a certain amount of attention. When I got to school, I wanted that same attention and developed my own ways of attracting it. It only landed me in trouble. My life would never be the same. Somehow I knew my carefree days of loving fun with Dad had come to an end. I had provided my sisters and mother with an opportunity to ensure that. A distance had been created and there would never be a chance for Dad and me to draw close together again.

5

KARL AND KANDY – ADVICE AGED 5

Now, darlings, on the occasions I've collected Karl from school (at this time you have been attending first year for a couple of months) I have noticed similar patterns of behaviour to Mummy's. You, Karl, were shell-shocked to learn that you had to abide by a new set of rules, unlike the rules at home. You are going to experience this as well, Kandy. Both of you will realise that this is called discipline. You are now learning about social behaviour and what is accepted in society. Up to date, Mummy has allowed a lot of leeway in this, inasmuch as I spoiled both of you because I was so ill. I didn't want to spend our precious time together making you abide by military house rules. I just wanted to have fun with my babies.

However, for both of you to grow into fine, upstanding citizens, this is the time to understand life's dos and don'ts and what is accepted in society. Mummy wants both of you to grow into very fine, well-educated adults. I know this might sound hard, at the age of five, but this is when it begins.

At this age, you will develop a keen sense of right and wrong and justice. It is at this time that children tend to latch on to rules and start to enquire about religious beliefs. You may meet a child who is a vegetarian and the youngster will explain that he or she doesn't eat meat because of their religion or conviction. You will want to know all about it. Karl, you already said to me that you thought it was a pity that cows have to die to be turned into food. This is your sense of justice developing.

You will both develop a sense of pride in being able to abide by certain rules, such as queueing properly before entering your classroom in the mornings. You will feel proud that you belong to a group of children who attend the same school and wear the same uniform. It is a sense of *belonging* that is now developing.

You will compare things with other children, such as what their parents do for a living. How big their room is. Do they share it? This is a sense of equality developing. Never feel that anyone else is better than you or luckier because they have something you don't. Never feel resentful or jealous. In time, if you study hard and work towards what you want in life, there is no reason why you can't eventually have everything you ever dreamed of. You will realise this in the later stages of growing up.

Your sense of the family unit will be very strong. You will put your toys into families and want to do very grown-up things like cook, keep house and go out to work! That is because, from the moment you start school, you are growing towards being an adult. It is a long process which will take many years but it starts here.

I have made the decision that you will share the advice letters. Kandy, you will always receive the same letter as Karl, only he will see it a year earlier as he is a year older. It will help him to understand what you are experiencing as a girl. It will help him to understand women as he grows into an adult.

The same principle will apply to you, Kandy. You will

have a better understanding of boys and the things they go through at different phases of life. It will help you both to gain a better insight into people and human behaviour in general. Perhaps it will help you to respect those of the opposite sex as you grow, for you will have a much better understanding of them than most young people.

You are only small at this point and the advice and information I have given you may be hard to digest but what I have explained above is the normal pattern of life.

Welcome to the future.

6

MUMMY – AGED 6

There is an old saying that there is no point in locking the stable door once the horse has bolted. That saying was true for me.

The only person who still struggled to maintain some sort of relationship with me was my father, but his shift work increasingly switched to daytime hours and I felt more and more isolated from my family. I sorely missed his presence as my sisters and mother seemed to have very little communication with me apart from telling me off.

At this point of my life, I was taking myself to and from school every day. Mum stopped walking with me and it used to hurt to see other parents happily escorting their excited children to school every morning. I used to latch on to some mothers and their children for I felt ashamed that I was the only one on my own. I would pretend to myself that whoever I walked with was my family.

I went through phases when I lived for playtime with other children, the half-hour daily recess after lunch and the few free hours I occasionally got after school. I developed a very real and desperate need for company and attention.

My sisters, who were so much older than me, had their own social life. My mother didn't get home from work until 6 p.m. and, once at home, spent her time cooking and chatting to the twins. At times, I was ignored to the point where I didn't even feel that I was present in the household. Sometimes I felt invisible.

Mum and the girls formed a clique of their own and it was impregnable. Even at six years of age, despite Dad's efforts to make me feel loved, I sensed I didn't belong with the Donaldsons. I just wasn't a part of their lives. I felt like a stray cat that had wandered in and was just about tolerated and allowed to take up a bit of space. I hated the feeling of being trapped in a house where there were people but no company. I wanted to be outdoors, playing with my friends.

I would find ways of keeping myself amused. Often I got up to mischief to accomplish this, which inevitably led to trouble. I settled for getting into trouble, for at least it attracted Mum's attention. Sometimes I did things quite innocently that led to trouble, simply because I didn't know any better. If Mum and Dad weren't there to correct me about what was right and wrong, I just got on with it. I'd often play on my own. There were slabs of concrete at each side of our front door. I used to play teacher and pretend the slabs were a blackboard. I'd write on them and then my mother had to clean it off. I'd get punished for that. If I got told off, I would sulk and then I got into trouble for sulking. If I answered back, I got into trouble. If I didn't answer back, they would demand that I explain myself. I would be too scared to and, you guessed it, I got into trouble again. I couldn't do anything right. Often, I was punished many hours or days after an event. When they discovered something I had done, such as rummage through my sisters' cupboards, I would be told off or grounded.

I remember being in the house on my own one Saturday

morning. I had two piggy banks called Pinky and Perky, in which I had saved coins. Pinky was pink and Perky was blue. In one, there were threepenny pieces. That's old money. There were sixpence pieces in the other. In today's terms they were worth one penny and three pence, respectively.

Those piggies were kept in Mum's china cabinet. On this particular Saturday, I was playing with other children in the street. We heard the ice-cream van and I decided to use some of the piggy money to buy all the children an ice-cream. After we had feasted on our treat, all the children came indoors with me. When my sisters appeared, my little friends were gathered in my Mother's front room. The youngsters tried to hide behind the sofa because they knew they weren't meant to be in the house. They were discovered and marched out into the street like prisoners of war.

I was then beaten by my sisters and any remaining ice-cream was confiscated. I was sent to my bedroom, yet again, for the rest of the day and evening. I thought I had done a good deed by giving the other children ice-cream. Mum and my sisters saw it only as stealing. There was never any discussion about the rights and wrongs of what I had done. There was no reasoning over the fact that it was my savings anyway. It made no sense to me at the time. Over the next few years, I would find myself spending more time being punished in my bedroom than I did playing outdoors. I spent a lot of time curled up in my room, wishing I could run away or hoping I would die.

I have many memories of being sent to my room without supper. I would sit there and stew in my anger, while smelling the scent of a hot meal on the table downstairs. I would also feel hurt to have to look out of my window and see the other children playing. That would frustrate me as I had a great need to be free. I wanted to be out there instead of locked in a bedroom. Sometimes Mum and the twins' methods of discipline were cruel and unnatural.

For example, I remember coming home from school one day bursting for the loo. Being a child, I was unable to control it and wet my pants on the way home. Because I feared being punished by the twins, I attempted to dry my knickers in front of the fire. I was so young and panic-stricken that it didn't occur to me to rinse them out first. When my sisters walked into the living room, they smelt the urine. I'll never forget that day. One of the twins grabbed my soiled knickers and rubbed them in my face. I struggled and screamed but that only earned me a slap.

In those days, if I wanted a biscuit or food I had to ask. If I helped myself to food, I was called a thief. I was called that on many occasions simply because I foraged for food when I was hungry. My mother had a passion for Vienna wafers, which I confess to adoring myself. When the rest of the household were asleep in the mornings, I would creep out of my bedroom, climb up on a kitchen stool and help myself to the biscuits. I didn't do it to annoy my mother, I did it because I liked the biscuits. I would get punished for a single missing biscuit. As a mother and adult, I find the denial of food to anyone quite disgusting.

When I think of you two darlings today, you both help yourselves freely from the fridge, fruit bowl or biscuit tin. I never classed it as stealing. It's not. It's just my babies nibbling when they are hungry. It's not a crime. I'm sure lots of mothers allow their children to do this within reason, as long as the children nibble healthy food and do not eat junk all day.

I was made to feel that whatever I did or said was wrong, so much so that I became unnaturally unhappy at the age of six. I lost all identity. I felt as if I didn't belong there – or anywhere.

Because of my own childhood, I made very sure that this would never happen to you two. You will always have a sense of belonging, identity and lots of space to develop your own characters.

I developed an uncontrollable need or desire which I couldn't put a name to at the time. I didn't understand what the urge was but there was a need for *something*. I got into a tremendous amount of trouble through chasing this unknown desire or trying to discover what it was that I lacked. I was searching for something but I didn't know what. It affected my schoolwork because my mind was always elsewhere. Then I discovered what I was looking for. *I needed to be loved and I needed to be wanted.* I had had that sense of love and belonging before the age of five, therefore I knew what I was missing although it no longer existed in my life. My father, whom I relied on greatly, had developed a fear of showing too much attention to me. If he was kind to me, it was met with disapproval. He started backing off just to ensure a peaceful life.

I felt I was unwanted and nothing but a burden and trouble to all concerned. The more I lacked security, the more I did whatever I could to get attention from my family. It always ended in tears – mine. I started becoming a problem at school. The other children seemed to irritate me. They all had parents who clearly cared about them and it hurt seeing everyone else belong to someone except for me. I was cheeky to my teachers because it got their attention. Although not favourable, it was attention none the less. It was obvious that something was wrong. I showed all the signs of anxiety at that early age. I wet my bed and chewed my nails, both signs that any mother would pick up on and question instantly.

When I went to bed at night, I'd be warned not to wet the bed. I became paranoid and would tell myself constantly that I mustn't wet the bed. Worrying about it would keep me awake into the early hours. Through tiredness and confusion, I would sometimes end up wetting the bed no matter how hard I tried not to. I would climb out of bed and try to hide my sheets. I knew I would be made to feel ashamed of what I had done. Apart from my father, my family would tell everyone about my bed wetting. They would hold me up to ridicule in front of anyone who would listen. It didn't matter to my mother and sisters that I had to live with this. At school, the other children started calling me 'pee the bed'. I dreaded going to school because of this. Some mornings I would be bathed and on other mornings I would not. Consequently, I would sometimes go to school smelling of urine. The other children refused to sit by me because they said I stank of wee.

I started feeling like an oddball at school. I listened to the other children talking proudly about their mums and dads. I had nothing to contribute. I would think, 'My mother doesn't do that with me.'

I adored Dad and he me, but my mother ruled the roost. I could see how pained he was to know what I was going through but he was powerless to do anything about it. When he stood up for me, it would automatically be thrown in his face that he was showing favouritism and that I was a little devil who had him wrapped around my little finger. It was an unspoken rule with Dad and me, but I preferred him not to defend me and have to suffer for it later. There was no point in both of us being made to feel unhappy.

I started disappearing for hours. I would go out to play and find refuge and happiness anywhere but home. There was a small river nearby called the Burney. On the bank there was a tree with a big rope tied to it with a tyre attached to the end to make a swing. I sat on the tyre and swung back and forth across the river, sometimes for hours. I loved being near water and still do. I found refuge and tranquillity down at the Burney. Maybe you will go there someday and, if global warming hasn't made it evaporate, you may feel your mum's presence there and the peace and happiness I received from the Burney.

I was nearing my seventh birthday but I knew, once again, that there would be no party for me this year. Through some sort of self-preservation, I had at least learned how to find some peace.

7

KARL AND KANDY – ADVICE AGED 6

Karl, you have already developed an interest in girlfriends. For you, it doesn't matter what age they are. You took a keen interest in Maria, the girl who helped Mummy to write her book. Whenever she rang the house, you would never say, 'Maria is on the phone,' you would say, 'Mummy, my girlfriend is on the phone!' I remember how proud you were when she started calling you her boyfriend. You told everyone who would listen that you had a girlfriend. In reality, you will take a shine to girls your own age, not ones who are 31 years older than yourself.

At the age of six, Karl and Kandy, your romantic interests will increase. This is influenced by how you saw Mummy and Daddy behave as a couple and things you will see on television. You will notice boys and girls holding hands and showing affection to each other. At the age of six, you will want to copy that part of adulthood. It is all very innocent because at this age you will probably only want the display of it. It will be many years from now before you will want to carry out the actual functions of a relationship. All that information and advice comes later, at the appropriate time.

Karl, you seem already to have developed a respect for the more delicate creatures in life, girls. I'm very pleased, for this is very important. You must always respect other people and must understand that you can't be as rough with some people as you are with others. You already seem to know that you can't play boxing games with girls, as they tend to be more fragile than boys. By your own choice, you have noticed the difference and responded accordingly.

As I write this, you have just celebrated your fifth birthday. You have already become fussy about your appearance. You want to have a shower every day and keep insisting to Mummy that you want to use aftershave. Oddly enough, you have developed an expensive taste. Your favourite scent is by Calvin Klein. You had better work hard because I have a feeling you will need a great deal of money to keep yourself in the style you have already acquired a taste for.

When you went to visit Auntie Iris, you commented that her sons used Calvin Klein as well. I had to remind you that they were much older than yourself. You simply shrugged your shoulders and replied that you just wanted to smell nice. I had to laugh.

You admired Auntie Iris's sophisticated taste for the fine things in life. I remember her promising to give you the best education and all the love a person could offer. You admired and loved her dearly. I imagine this relationship will continue. I knew by watching you two together that she was determined to do these things. It was a great relief to Mummy.

You were also manic about gelling your hair. I'm not surprised. Mummy was always very fussy as well. Then I remember you saying that you wanted to use the aftershave and stating that you were a man. In reality, I believe that what happened was that you took it upon yourself to be the man in the family because you knew Mummy wasn't well. You seemed to decide to take on certain responsibilities.

These senses are likely to increase with each year. I'm guessing they will be even stronger now at the age of six. You have always been protective about Kandy and it is likely you will become even more so as the years roll on.

Kandy, I couldn't keep you out of my make-up or clothes. You always wanted to improve your appearance and fuss over pretty things to wear. You were very much a girl at the age of four and this behaviour is likely to continue as you reach five and six. You may develop the desire to play motherly roles and make all your dolls your own children. You have already shown a very strong bond with your brother. You have always told him you love him and made sure he told you the same. You are likely to develop a strong sense of responsibility in a family sense. You may always want to take on the role of the lady in the house.

This change that you both may experience will coincide with a sense of responsibility that develops at school. You will be in year two and that is when you get down to real work. During your first year at school, you would have played and socialised a great deal during school hours.

The second year involves learning to read, write, do maths and learn about history, music and many other things. There will be less play and more studying. It is a responsibility coupled with discipline. However, it is such a slow process that you will easily adjust after the shock of less play and more work wears off.

At the age of six it is likely that you will want to be more independent and get on with certain things yourself. You will want to choose your own clothes for the day, comb your own hair, play outside without an adult hanging around. This is all part of natural development.

I have arranged for you to start receiving an allowance at this time. You will receive 50 pence a week spending money. Around this time you will learn at school about the face value of money and spending. You will make your own choice on how to spend your allowance. This will help you to learn about handling money, which should coincide with this part of your education at school.

You will now take on chores in the house to coincide with your sense of independence and responsibility. You are likely to be asked to set the table at meal times and to make your bed every single morning. These chores are *not* in exchange for your allowance. They are simply to feed some senses you are developing.

You may start experiencing the odd bad dream at this point. This is natural and you mustn't let it frighten you. Reality will now be combining with your active imagination and scenarios will develop in your dreams. Most dreams are good, by the way.

Perhaps you will see a film where a man gets chased through a forest by a bear. You may fall asleep that night and dream that you are being chased through the streets by wild animals. This is because things you see during your waking hours can mingle with your imagination and develop into a dream. I emphasise again, most dreams will be good.

I'm sure, and I pray, that there will always be someone around to give you comfort if you experience the odd bad dream. I have made arrangements for your future with loving people. Don't be afraid to ask for comfort. Bad dreams happen even to grown-ups because the subconscious mind can play funny tricks on us when we are asleep. Never be frightened as this happens to everyone and it is very natural throughout life.

Karl, you will probably want to walk to school by yourself every morning, unlike girls who tend to want to make a social display and show off an adult. Boys tend to feel embarrassed by an adult's presence at this age, whereas girls seem to like hanging around grown-ups.

In my day, it was safe for children to walk to school by themselves. Sadly, in today's society, it is not so safe. An adult will watch you safely to school but respect your wishes should you feel the need to appear as if you got on with it yourself. There will always be someone a few paces behind, keeping an eye on you.

Should you feel the need, at this age, to want to be in the company of an adult and enjoy a good chat on the way to school, that is perfectly fine as well. For boys, the sense of independence tends to be strong around this age, but it may happen next year instead. Kandy may surprise everyone and want to be the independent one instead. Who knows? This is only an insight into what happens to most people. You don't have to live by this pattern. Just be yourselves. This information is only to help you to understand what these feelings are when they do pop up. They won't necessarily happen at the exact times I suggest or even in the ways I suggest.

If you have a problem of any description, talk to Daddy,

your guardian, teacher, a friend's parent, anyone who will lend you an ear but do not, as Mummy did, disrupt classes at school. It is vital that you learn as much as you can.

Karl, you have already surprised your teacher, who sent a glowing report home last year about your incredible learning abilities and talent. I ask both of you, please, for Mummy, do not waste your abilities. Your future depends on you. Your life will only be as good as its foundations. Please cherish and nurture your talents. Do it for yourself. Do it for each other. Do it for Mummy. Your whole future depends on all your todays. Just do your best. You *will not*, and *mustn't expect* to be, the best at everything. Just give everything your best effort.

There is so much fun to be had at the age of six. You will have more friends and socialise so much more. You will stay overnight at friends' houses and they may stay overnight at yours. You will start attending an endless round of birthday parties. There will be school parties and school fêtes. You will get involved in school plays and sing in groups and put on shows. It is just a small taste of all the fun that the future brings.

Happy travels through the age of six!

8

MUMMY – AGED 7

It is said that childhood is the most important part of life – the special years when a child is brought up. In my case, I was dragged up.

My seventh birthday was a non-event. There was no party and I was given the same things I had received the year before – colouring books and crayons. I noticed at this point that a lot of thought went into everyone else's birthday except mine. It was as if I didn't really exist. At this stage of my young life no one in my family enquired as to how I was getting on or what I did at school. There was little communication with, and no interest in, me whatsoever. At times, Mum and the twins even stopped questioning me about the things that I did wrong. It was useless trying to attract their attention. I became a bit of a loner and a hermit within my family. I didn't even bother much about my friends. I went through a phase of wanting to be on my own.

I developed an undisguised dislike towards my sisters. I was also petrified of them. Cinderella and her horrid sisters was one childhood story I could clearly relate to. I just longed for a happy ending like in the fairy tale. It was awful – the feeling of being shut out – the feeling of no purpose in my little life. Why did Mum and the twins dislike me so much? I didn't ask to be there. Why couldn't I be treated like other little girls who are part of a family? Why didn't they praise me for the things I did that were right? Why didn't I matter to them? It wasn't a crime wanting to be loved and wanting to give love. I only wanted them to love and care about me. Why didn't it matter to the twins and Mum whether I loved them at all? I remember the lonely nights in my bed, worrying that I was living a pattern that would continue for the rest of my life. The thought horrified me.

The twins and Mum developed a new game to torment me. They took great joy in belittling me in front of anyone who would listen. I used to dread aunts and uncles visiting because I didn't know what my sisters and others would say about me. I hated the feeling of always being the centre of their cruel conversation. I hated being a laughing stock. I wondered if they had any idea how their behaviour would affect me in my future years. If they did, then what on earth were these people made of? I feel very bitter and angry that my early years were filled with shame and torment at their hands. It is a pity that the only emotions I felt towards those women were balanced between sheer dislike and fear. I remember needing stitches above my left eyebrow due to a beating I received from one of the twins when my parents were out.

One of the girls struck me because I was chattering on about something. The sting of the slap made me cry. She demanded I shut up and hit me again. The more she hit me, the more I cried. Finally, she threw me against the bathroom sink and I cracked my forehead open on the enamel basin. When I started bleeding, she tried to clear up the mess so that Dad wouldn't question her. She told me I had to say I had fallen or else she would make my life not worth living. I believed her and did as she said.

A couple of months later I was in Mum's bedroom, rooting through a cupboard for my baby doll cot. Suddenly I felt a blow on my head. One of the twins had broken a thick, old-fashioned gramophone record over my head. I looked at the twins and my hatred for them engulfed me – and my fear. There was no one I could turn to. Anyway, who would believe me as my sisters and mother had made out that I deserved everything I got?

Then, one day, I overheard something that would rule my following years. It was the catalyst that was responsible for me becoming a very deep thinker. The twins and my mother had been gossiping. I heard one of them say, 'Anne is just like Isobelle Anderson – a born liar.'

I wondered what Auntie Isobelle had to do with me. Their conversation puzzled me. I went to my schoolteacher and asked her what a liar was. She told me it was a person who made up stories that were untrue. I couldn't believe what my mother and sisters were saying about me. I couldn't understand it. The only thing I was sure of, suddenly, was that I hated them.

I started thinking deeply about Aunt Isobelle. She hadn't visited for a while because Mum had had a quarrel with her. It had been at least a year since I had last seen her. Suddenly, she started coming around again.

It was then that I became more aware of Aunt Isobelle's affection for me. I remember her telling the twins that if they ever laid a hand on me again, they would have her to deal with. This bewildered me. This woman, who was only an aunt, showed more of a caring nature towards me than my own mother. I looked forward to Aunt Isobelle's visits because she gave me a sense of security. I felt safe when she was around. I relished day trips out with her whenever they arose.

Aunt Isobelle was very short. She had a very loving smile on her face when she looked at me. When she smiled at me it was like a beam of light. I felt good all over. When I was around her, I felt like a real person, not the person the Donaldsons would have me believe I was. Deep in the back of my mind, I had a terrible fear that Aunt Isobelle would go away again and I wouldn't see her. The bond between us was far greater than anything I had with my mother.

At this stage I developed an extra sense of awareness and a keen sense of survival. I had to be on my guard when Mum and my sisters tried to humiliate and embarrass me in front of others. I built a protective shield around myself to preserve my own sanity. At this age, my life revolved around Aunt Isobelle's visits.

I never forgot the remark the twins and Mum made about me being a liar like Aunt Isobelle. I shared my secret with a girl named Beth who was five years older than me. I also told her about the affection between my auntie and me. Beth said I looked more like Isobelle than like Mum, Dad or my sisters or brother.

I asked her what she meant. She replied: 'Anne, I don't think those people are your parents.' I was mortified at her suggestion. As much as I disliked them, it would be a most unacceptable blow if something like that were true. I asked her how many years' gap there was between her brothers and sisters. She replied, 'Only a few years, but your brother is old enough to be your dad.'

I was rooted to the ground. I felt like being sick. She said it would certainly explain my feeling of not belonging. It would make sense of the fact that the Donaldsons tolerated me instead of loving me.

I screamed, 'Shut up! Shut up! They are my mum and dad!' I stood up, my legs shaking, but somehow I managed to run off. I ran to the Burney, my river refuge, and stayed there for hours and hours.

The police were called because I stayed at the Burney for so long that I was reported missing. When they found me by the stream, I didn't utter one word of what I had been told. I was punished for the worry I had caused but the punishment they gave me could never compare with what had been planted in my head that day.

I continued my life as normally as I possibly could while carrying the burden of Beth's words in my head. I never gave any indication of my suspicions but I kept my ears and eyes open more than usual. For the first time in my life I started noticing certain things that made me think that what Beth had said might be true.

I called myself Anne Donaldson but my surname at school was different. It was Anderson. It was the first time in my young life that I questioned the difference and noticed it was the same surname as Isobelle's. Also, one of the twins had the same first name as me. Why would anyone give two girls in a family the same name? I kept everything to myself. I started questioning my bond with Aunt Isobelle, which was far greater than it naturally should have been. I stored it in the back of my mind and decided I would find out a bit more. My family never suspected a thing. I hid it well, but, thinking back, they were so distant from me that they wouldn't have noticed if I wore my feelings written across a T-shirt.

There were times when I nearly blurted out my suspicions in temper. I wanted to shout that they were so hateful they couldn't possibly be my family. However, even at such a young age, I knew I had to keep my mouth shut and watch, listen and eavesdrop on conversations that occurred behind closed doors.

As the months passed, I became more wrapped up in myself. I barely spoke to my family and chose to be outdoors as much as possible or shut myself in my room. I didn't want to have an encounter with them and reveal what I suspected. It would only inhibit the possibility of finding out the truth.

My young brain constantly ticked over. I came up with many ideas and theories. Although I didn't want to accept it at that time, Beth had been right in saying if the Donaldsons were not my family, it would explain why they behaved in such a manner. There was no bond of love between Mum and myself although it was clearly there between her and the twins. I was just a little person living in their house. A little person they had once attempted to love but couldn't – not once I had passed the age of being a little doll. I was no longer a toy once I started growing up. It's like people wanting kittens because they are so adorable, without realising that they will grow up to be a responsibility someday. They acted as if I did them wrong by not being a little toy any more.

Mum always sang the twins' praises, tagging them as the sort of daughters most mothers only dream of. I was nobody, just a child who gave them endless problems. In reality, I was a child screaming to be loved.

The year was nearing an end and Christmas was coming. One thing I can honestly say for my family is that they did make a great effort to create a joyous and merry Christmas for everyone under their roof. At Christmas I was always spoiled with toys and other material items, while, in actual fact, a cuddle at any time during the rest of the year was more important to me than all the toys in Toyland. I now realise that showering me with Christmas presents was their way of alleviating their guilt for giving me nothing of themselves.

The year was 1964 and I now dreaded school, home and anything that had to do with being a part of life. I sorely missed the guidance that other children received from their families. I spent a lot of time thinking. I became aware of how much people underestimate young children. I wondered what they would do if they knew the thoughts that swam through my head. I wonder what they would do when I finally discovered that it was they who were the liars. I knew I would prove it one day.

I was deeply unhappy. I would have liked to have spoken to Aunt Isobelle but, for some reason, Mum made sure that I never had any privacy with her. I would lie in bed at night and think of Aunt Isobelle. I wondered where she was, what she was doing and when I would see her next. I wondered if she was thinking about me. I had a deep affection for her and not only because she clearly cared about me and was the only person who wasn't afraid to show it. It was deeper than that. I carried those thoughts into my eighth year.

9

KARL AND KANDY – ADVICE AGED 7

By now you will be developing a keen sense of belonging. You will both have chosen a few young people, likely to be of your own gender, who you consider to be your best friends. It is rare, at this age, to have a best friend of the opposite sex although it does happen and it is very special when it does. You will have started forming an exclusive circle of friends and will want to keep them to yourself rather than share them with other children.

Comparisons will be coming along fast and strong. You will want what other children have and they will want what you have. You will wonder why some other people of your own age are taller than you. You may experience a sense of one-upmanship if someone is smaller than you. There is a saying that the grass always appears to be greener on the other side of the fence, the whole point being that it is not true. It is human nature to want what we don't have and you will be experiencing a lot of these feeling at this age.

Boys, especially, tend to compare themselves physically with other boys, from the size of their feet to the size of their personal bits. This is natural. Everyone grows at different rates and, on average, you all tend to catch up with each other eventually.

Interestingly enough, it is roughly between this age and eleven that your romantic interests will subside. This is because other things take over, such as interest in sport, school activities and socialising. Karl, science may become fascinating to you now as well as other school activities. Boys tend to develop an interest in dinosaurs, how cars really work and subjects of a scientific nature around the age of seven. Girls may suddenly seem rather uninteresting. Having said that, you are likely to become wildly interested in them again nearer to your teen years.

All boys tend to explore their bodies. Touching parts of your own body would have started as far back as infancy. This exploration is all part of natural development. Boys of your age continue to explore. Again this is because of an interest in your own physical changes. You are growing and you will probably wonder if every single part grows as well.

It is also because you will sometimes wonder how you are developing in comparison with other boys. It is natural and not harmful to take this sort of interest in yourself, within reason. There should be no guilt attached to it as it is all part of growing up.

However, you should never explore your personal body in front of other people as it may make them feel embarrassed or uncomfortable. That applies to you as well, Kandy. You shouldn't touch your private parts in front of anyone else as this will make them feel ill at ease. That is regarded as bad manners and these sorts of things are best done in privacy.

Don't ever believe anyone if they say that touching your private areas will make your hands fall off or you will grow hairs on your fingers. These are what are known as 'old wives' tales' and they were once used as threats to stop children from touching their own bodies in public.

It is natural to want to know about your own body but this is always done in private. All children are curious about their physical changes. Again, I emphasise that it is natural.

It is slightly different for a girl. She may notice that grown-up women have breasts. Some little girls stuff socks or paper hankies down their vests and then look in the mirror, imagining what they would look like with breasts. This is natural, Kandy. Girls tend not to explore as many bits of their bodies as boys do. Girls usually just want to experiment with endless make-up, hairstyles and things like that. You may also develop an interest in poetry, singing and music. Girls seem to like this sort of thing around this age and, if you do, I encourage you to pursue it full force. Learn an instrument. Sing. Do it if you want to. It will bring you and others great joy and satisfaction in years to come if you can express yourself through music or poetry.

Around this age, both of you will want to be with your best friends more than anything else. You may feel uncomfortable if your meetings are too organised, such as your friends coming over specially for a picnic or an organised game. You may start feeling that you want your friends to come around but you want to get on with doing your own thing with them. That is because your imagination, creativity and inventiveness should be very active around this age. You and your friends will want to come up with your own ideas and carry them out.

You will have a lot of fun inventing your own activities at this age. You will also experience a lot of trial and error, which, when you look back later, will probably bring a smile to your face. Around this time, you will probably go on school trips and you may develop a keen sense of adventure and want to travel to faraway places. All this happens in time.

About now, you may notice that some children are brighter at certain subjects at school than you are. You may turn out to be brighter at some things than other children. Either way, never feel threatened or envious if another child can draw or write better. Everyone develops at a different rate and you will all catch up with each other eventually. If another child doesn't do as well as you, you must never harass them, make fun of them or call them dumb or stupid. Don't ever believe it if someone says that of you. Just remember, everyone develops at a different rate but it all balances out in time.

By now, you will have realised how different your life is to the way Mummy's was at your age. I endeavoured to provide for you all the things that I didn't have – the really important things, like love, stability, confidence in yourself and recognition and nurturing of your natural gifts and qualities. That is why the treasure chest is so important. You have a chance in life and I pray you are never held back like Mummy was. The treasure chest may give you all you need to believe in yourself and make your own dreams come true.

You were given, and will always be given, a lot of love throughout your lives. Remember to carry it with you for ever and return it to the world by doing your best and respecting other people's feelings. You never know what life is really like for them at home. Maybe they are not as lucky as you are.

My love is with you always. Have a great time adventuring through the age of seven.

10

MUMMY – AGED 8

Four very important things happened in my eighth year. I developed some sort of relationship with my mother, I discovered a love of horses and I learned about loyal trust and about responsibility.

As a person, I hadn't changed much. I was still getting into the odd scrape over things I did and didn't do. The major change in my household came in the form of chores. I was appointed certain duties and responsibilities, such as keeping my room tidy and washing the dishes after meals. I didn't mind washing up but I had a peculiar aversion to drying dishes and cutlery. Mum showed me how to carry out this task and someone was always on hand to help out because it was unreasonable to expect an eight-year-old to do the whole family's dishes by herself.

Because of the washing-up routine, Mum and I found ourselves spending up to twenty minutes a day in each other's company without any interruptions. I realised that Mum treated me differently when the twins were not around. As soon as they appeared, she became another person.

I began to enjoy our washing-up sessions. It was the first time in ages that Mum and I had laughed together. I sensed that she felt she was betraying the twins if they caught us having fun. For the first time in years, Mum and I were learning a little bit about each other. This intrigued me.

Miraculously, things were going well at school too and, although I still had a need to attract attention, I managed not to interrupt lessons and interfere with the educational progress of other students. Glass-eyed Brian Bunter and I were still friends and we started going to Saturday-morning film matinees every fortnight at the Gaumont Cinema. We'd watch Flash Gordon and share popcorn and drinks. Mum gave me enough money for the film ticket, sweets, drinks and bus fare.

Of course, trouble still followed me about. There was a long, fluorescent light tube under the ticket counter. I wondered where the light was coming from and Brian pointed it out. I had my gloves on but I had to make a closer inspection of this fascinating light. I started twisting and fiddling with the glass tube that reflected such a brilliant blue light. Unfortunately, it came loose and crashed to the floor. I didn't mean to break it; it simply slipped out of its brackets. I was distressed over what I had done as I had made a concerted effort not to get into any trouble lately. I felt very sorry and was worried that my parents would stop my cinema excursions but I was lucky as the cinema manager understood it was an accident, much to my relief.

As a routine, after the matinee Brian would go his way and I would go mine. One afternoon, during my journey home, I heard two people on a bus talking about stables near Grassy Beach, a place I knew.

I was fascinated by their conversation and decided to have a look at the stables one day after school. I went on my own. It was about four miles from my home and I walked the whole way. I found the yard. It was called Mr Conky's Stables. As I neared the gates, my heart raced with excitement. I could smell the horses, the manure, the grass, the feed – all very horsey smells and, to my nose, all so attractive.

I found myself walking down a muddy gangway with rows of stables on each side. Some of the stalls were vacant and some had horses or ponies inside. Scruffy old cats, dogs and chickens wandered freely around. I could feel my pulse racing faster and faster. Even the cats, with their matted fur, sent thrills through me. I had found my paradise on earth.

There was one horse, in particular, to which I was attached. His name was Goldie. He was white with golden-brown patches and belonged to a very lucky girl the same age as me. I fussed him and rubbed his large nose. Curiosity got the better of him and I burst into giggles as he pushed his nose into my face and hair. I had never been so close to a real horse. He seemed so large and powerful. He wiggled his big lips against my neck, snorting with approval, and my heart melted. I stroked the soft area on his nose and we instantly became firm friends.

I must have been there for half an hour before a gentleman enquired who I was and what I was doing on the property. I told him my name and explained that I had walked four miles to the stables to look at the horses. He said that if I wanted to go riding, I needed to wear the proper kit: a safety hat, boots, jodhpurs and so on. I explained that I didn't have any such items and I doubted if my parents would buy them for me.

At that point I wasn't bothered about riding but was desperate to visit the horses again. I didn't tell my parents anything. The stables could become another haven I could go to when things were unsettled at home. It could be my secret place that no one knew about.

During the weeks that followed, I spent most of my free time at the stables. I learned how to groom horses and muck out the stables. I learned never to stand behind a horse as its kick could kill. I knew that I would never own my own riding kit and take classes but it didn't discourage me from wanting to be near the horses. One day the riding class went on a 22-mile trek and I walked and ran alongside the horses for the entire way. People wanted to give me a ride but they couldn't as I didn't have any safety gear. It didn't bother me at all.

At my young age, I earned the respect of everyone at the stables. I proved my dedication to the horses when I followed them on foot on that gruelling trek. I felt as free as the birds in the sky but I was completely shattered after the trek and broke away when the riders neared the road that would take me home.

I had been gone the entire day and knew I would be in deep trouble but I wasn't worried at all. No punishment could ruin my magnificent day. As I headed home, I conjured up images of how angry my parents might be. I had left the house at 8 a.m. and was returning home at 8 p.m.

Although I say I wasn't worried about the trouble I would get into, I was just a little scared. It was simply that I felt any punishment was worth it. As I neared the front door, I could see everyone pacing in the front room. The lights were on and the curtains were open. I turned the door handle very quietly. God knows what I was hoping to achieve by this. As I walked in, everyone began to hurl questions at me all at once. I said I had been with horses all day and excitedly told them about the trek. They didn't believe me. I later found out that Mum called the stables afterwards and checked up on my story.

I was beaten for causing them so much worry, told off and sent to bed. The great part was being sent to bed as I was exhausted. I lay in bed thinking of my day. I was worn out. Even my hair seemed to hurt. I felt as if all my limbs were going to drop off. I soon drifted into a very deep sleep.

When I woke the next morning, my whole body ached. The twins said it served me right. I looked at them and thought they would never understand what real joy is. I knew I had found it the day before.

The following Monday at school, I excitedly told all my classmates about the trek. One nasty girl said, 'All you will ever be able to do is run next to the horses. Your parents won't ever let you get on the back of one.' I leapt to my parents' defence and said they planned to buy me a riding outfit. Some children jeered at me. I said, 'You wait and see, I'll come in and show you my new riding hat.'

I didn't go home after school. I ran straight to the stables in my school uniform. I was determined the children at school wouldn't ridicule me. When I got to the stables, I saw a riding hat sitting on a bale of hay. I picked it up and stuck it in my school bag. I thought I would just borrow it and take it back the next day after I had showed it to my classmates.

The hat never made it to school. As I approached my

house, I hid the hat in a bush. Two hours later someone from the stables appeared at my house, saying I had stolen a riding hat.

I remember my mother saying that I had never come into the house with one. My parents questioned me for ages. There must have been a change in me. I had never lied to them before, although I had been accused of it in the past. They must have seen the discomfort the lie was causing me. I admitted I had it but refused to give it to them until the following day. Finally, my mother threatened to call the police if I didn't produce the hat. I never explained to anyone why I took the hat. I simply went to the bush and retrieved it. I told the man from the stable that I was very sorry for the trouble I had caused and I hoped he wouldn't stop me from visiting the horses.

He told me that if I ever did anything like that again, I would be banned from coming near his property. I was so embarrassed and ashamed. They had no idea about my ridicule at school because of my passion for horses. Maybe, if I had explained it, they might have understood my actions. At the end of the day, however, it was stealing, no matter what the reason. I realised there would never be a good enough reason for taking what wasn't mine.

I was so ashamed that I didn't return to the stables for four weeks. Then my love for the horses drew me back. I bumped into Mr Conky, the man who had come to the house to retrieve the hat, and he cast an uncertain glare my way. I told him it would never happen again. He pulled me to one side and told me that he understood why I took the hat. I said, 'What do you mean?'

He said, 'You have been coming here for a long time and

I feel your love for horses is very deep. I know you would genuinely love to ride.'

I looked at him with tear-filled starry eyes. He took my hand and led me to the stables where he saddled up Goldie. He said, 'If there is anyone entitled to a free ride, it's got to be you, Anne.'

He put a little black-velvet riding hat on my head. It fitted like a glove. I felt so proud. He said it was a spare hat that his daughter had grown out of and that I could use it any time I came to the stables. He warned me that I must never get on a horse without it.

I spent the rest of the year mucking out stables and learning to ride. I never even bothered to share this with Mum or the twins. I loved what I had so much that I was scared that if anyone knew about it, the magic might disappear.

Christmas drew near and I was old enough to start going to Mum's annual Christmas party, which was held for the children of staff. I was so excited to be grown-up enough to attend the party. It was something I had always heard about and wanted to do for years. Mum bought me a new outfit for the party, everything from shoes to a new hair ribbon. She bathed me and dressed me like Cinderella going to the ball.

I felt extra-special because Mum beamed with pride when she saw me dressed so beautifully. I realised now that all the extra effort went into my outfit because children are a reflection of their parents. As long as I looked good, she looked good. It was the first time in years that I felt any sort of warmth and approval from Mum. I thought, for once, I was a part of her.

All of Mum's co-workers spoke to me and told Mum

that I was witty and charming. Mum looked at me as if it was the first time she had ever seen me. I started getting her undivided attention because the twins were not around and her workmates found me rather cute. Mum began seeing me in a different light. I remember one of her colleagues saying I had a lovely, cheeky, little face. I'll never forget how Mum beamed at the compliment. Then, when I started to chatter, I remember Mum saying, 'My, that bairn can blether,' which was Scottish dialect for 'That child can talk.'

I started visiting Mum at work and would spend roughly half an hour there before my sisters collected me. We would either go home or stay in the area and meet Mum after she finished work. Having spent 30 glorious minutes revelling in Mum's attention, I dreaded going home for, once we were indoors, the twins came first and I came second-best or not at all. Mum didn't dare show me any favour in front of the twins.

Even as the years wore on and I became a teenager and, later, a married woman, I still got along with Mum much better when we were left on our own. As soon as the twins arrived, the change was as obvious as it was when I was a child.

Whenever I had spare money for the bus fare, I took to visiting Aunt Isobelle on my own. I managed to see her at least twelve times during my eighth year. If I had had my own way, I would have been with her every day.

Aunt Isobelle had two sons by her husband, John Wilson, and she was raising a further six children from his first marriage. She had her hands full but would drop everything when I popped over. It never occurred to me to ring and say I was coming. I would just show up.

I never let my parents know I had visited Isobelle. She rarely came to our house during this period of my life and I missed her sorely. Whenever it was time to say goodbye to Aunt Isobelle, I felt as if I had left a part of me behind. When I visited her, I sensed tension between Aunt Isobelle and her husband. He gave me the feeling that he didn't welcome me into his house, although he tolerated me for some reason. Aunt Isobelle was nothing less than welcoming. She swooned with joy at my visits and her husband looked on disapprovingly. He came across as a very dedicated father to his own children and I genuinely liked him. I would daydream of what it would have been like to be a member of his large family. I would have lots of brothers and sisters who got along and I would have Aunt Isobelle as a mum. But daydreams like that never come true. Well, they never did for me, anyway. In reality, I belonged to the Donaldsons and the jealous twins. That was my lot.

As I neared my ninth year, the twins brought their future husbands to meet Mum and Dad. I have no recollection of any other boys ever being brought home by the twins.

Annie's fiancé was a heavy-set man named Jake. The first time he came to the house, he wore a greyish-green suit, a white shirt with a deep-coloured tie and brogue-type shoes. I thought he was very good-looking and well turned out. He travelled a lot and spent most of his time journeying up and down the country.

Jake had a nickname for Annie. He called her Blue because of her stunning, deep blue eyes. He thought the world of her. As I write this, they are still happily married after 26 years.

When Jake went off on his trips, he would always return with lovely gifts for Blue. He gave her very feminine presents. My parents approved of Jake and it was moving to see how deeply in love he and Annie were.

In the beginning I found Jake to be a warm person but my instincts told me that he had heard things about me – that I was cheeky, mischievous, ill-mannered – all the standard stuff the twins used to tell people.

At the same time the other twin, Sheena, was courting a man named Harry whom she would later marry. Visually, he was the complete opposite of Jake. Harry was small with black curly hair. He didn't seem really devoted to Sheena nor as deeply in love as Jake was with Annie.

I didn't like Harry from the start. He always seemed false, whereas Jake was straightforward and open.

Soon after Jake and Harry came into our lives, the twins announced their plans to marry. The house was abuzz with the excitement of the two upcoming weddings. I got caught up in the romance of it all for, suddenly, everything seemed beautiful. The twins were too busy to harass me and I welcomed the idea that they wouldn't be breathing down my neck any longer. I was nearing my ninth birthday.

11

KARL AND KANDY – ADVICE AGED 8

At this stage of your life, you may feel frustrated because there will be material things that you feel you really must have but can't. Perhaps, Karl, you can't acquire a new cricket bat or you, Kandy, can't have a new sticker album because your guardians refuse to replace certain things that you may have left behind in a park.

This does not give you the right to help yourselves to anything that doesn't belong to you. That is what we call stealing and, by this age, you will know only too well that it is wrong. If you ever take away any item that you haven't paid for in a shop, or that belongs to someone else, regardless of how small or big, you will be branded a thief by others and, once that happens, it will be difficult to regain other people's trust in you. If anything went missing when you happened to be around, people would immediately assume you had taken it and refuse to believe that you haven't. They would start calling you a liar as well as a thief.

As you read about my life at the age of eight, you will see that that was when I stole the riding hat and told lies to try to protect myself. It then became difficult for others to trust me. I hope you will learn by Mummy's mistake, and never need to experience this. No matter how desperate you are for something, never take anything without asking for it or buying it. The combination of being branded a thief and liar is hard to shed.

Perhaps, at this age, the responsibilities of school will start to show. You will have more homework but all you may want to do is play with your friends. This is when you will start learning about priorities. It may seem very boring at the age of eight but, believe me, through the rest of your school years and life you will benefit by learning to get your priorities right. I was less fortunate and didn't have the guidance that I left for you, nor people to raise me who really cared. I refuse to let you grow without those things or to let you miss any opportunity to further your education and talents.

I hope my advice and openness about my life will help you to decide to achieve the things in life that are very important. This starts at an early age. I have faith in you that you will grow into decent, honest adults.

Of course, life is not always so serious. By the time you read this, you will have got into more hiccups and scrapes than I care to think of, just through natural development.

I know what you are like, Karl. You were the sort of child who would try to turn the bathroom into an indoor swimming pool and flood the whole house in the process. By now you know the difference between right and wrong and, hopefully, your experiments won't be as costly as they were in your younger days.

Kandy, you used to cut new shapes in Mummy's painfully expensive hats and get make-up all over the house and my clothes. By now, I hope you realise the importance of taking care of anything you touch, especially if it is not yours.

I believe the adventure in your souls will never subside and that is a good thing. Just don't put yourselves in dangerous situations along the way. The older you get, the sharper your ability will be to carry out your adventures successfully. Have fun doing it.

If you join the Cub Scouts or Girl Guides at this age,you will be able to exercise much of the sense of adventure you were born with. I hope you do this. It would really suit you both and you would have a wonderful time. Cubs and Guides go on adventure trips to camp, hike and learn how to survive outdoors. It is a great lesson in learning how to be friends with the earth.

You may find that you are good at a particular sport, such as tennis, or a game, such as chess, or gifted in playing a musical instrument. If this happens, provisions have been made for you to spend extra time in classes to develop something you are particularly keen on. Have fun. If you can't be careful, I've made sure your guardians can provide you both with a lifetime's supply of sticking plasters! Good luck!

12

MUMMY – AGED 9

My ninth year saw lots of changes in our household. The twins were to marry soon and I would find myself living alone with Mum and Dad. The whole family seemed to talk about little else except weddings. Most of the activities within the household revolved around these events.

I don't remember which twin married first but the weddings were within months of each other. The twins had a joint hen party, when both girls celebrated their final days as single women with their friends and colleagues. I remember it well because I cried to go with them but it was impossible as I was too young.

The girls were brought home from the hen party all dressed up to look like babies. From what I can remember, they had had a smashing evening.

I was more excited about the outfits chosen for me to wear at the wedding services than the actual events. A pink and white one, chosen for Annie and Jake's wedding, was my favourite. It was a two-piece suit with a little white hat and pink ribbon. My gloves, shoes and socks were white. I wasn't a flower girl at their wedding but I soon forgot how upset I was when everyone told me how pretty I looked.

The church service was held in Charleston. I remember that morning so well. The house was chaotic. Flowers were delivered by the dozen and the girls went dashing off to the hairdressers. Annie finally appeared at the top of the stairs looking absolutely gorgeous. The car arrived just in time to take her to the church.

At Sheena's wedding I was a flower girl. I wore a long, lemon-coloured dress with matching gloves and lemon and silver shoes. My hair was set in a curly style for the wedding. I walked out of the church to have photos taken and I stood behind Sheena to hold her long veil. With her high-heeled shoes on, she was taller than Harry. They never seemed as well suited as Annie and Jake. I overheard a relative saying that they thought Sheena was making a mistake in marrying this man. They couldn't have been more right.

However, all I could think of on the steps of the church was that I would soon have Mum, Dad and the house to myself. I was relieved that both twins had started their new lives and was looking forward to taking over the twins' bedroom, which was much larger than my own. My brother John, who was twenty years older than me and had been married before I could remember, was long gone.

I continued going to the stables as often as I could. Mr Conky's daughter Caroline (whose hat I had taken) gave me an old pair of jodhpurs and riding boots two sizes too big but I loved my hand-me-downs. I always brought two pairs of socks with me to give the boots a better fit and left the gear at the stables as it was only on loan and not my property. I would return to find everything clean and ready for use.

I became a good rider, thanks to Mr Conky and Caroline. I never told my parents how kind the Conkys had been to me. I didn't want them to know I was riding at the stables for fear that they might ban me from the horses as a form of punishment someday. I also resented the fact that, although they could afford to, they never offered to pay for riding lessons.

Some things only make sense years after the event because you are then able to call on the wisdom of the intervening time and see things for what they really are. It upset me deeply when I saw other parents proudly watching their offspring show off their skills on the back of a horse. I used to watch the children being praised by their parents as they dismounted. Mr Conky always knew what was going through my mind. He once told me that my parents didn't know what they were missing. I loved being there and didn't want anything to jeopardise it. When Mr Conky said those words, I sat down on a bale of hay and wondered why my parents showed so little interest in me. It was hurtful. Little did I know at the time that all my questions were soon to be answered. As I walked home I felt desolate, empty and blank. It seemed that wherever I found happiness, it was always in someone else's home. When I left the Conky fold, I always felt depressed. Most people are pleased to go home. I dreaded it.

I stopped talking about my love for horses at school. I hadn't mentioned it since the riding hat incident. My classmates never saw the hat I promised to produce so I thought it was pointless to tell them I was riding. I was still best friends with old glass-eye Brian Bunter. He made the other children stop picking on me by telling them he would knock the socks off them if they tried to make fun of me or my parents again.

I was very busy with the horses and visiting Aunt Isobelle so I rarely had a chance to get to the cinema with

Brian any more. He came with me to the stables only once but still managed to get into trouble. He found a bird's nest as soon as we were on the stable property. Not realising that nests should remain undisturbed, he removed the eggs to have a closer look. When he was told to put the eggs back, he dropped one in his haste and broke it. Brian was immediately told to leave the property by the bird-loving owners. He didn't even have a chance to see the stables, let alone stroke a horse or see me ride. His visit lasted all of three minutes. I was so angry with him. I had wanted him to marvel at my riding ability and see me in my smart riding clothes.

I didn't stay angry with him for long, though, because daft glass-eye Brian was my only real friend at this time who was of my own age. In retrospect, I now realise that all my other friends were much older.

It was around this time that my brother John had difficulties in his marriage and returned home for a short period with his two children. I loved the idea of having smaller children in the house. I became very attached to both of them. However, John soon met another woman and moved in with her, so she raised his children.

I found myself alone with Mum and Dad once again. I felt it was very important to have my parents to myself. There was a lot of good in me as a child and I welcomed the idea of displaying it without having to worry about interference from anyone else. I felt I could make up for all the lost years. I was very devoted to my father and, naturally, loved my mother dearly and I was eager for a chance to show it. My plans were very short-lived.

About this time, a married couple came into my parents'

lives. I shall call him Steve and her Susan. They often visited our home. Steve would make strange remarks to me which made me feel uncomfortable. He never made these remarks when there was anyone else around. He would ask what colour underwear I was wearing and personal things like that. Being a child, I would innocently answer 'white ones', not realising what his line of questioning was leading to. All I knew was that it made me feel frightened of him.

I was relieved when Susan and Steve went to live in a small flat in Dundee. Now, at least, they didn't pop over as often as they had before their move. I felt relieved that Steve was no longer around the house on a regular basis.

My dream came true. Mum, Dad and I had a couple of uninterrupted months together and they were very good months indeed. We spent many cosy evenings at home. Mum was an excellent cook and I would watch her while she prepared meals. I loved helping her to bake a beef pie. She would put a very small glass under the centre of the pastry to help it to rise in the oven. She shared her cookery secrets with me and sometimes allowed me to assist her. I was truly grateful for that time we had together.

For the first time since I was preschool age, life was once again enjoyable for me. During my ninth year, my feelings moved from low to highly optimistic. My happiness became consistent. I was in my element.

Then Mum suddenly suggested that we should find a smaller house. As the months wore on, she stunned me by choosing a flat very near to Susan and Steve. I was absolutely horrified to learn that we were about to become their neighbours. I dreaded the move. I kept trying to discourage my parents by saying that I didn't want to change schools and I would miss our old house. As a child I found it difficult to explain why Steve scared me. I didn't know why myself. Instinctively, though, I knew something wasn't right.

Mum and Dad started packing. All of a sudden, I felt like a condemned person. I couldn't understand the terrible fear within me. Just when I felt so very safe in the big house with Mum and Dad, my life was to be turned upside down. Little did I know that the instinctive fear that dwelled within me was well founded because Steve would soon ruin my life for ever. I had just turned ten years old.

13

KARL AND KANDY – ADVICE AGED 9

At this age, you may be involved in certain things, like sports days at schools and other activities, that parents attend. It is important to children that their parents are present on these occasions. In your circumstances, however, this may not be possible, for obvious reasons. Daddy, who was not very healthy when I wrote this, might be too tired or unwell to become actively involved in some school activities. Please do not feel offended or upset in any way. My love is with you and that you can be sure of. Your circumstances are different to those of most other children and you know it. Wherever you are and whatever you do, my heart and spirit will always be with you. I promise you that you are never really alone.

This is also an age where a child's behaviour changes radically. You two may become slightly rebellious or even eccentric. You may start becoming aware of injustice in society and you may regard it as shocking. For instance, if a male student is not allowed to attend school because he decides to grow his hair and wear it tied back, you may consider this radically unfair.

You may dwell on such matters throughout the day and this can prey on your mind and make you sulky and withdrawn. You may want to change the entire school system and make some sort of stand or statement. Desires like these creep in as early as the age of nine or they may come later in life but strong feelings towards society are sure to occur during the next few years.

You may start to feel that you want, or need, more freedom than you are permitted at your age. That is because you are developing strong viewpoints and want to be seen and heard. You may feel that you are being held back because of your lack of freedom. All this is natural and can occur anywhere from now through the next couple of years. Bear with it. You can make all the points you want to in life all in good time. If anyone ever tries to hold you back from doing anything, just hold on hard to your dreams until you are old enough to carry on with your own life independently. You are still young and need guidance and safeguarding. This may seem restrictive now but it is something you will understand when you get older.

It is around this age that most children start thinking about life and wondering how they evolved. They are curious as to the finer details about their parents' and relatives' lives. You will learn in school about the evolution of humans. Through the treasure chest, you will learn about your own roots.

You may start feeling that you are different from other children or comparing your neighbourhood to theirs. This is all part of wanting more and more out of life. It is natural to experience these feelings. As you grow, you will realise the only way to have what you want is to work towards providing it for yourself.

You will become more aware of physically attractive people. You may find that some boys and girls are very popular simply because of this. Believe me, it doesn't mean they have the best qualities, although many will have good qualities as well as good looks. Children who are not good-looking are just the same inside as anyone else. They have feelings and needs like any other child. Respect that.

Karl, by this age you will probably have had discussions with other boys about the personal parts of girls and kissing. You must never feel ashamed about discussing matters like this as it is a phase all human beings go through during their development years.

Kandy, you are likely to have giggled with your girlfriends about boys whom you like. You may even have discussed kissing games.

Either way, by this age most children start to learn in school about human bodily functions, sexual anatomy and reproduction. The most important thing I wish to stress is that while having these discussions, albeit with a boy, girl, teacher or guardian, matters of this nature should be spoken about with respect. I know that when children are together they have their own language and ideas and that they also use slang words for the personal parts of bodies. Avoid using silly terms for these parts or for the act of reproduction because that is just as common as using bad language.

When these subjects are discussed, I would prefer you to have the integrity to regard them with respect and intelligence. Never become involved in discussions that insult the act of reproduction or anything to do with the physical or sexual side of people's natures.

I know from my own past experience, when I have used bad language, that it is most frowned upon. It fails to gain people's respect. It is a display of a lack of intelligence and vocabulary. I believe you two will be much brighter than that. All of this will make a lot of sense in the very near future, I promise. I am sorry if some things sound confusing. I don't know what you can absorb at your age and I am only guessing that you are ready for these things.

Mind you, life progresses so quickly these days that you may read my advice and sigh as you think, 'Poor old-fashioned Mummy, I know about all these things already!'

14

MUMMY – AGED 10

The move to the flat was on. Mum had a huge clear-out and a removal truck arrived to carry away what remained. We couldn't take everything as we were moving to smaller premises. I didn't miss anything that was left behind because I was too busy dreading the prospect of having Steve as my neighbour. I took one final look at the house I grew up in – the house in which I had spent the last two months of my life recapturing some sort of contentment – and knew I would miss my newfound happiness. After so many wishful years, I had finally achieved the feeling that I really belonged there, only to have it torn away like a rug pulled from under my feet. We drove to the place that was to be our new home and, although I was familiar with a couple of them, the broad streets suddenly looked grey and dark. During the journey I began wishing that Annie and Jake were to be our neighbours instead. The prospect of having Steve so close left me feeling like a cornered animal with nowhere to run. Fear and dread overcame me.

It was eating away at me. I wished I could explain it to my mother. I wished I had been gifted with the ability to express my feelings at that time. I also knew that I would lose the bond I was forming with my mother once Susan was back on the scene. But that didn't bother me half as much as my thoughts about Steve.

The van pulled up on the main high road which was a

very busy thoroughfare leading into town. I stared blankly at the rows of little shops. We arrived at the flat and I saw it for the very first time. As I walked up the stairs, the first door I encountered was Sheena and Harry's. To the left was a landing which led to our flat. As Mum proudly opened the front door, I was instantly taken aback by the size of the rooms. Everything seemed so small.

The sitting room and kitchen were open-plan. There was a very small sink in front of the window and, in the corner, a cooker. There was a gas fire and a further door which led to a bedroom. I stood there, wondering where my bedroom was. Mum noticed the quizzical look on my face and announced that, in fact, I didn't have a bedroom. My bed was to be the sofa in the front room.

I realised at that moment that she had never included me in her thoughts. Suddenly, it all became so clear. Mum would do, and settle for, anything just to be near one of her precious friends. My feeling of belonging over the past couple of months had been quite without foundation. Mum clearly planned to make my next few years as uncomfortable as possible to ensure that I would move out as soon as I was legally able to do so at the age of fifteen. I instantly planned to do just that. I had been right my whole life. I didn't belong.

Everything fell into place. Sheena was pregnant with her first child and Mum had moved near to her at break-neck speed so that she could care for her through the whole event. I resented the fact that everything was happening at my expense. I had had to leave the school I had spent the last five years in. I was going to have to start all over again.

It didn't take long to unpack our boxes and settle in. I

knew this would be a major turning point in my life. I had an uncanny feeling it wouldn't be for the best.

In the weeks that followed, I became totally isolated. I was much too far from the stables to continue riding on a regular basis. It broke my heart to lose the horses and the Conky family whom I had grown to adore. I started at a new school called Glebelands. I remember approaching the school gates on my first day. It had the overall look of a large prison. The saving grace was my teacher, Miss Moyer, who had a warm, friendly face and a personality to match. We were introduced and she took me to my class. I felt embarrassed when I entered as a roomful of curious eyes followed my every move. I didn't fuse with anyone that day. Moving had left me in a deep rut. I longed for someone close to talk to, not a bunch of strangers.

The feeling of insecurity proved far too great a burden for a child of ten to carry. I wanted to run away. I was deeply unhappy and hated my life. I began to hate myself. I had no spirit and my bubbly personality started to dwindle. It was as if the Donaldsons had finally broken me. However, I had nowhere to go and no one to turn to. Both my havens, the stream and the stables, were gone. I was often a million miles away in my thoughts. I had no concentration to speak of during school lessons; I was too busy wondering about what had gone wrong in my life.

The other pupils in my class sniggered at the shoes I wore. They were a man's type of brogue which looked like enormous boats on my tiny feet. They were originally brown but Mum had dyed them black. I could feel the hairs on the back of my neck bristle. Anger rose within me and I silently promised myself that I wouldn't stand for any form of ridicule. I had been through enough in my life and I wasn't prepared to take any more. I knew straight away that I wouldn't settle down in this school. I was certain I would encounter problems. Often, I returned home from school having no recollection whatsoever of what had been taught that day. All I could think about was Aunt Isobelle, the Conkys, Goldie and the stables. I didn't have a clue how to go anywhere. The bus routes were new to me and I would have to learn how to use them. I had even lost the Burney – no more tyres to swing on and no more water passing below my feet. The Burney was definitely too far to visit.

As the weeks wore on, I made every effort to fit in with my new environment. It was hopeless. When we left Douglas, a huge part of me was left behind. Eventually, I became friendly with a girl at school called Lorraine. Her nickname was Lala because she was tiny and the baby of her family. She had an older sister called Jackie who was six years her senior.

I told Lala about the stables and my passion for horses. She laughed and said she was frightened of horses. She asked if I would like to come back to her house for tea after school, with her mother's permission. When we got there we went straight to the kitchen which smelled of good home cooking. There was a lovely, homey atmosphere in the flat. Lala removed her school coat and rucksack which she dropped on the floor next to her shoes. I cringed in horror at the thought of doing something like that in my home. Mum would have gone mad.

Lala showed me her bedroom, which was a horror story in itself. There were toys, books, crayons, clothes, you name it, all over the place. It was clear that Lala was spoiled and very much loved. For the first time in my life, I was overwhelmed with envy. I looked at all the items she had taped to her wall, most of which were her school paintings, of which she was very proud. I had nothing to show for the years I had spent at school. Nothing I did seemed important enough for my parents to keep, and I could never display my work so proudly.

When Lala and I had settled down in her bedroom, she told me all about her dolls and how each one came to be hers. Some were Christmas gifts from years gone past. Others had been given as presents at the many birthday parties that had been held in her honour. She asked me about my room and toys. I remember sitting there telling her a pack of lies. I led her to believe I had just as much as she did. She said that she hoped to come to tea at my house and then we could play with all my toys. I felt sick, but I decided I would deal with the problem if and when it arose. I was surprised at the dishonest thoughts that shot through my mind and the number of fibs that fell easily from my lips. I knew I was creating the lies because I felt left out.

As I was deep in thought, Lala's mother called us for tea. We sat round the table and I met her big sister Jackie, who had carrot-red hair. It was obvious that she was just as fond of Lala as her mother. Again, pangs of envy overwhelmed me. I wanted to adopt Lala's family and make her home a haven. I wanted it to be another happy place for me, just as the stables had been. I decided I would never tell Mum about Lala. I would keep her to myself and Lala would always be there when I needed her.

Everyone sat around the table laughing and joking.

Lala's mother was really interested in what Lala had been up to at school that day. Then she started asking me questions about my family. She wanted to know where I had lived before and where I had moved to. I started telling them about the stables and got so carried away with my memories that they must have thought I had been wound up by means of a key in my back.

Finally, the time came to make my way home. Darkness was falling quickly. Lala's sister and mother escorted me to the top of the hill. Once I left them, I ran as fast as my little legs could carry me. It was pitch-dark and the streets were dimly lit by the light from gas lanterns. As I ran down a cobbled road, I could feel my heart beating faster and faster. I didn't like the dark and it seemed even more scary as I approached my road which was engulfed in blackness.

I made my way to the flat and climbed the stairs as fast as I could. Both my parents were watching television. As I entered the room, Mum asked where I had been. I casually replied that I had joined a friend for a game of volleyball. It was already time for my wash and bed. I climbed into my pyjamas and settled on the sofa. I lay there thinking of Lala's bedroom. I looked around our front room, thinking about all the things Lala had in comparison to me. I had so very little, both materially and emotionally. I wondered if my parents realised what they were doing to me. How could they be so cruel? The twins always had their own bedroom. Why didn't it matter to my parents whether I had one at all? I had often heard it said that blood is thicker than water and that thought played around in my head. I wondered once again if they really were my parents.

I found myself comparing Lala's mother to mine. I suddenly had an urge to find out whether the Donaldsons were my parents or not. I was determined that nothing would stop me. It suddenly occurred to me that Aunt Isobelle would know the answer. Another thought entered my mind. If Mrs Donaldson turned out not to be my mother, then who was my father? At that moment I knew in my heart that I had spent my life with a family that really wasn't mine.

I remembered that, in Douglas, my mother had kept a black handbag in her wardrobe. I had seen her put what appeared to be important papers in the black bag on numerous occasions. I decided to make it my business to find this handbag. I knew I would have a couple of hours alone in the flat the following day. I planned to spend that time searching for the handbag.

The next morning was Saturday and Mum and Dad left for work. Dad wouldn't be back until noon and Mum was due at 6 p.m. I started my hunt in their bedroom. Within ten minutes I found the black handbag at the bottom of their wardrobe. It was packed with photos and I looked through them all. There were lots of papers as well. There were insurance policies, a marriage certificate, an old rent book and, finally, birth certificates. I wasn't interested in anything but my birth certificate. I wanted to see for myself if the Donaldsons were my parents. At last I found it. The worn old paper read Anne Anderson. Sex – female. Born – 14 August 1957 at 11.25 p.m. at Merryfield Hospital, Dundee. Mother – Isobelle Anderson. Father – unknown. Aunt Isobelle *was* my mother.

I knew then that no one would be able to stop me from finding out why I had been left with the Donaldsons.

Everyone had lied to me, including Isobelle. I knew then why, when Isobelle caressed me, her warmth was so overwhelming. Her touch always went straight through me. I realised why, when I used to leave her I always felt as if a bit of me was left behind. It explained her kindness towards me and the light in her eyes when we were together. Everything suddenly made sense. I stood frozen to the spot with the piece of paper in my hand.

This was something else that I didn't really know how to deal with. It explained a lot of things. How was I going to deal with all those grown-ups who had lied to me about my real parents?

Knowing that Isobelle was actually my mother led to a bigger question. Who was my father? Did he know I existed? What had happened between Isobelle and him? Why was I raised by the Donaldsons when Isobelle was raising six children that weren't hers? Why did she choose to keep the two boys that were hers but not me? It also confirmed, for certain, something I had always known. I didn't belong anywhere. It also explained why Mr Donaldson, who I wrongly thought was my father, always sang me a song called 'I'm Nobody's Child'. The picture was so clear.

I didn't know what to do. I wondered whether to reveal what I knew or keep it to myself and try to learn a bit more. My fear of my neighbour Steve, the dreadful move and discovering Aunt Isobelle was really my mother brought on a raging battle in my head. I felt as if I was going to crack up. I knew it would be difficult for me to continue looking on the Donaldsons as my parents and pretend that I didn't know otherwise.

What had I done to deserve all this? I didn't ask to be

brought into the world. I felt that I was a living mistake that should have never happened. I was faced with problems that belong to adults. Surely these things were never meant to happen to children. I remember sitting there unable to pull myself together. I also had to deal with Aunt Isobelle. Should I tell her? Should I keep my silence? What, oh what, should I do?

I started to feel great resentment, bordering on hate, towards all those concerned. I made up my mind that, on my return to school the following Monday, I would ask my teacher what a child is called who is born without a father. Waiting for Monday would be like waiting to reach the other end of eternity. I also decided to keep my silence for the time being.

I suddenly heard my father whistling as he approached the front door. I scrambled to get the papers into the bag and back into the wardrobe so that no one would know they had been disturbed. My mouth went dry and my hands shook as I stuffed things into the bag. My heart beat faster than I could ever remember. I found out years later that these physical reactions are simply the result of panic.

In the nick of time I just managed to be seated in the front room as my father's key turned in the lock. He looked rather surprised to see me sitting there without the TV on. He made tea straight away and opened his newspaper at the racing pages. I couldn't look him in the face when he spoke to me. I wanted to blurt out what I knew but I didn't, not out of fear but because I suddenly felt sorry for him. I didn't want to upset him as he was always the one who was good to me. At the same time I thought, what on earth do I have that I should be grateful for? My life was in complete tatters.

Adults say things in front of children and assume the youngsters don't understand. It just shows that adults can be wrong. Children gather information from adult conversations and can put a jigsaw puzzle together no matter how long it takes, just as I had.

My father looked at me and said, 'Come on, Anne, pick a winner.' I just wanted him to explain himself. Why had I been denied my birthright? I said nothing. He sensed there was something really wrong with me and asked why I was being so quiet. I told him I had a headache and it was a big one. I told him I was going out shortly to call on a friend but would be home early. I made my way to the beach and walked for hours along the seafront. I always found a sense of tranquillity when I was near water. It was a place where I could gather my thoughts. All I could hear was the rush of the waves and their steady beat against the rocks. Out there was a great, big, open space. I let the clear, fresh air soothe me.

My head was so mixed up inside as I struggled to put things into some sort of order. My thoughts were coming steady and fast, like the waves. The Donaldsons, Isobelle, everything. I remember children in class talking about what they would like to be when they grew up. I just wanted to be someone's child. There was no future for me. I had never even thought of a career. Was my life to be plagued with one disaster after another? These were strong feelings for a child of ten; strong thoughts to be going through a young mind. It was a crime to let a child go through so much emotional trauma. I bet Lala's biggest problem at that time was what to dress her dolls in.

I had completely forgotten about the time. I asked a passer-by. It was 5.45. I had been at the beach for nearly five hours. I raced home and was indoors ten minutes after my mother. She asked where I had been. I lied, and I didn't feel guilty. They had been doing it to me for years. Furthermore, I didn't want them to know about my day-to-day activities any more. I felt it would be an intrusion on my privacy.

As the day wore on, I managed to put what I knew in a corner of my mind. I had to so that the Donaldsons wouldn't suspect anything.

Finally, Monday morning arrived and I had an important question to ask my teacher. School took on a new meaning. It was now the place I could escape to for a few hours a day. When we were lined up in the playground to go in, I decided on what would be the best moment to speak to my teacher. I didn't want the other children to overhear what I was going to ask her. I waited until lunchtime and watched as the children filed out of the classroom. I stayed behind. I said, 'Please, Miss, can I ask you a question? What is a child called that does not have a father?'

Miss Moyer replied, 'It depends on what terms you are talking about.'

I said, 'What if the parents were not married?'

She explained, 'If the parents are not married, the child is referred to as illegitimate or a bastard.'

I could see by the expression on her face that she was

curious as to why I had asked such a question. I wondered what I would say if she asked. I wouldn't be able to answer, which meant I would have to tell a lie.

She did ask and I told her I had overheard my family discussing a cousin of mine. She replied, 'Have I enlightened you?'

'Yes,' I said and thanked her before running off.

Now I understood why my sisters and mother would call me a little bastard when they were angry with me. I decided that the quicker I got out of there, the better it would be for all concerned. I knew trouble would follow. Every day seemed harder for me to get through. My school work suffered badly. I had no interest whatsoever in learning because I was so preoccupied with all the other problems in my life. Then I overheard a conversation about me between two teachers. They said if I stuck to my work, it wouldn't surprise them if I ended up at university. If only they knew I had far too much going on in my mind to think about such trivial matters. I knew what my abilities were. I could learn things effortlessly but no longer had the time or space for such things. It was going to be impossible for me to achieve anything until I had sorted out my personal life.

I was now faced with the dilemma of not being the Donaldsons' child and, worse, being a bastard. I was sick and tired of seeing everybody's life complete but mine. Isobelle, with her eight children, was settled and happy, the twins married and happy, my friend Lala happy. I could be dead for all they cared. There I was, like a lonely ship sailing through the night. I made a conscious decision to take control of my own life because no one else cared enough. I would create my own private world to live in.

After I had spoken to the teacher, I decided it was time to pay Aunt Isobelle a visit. I decided to ask Lala if she would join me when I visited my 'Aunt'. She asked why it was suddenly so important to visit this aunt. I told her it was normal for people to visit aunts. Didn't she visit hers? I told her it was no big deal if she didn't want to go. Then I had second thoughts about taking her with me. I had felt I needed some sort of support, even though she didn't have a clue as to what was going on. It would just be comforting to know someone was there.

It was a silly idea and I was glad when she declined. I had only known her for a couple of months at this point and she was my only friend. She still hadn't been to my house and, in fact, never did come in all the years I knew her.

In the few days that followed, I made an excuse that I would be home late from school. In fact, I was going to make my bus journey to Isobelle's. I knew she would be at home because she was always there to look after her children when they came home from school. There was no need to forewarn her. As I got off the bus, I dithered along the road. Just before I got to the door, I considered turning back and going home. I rang the doorbell and could hear her footsteps. When she opened the door she looked astonished to see me. It had been at least half a year since my last visit.

In a very welcoming way, with a beaming smile, she hugged me close and said: 'What are you doing here?'

I told her I had nothing to do, I was bored and too much time had passed since my last visit. She made tea and put cakes on plates. We chatted away and I talked a load of nonsense. Then bitterness filled me when one of her boys returned from school and she made a big fuss of him, asking if he had been a good boy and how his day had gone. It suddenly dawned on me that I shared the same mother with two of the boys, although we had different fathers. They were my half-brothers. It was obvious that they didn't know anything about me.

Just before half past five, Isobelle said I should make my way home as it would soon be dark. Oddly, she added that if I ever needed her, I could find her at a local club called the Rialto in the afternoons. I thought it strange for her suddenly to say such a thing. I did not question her, though, as I didn't want her suspicions aroused in any way. I knew it was only a matter of time before I broached the topic of her being my mother. I felt it was necessary to pick the correct moment.

I kissed her and bade her farewell. I felt relieved after leaving her home. I found myself skipping and hopping down the road, something I hadn't done in a long time. In doing this, I completely forgot that Aunt Bella, Mum's sister, lived directly across the road from the bus stop. As I stood at the bus stop, I realised how close Aunt Bella was and thought it best to walk to the next stop as I didn't want her to see me. I feared she might inform the Donaldsons that I had been to Isobelle's.

I climbed the stairs to the top of the bus and sat at the back. I felt proud that I had made my first trip from the new flat to Isobelle's on my own. I knew that if she was unable to come to me, I could get to her. I started wondering if I could trust her. After all, she was the woman who had denied me as her daughter. Yet she had never really let go of me, not completely. I realised that and tried to make sense of it. How could she give a child away and then bring up six step-children and two of her own? It bewildered me. I once heard it said that humans can be very cruel. I thought it was very true.

For some odd reason I didn't get off the bus at my stop but continued to journey for a further four stops along the Arbroath Road, which brought me to the local cemetery. I don't know what possessed me. I walked around the cemetery looking at headstones and reading the engravings. It was very peaceful. I came across the headstone of a baby who had died shortly after birth. It read: 'In loving memory of our dear daughter who was taken away from us so early.' I thought it would have been better if I had been taken at birth too.

There were fresh flowers on many of the graves. I wondered what the point was of giving flowers to people who were no longer alive. Wouldn't it have been better to have given them to people when they were alive?

I began to feel sad again. I left and walked home, searching my feelings. 'Who am I? What am I? Where do I belong?' I was so wrapped up in my emotions that I didn't care about what was going on around me. I was in a world of my own without the moral support, love and care that is needed to help us through life. Because I was a little person, I had no rights. I thought if I was able to write a book, I would express how I really felt. I had never been able to do it with my tongue. I once told Mum Donaldson that I wanted to write a book when I grew up. She only laughed at me. It made me feel my wishes were of no importance. Of course they weren't. She didn't care about what wasn't hers.

A few months passed and I had reached a stage where I didn't give a damn about anyone, not even Isobelle. My feelings towards her had become hostile. Everyone was so wrapped up in their own lives and I was left to my own devices.

My school work continued to go downhill. One frustrated teacher sent home a report suggesting I might be backward. I knew what that meant and I hated her for it. I felt that I had been branded once again when, in fact, I couldn't think straight because of my problems.

My whole attitude became negative. I didn't care about being disciplined or smacked. It was water off a duck's back. I had grown immune to insults. No one could see the damage they were doing to me.

As I sat indoors on the evening of the report, I felt uncomfortable. I was unsure of everything and my confidence had dwindled. I started thinking about the graveyard again. The thought made me shudder. I saw goose pimples rise on my arms. There was nowhere for me to hide in the flat so that I could be alone with my thoughts. I just sat and stared at the TV as if I was watching it. I hated being there. Dad asked if I wanted a drink of hot treacle. I didn't even answer him. I found it difficult to say the word 'dad'. I did not want to arouse their suspicions, but it was difficult.

On my way home that day there had been a putrid smell in the street. I asked Dad if he noticed the smell. He said, 'Strangely enough, there's a slaughterhouse in town. I'm sure the smell came from there.'

I didn't understand what a slaughterhouse was, so he

explained it to me. I decided I would visit the slaughter-house one day. Perhaps I could find a cubby hole there that I could escape to whenever I felt it was necessary.

It was 9.30 in the evening. I just wanted to go to bed and try to forget the events of that day but I couldn't settle to an easy sleep that night. I got up and made myself a hot drink. My whole world was torn apart and I could no longer escape from it, even in sleep. I thought things couldn't get worse, yet I had an eerie feeling that they would.

I wanted to tell someone about it but I was afraid it would get back to the Donaldsons. As dawn broke I was still awake. The chirping of the birds broke the night-time's silence. I had to go to school that day although I felt shattered and wanted to be left on my own.

Yet again, my mind was not on my education. I waited for the hours to pass at school. My hatred towards Isobelle escalated as I blamed her more and more for the situation I was in. Lala kept asking what was wrong until, at the end of the day, we had a fight. It wasn't her fault. She was trying to be helpful and caring. The fight got out of hand and we ended up ripping each other's clothes and pulling each other's hair.

Lala went home terribly bruised and told her sister what had happened. Rather than face a confrontation at my home, I took it upon myself to go to Lala's and explain. I expected a hostile reception and steeled myself against it, but when they opened the door I just broke down and wept. I apologised over and over again for hurting my friend. I explained that I had terrible problems and there was no one I could talk to. As Lala's mother bathed her cuts and bruises, I felt terribly guilty about my aggressive actions. I had never wanted to hurt my only friend. Now, I had only created new problems for myself, like having to live with the guilt of hurting Lala. Her mother tried to find out why I had done it but I just sobbed uncontrollably.

She asked Lala and Jackie to leave the room and then I blurted out what I knew about the Donaldsons and Isobelle. She told me that I must confront them and let them know I was aware of the situation. I said it wouldn't make any difference.

She said she had thought it a bit strange that I had never invited Lala to my flat but now she understood. She also said that if I ever needed someone to talk to, I should come to her. I never took her up on the offer. I just cried myself dry and left.

I was in more trouble when I got home for not letting anyone know where I was. Mum Donaldson boasted about how good the twins were and how they never brought problems into the house. Had they loved me as much as the twins, I might have been a golden girl as well. As Mum Donaldson stood there, ranting and raving, I remembered an incident that had happened when I was eight. She had taken a leather belt to me, leaving buckle marks all over my back. She even took me to the police station to show an officer what she had done. She pulled my pants down and my shirt up and showed the policeman the marks on my body. I don't know who was more embarrassed, the policeman or myself. What sort of woman would boast about beating a child that way? Back then, there were no laws to protect children from being battered. Today there are. Had she done that to me today, she would probably have been locked up.

As I stood there, being shouted at for being at Lala's, I wondered if she was going to beat me again because she was in so much of a rage, but she didn't touch me.

After she had finished, she popped over to visit Sheena. I thought that things might have been different if I had been the only child in the house. Then there wouldn't have been anyone to compare me to. I wondered what the following year would have in store for me. I felt it was time to approach Isobelle and see what she had to say for herself.

The following day I noticed that Sheena was out and I asked where she had gone. Mum Donaldson said that Sheena had given birth to a baby girl during the night. She wouldn't have told me if I had not asked. It was as if the event was none of my business. Even so, I was excited about having a new baby around. Sheena named her Wendy Anne Brown.

Wendy was absolutely beautiful. I would pop over to see her while Harry was at work and Sheena would let me feed her with a bottle. I felt like a little mother hen and it was something I really enjoyed doing. In the weeks that followed, the baby grew in leaps and bounds. Then, out of the blue, Mum Donaldson arranged to take Sheena and Harry out to give them a bit of a break. Wendy was about eight weeks old and Sheena hadn't been apart from her since she was born.

Steve was asked to keep an eye on me as well as the baby. I wanted to stay in my own flat and watch TV, but Dad was working on a late shift and wouldn't be home until 10 p.m. Steve said it would be better if I went to his flat rather than him having to pop in regularly to check on me. I felt very uncomfortable about the arrangement. I always felt uneasy around him because of the things he used to say to me about my underclothes.

Shortly after Sheena, Harry and Mum Donaldson left, Steve fed the baby, changed her nappy, and settled her back in bed. He returned to the sitting room and stared at me. He said I was going to grow up into a lovely-looking girl. I didn't understand what he was getting at and I didn't want to know. I noticed he had started rubbing his hands on his private parts and wondered what he was doing. I became strangely frightened. He asked me if I knew what he was doing to himself. I told him I thought I had better go back to my own home. He turned on me and firmly ordered me to sit down and do as I was told. Then he unzipped his trousers and pulled his penis out. At that time I didn't even know what that part of the body was called but I thought it was ugly and disgusting.

He came closer to me where I sat on the edge of the sofa, trembling. I had on a little red dress. He took my knickers down and pulled my legs apart and kept trying to push his thing between my legs.

I began to cry and begged him to let me go. I told him it wasn't right. I was scared to death. He told me it was natural and that all big people do it. He said there was nothing wrong in what he was doing but, instinctively, I knew it was not right. I whimpered and threatened to tell Sheena and Mum Donaldson. He told me that if I did, he would beat me and no one would believe me anyway. Then I managed to get away from him and ran to my own flat. I locked the door and was determined not to open it if he came near.

It was half past eight. I kept looking at the clock begging

it to go faster so that at least one of my parents would come home. I was quaking and petrified but Steve never did come to check on me. Dad was the first one home that night and he asked straight away where Mother was. I told him she was out with Sheena. As I spoke to him, all I could think about was killing Steve. Dad kept asking what the problem was. All I could think about was what Steve had done.

When Mum Donaldson returned, Dad asked her what was wrong with me. She said, 'How do I know, I've been out.' I wanted to tell them what had happened but I was frightened of being disbelieved.

From that day on I was so frightened of Steve that I would never go to his flat when he was there. He would come over to our flat and glare at me and it made me feel sick. It became the biggest hang-up of my childhood. In comparison, the other problems seemed irrelevant.

I started clinging to Jake and Annie, who had had a baby girl around the same time as Sheena. She was called Fiona. Because Jake was always on the road, I would keep Annie company when he was away.

When the twins weren't together, I saw them in a different light. I remember Annie saying I must learn to behave and I looked at her and thought, 'If only you knew what I know today and what Steve did to me.' I wanted to live with Annie and Jake. They lived a good five miles from disgusting Steve.

I don't think Jake had much time for me. That made me feel sad because I liked him and needed him. I helped Annie to do the dishes and polish and tidy. I wanted to prove that I wasn't the bad apple they all thought. I helped with little Fiona who was so lovely. I would watch Annie bathe and feed her. I thought how lucky the baby was because she certainly wouldn't have an upbringing like mine. I was happy and comfortable at Annie's.

I became a real handful at home because I didn't want to be there. It was too close to Steve. I became troublesome, argumentative and nasty. I would talk to my parents in a snappy tone and I was deliberately disrespectful.

Jake pointed out that my parents were getting on in age and that I should try not to cause them so much grief. I asked Annie if I could come and live with them but they said that although they didn't mind me visiting and staying the odd night, they wouldn't have me on a permanent basis.

My birthday was just around the corner. I thought the best gift I could receive would be honesty about my parentage and a life away from Steve. I never gave up hope.

15

KARL AND KANDY – ADVICE AGED 10

You are now at an age where I feel it is important that I advise you about drugs, smoking and drinking alcohol.

I will start with smoking. This makes Mummy feel hypocritical because I was a smoker. It was a weakness of mine for many years. There were many occasions when the cigarettes would make me cough. You both used to tell me how disgusting it was, although you were only four and five then. You used to beg me to give them up.

You may have already been told about this at school but I shall tell you of my own experiences. I can remember the very first time I started smoking properly. I thought it made me look grown-up to walk down the street with a cigarette but with every cigarette I lit, I threatened my future health. Smoking damages your lungs, trachea, sinuses, voice box, arteries, everything. Smoking kills.

Addiction in humans is a serious problem. I was addicted to cigarettes. If you start using anything at an early age, you can become dependent on it, including drink and drugs. Even at the age of ten, it is possible that such items will be offered to you. I hope you will have the will-power and intelligence to decline to use or even try any of these things mentioned above. Your friends and peers may tempt, ridicule and taunt you into having a go. Let them say what they will. At the end of the day, it is your body, your life and your health that you are taking a gamble with.

Many different types of cancer are related to the things we put into our bodies. I ask you to walk away – and not to feel ashamed about it – from anything that can threaten your health.

This covers a wide area. Drug abuse can come in the form of glue sniffing, smoking marijuana, snorting cocaine and taking heroin. These things will interfere with your personality, health and entire future. People who become dependent on drugs turn to crime to support their addiction. If this happened to you, you could kiss your whole life away.

You must have the willpower and strength to say no to these things. I cannot dictate to you on these matters. I can only advise you. I have seen these influences ruin people, even people in high and responsible positions. It is my duty as a loving parent to warn you about these things. I hope you take notice.

Many young people try these things because it makes them feel grown-up. They may say that you two are wimps for not trying. You are not weak if you say no. In reality you are the stronger ones. It is easy to say yes and go with the crowd. It is hard to say no.

I promise you, anyone who tampers with these items will have no future worth living for. Glue sniffing is life-threatening. One strong sniff can destroy so many brain cells that you could end up a vegetable after your first try. (A vegetable is a slang term used for people who become 'brain dead'. They damage their brains and end up like zombies. They have to live in institutions and can't even go to the toilet by themselves.) I have read so often about bright children with promising futures who took just one sniff that ended their lives.

Don't ever gamble with your life. Don't do it.

Alcohol can be consumed in two ways. One way is socially at parties. This is done in moderation at an older age. The law says alcohol consumption cannot begin until the age of eighteen. Some people start at a younger age.

If a time comes when you feel you would like to drink alcohol, I would prefer that you kept within the law and waited until you are eighteen. There are laws about drinking and driving, of which you will become aware by eighteen or when you reach the legal age for driving, which is seventeen.

The other side of alcohol is when people consume it until they become dependent on it on a daily basis. They are called alcoholics. I speak about this from personal experience, which you will learn about in later tapes and letters.

You have so much going for you. At this age, you know about your roots and you have love and security, unlike Mummy's life at your age. There is no reason for you to ruin all the good things you have. Instead, cherish what you have and take care of it.

Sometimes, even at the young age of ten, life can be as frustrating as it is good. I will ask you not to take your frustrations or anger out on other people, whether they are friends or not. Be dignified and composed. You will always have Daddy or your guardians to speak to about your problems. I had difficulties because I had no one to turn to and so I lashed out to relieve my frustrations.

Believe me, this gets you nowhere, as you have probably realised from my account of my life at the age of ten.

Take it out on a beanbag instead or just have a good heart to heart with Daddy or a teacher or guardian. Lucky you. You probably won't ever need the beanbag. I feel like patting you both on the head right now and saying, 'That's my treasures!' I'll give you both a big, spiritual hug instead. Love you, like crazy.

16

MUMMY – AGED 11

I woke up on my birthday immensely excited at the prospect of confronting Isobelle. I spent the next two days planning what I would say to her, imagining an assortment of different scenarios, depending on her reaction.

I told Mum Donaldson that I had a dental appointment after school hours at the school clinic. It was a fib, of course. I just wanted time to go to Isobelle's without any objections or interruptions.

It was a Friday when I raced off to Isobelle's, determined that I would find out everything I wanted to know. I didn't bother knocking on the front door when I arrived. I went round to the back and let myself in through the kitchen. Isobelle was delighted to see me and wished me belated birthday greetings. She had a card waiting for me and presented me with a beautiful case filled to the top with coloured pencils, chalks and crayons. I gave her a warm hug before putting the gift into my school bag. Isobelle put the kettle on and I made myself comfortable at her kitchen table.

It was a warm day and the kitchen was bright from the natural summer light that flooded through the window. Isobelle stood at the sink with her back to me. It made it easier for my words to flow. I said, 'Aunt Isobelle, there is something I must ask you.'

For a split second she froze at the sink. I'm sure she knew what I was about to ask.

I said, 'I know you're not really my aunt. Are you my mother?'

She turned slowly to face me. Her look was one of horror and embarrassment. I was unusually calm, but worried.

She asked me to wait until she had made the tea, which she did in complete silence. I guess she needed time for everything to sink in and to dream up some acceptable answers. When she was seated at the table I said: 'Well?'

She confirmed what I already knew by asking how on earth I managed to find out. I told her the story of the handbag in the wardrobe, of how things said to me in the past had fallen into place and that the way the Donaldsons treated me had also aroused my suspicions.

Her explanation went as follows. In Isobelle's young days, in the late 1950s, it was a terrible thing for an unmarried woman to give birth to a child. Isobelle had grown up without much money and times were very hard for her. She said I would have suffered and we would have had nothing if she had been left to bring me up on her own. No one would want to give work to a single mother and we would have been without food and clothes.

Mrs Donaldson, who brought me up, was, in fact, Isobelle's aunt. Isobelle had asked her to take me when I was born. I asked who my father was. She paused and said she didn't want to talk about him. I didn't press her at the time as my instincts told me to leave that subject alone.

I asked her why, if she had loved me so much, she hadn't taken me back from the Donaldsons when she settled with her husband? The question embarrassed her and I enjoyed watching her squirm. I raised my voice and told her she had messed up my life completely and that my whole world had been filled with misery as far back as I could remember.

She looked at me as if I was a Martian with two heads. I screamed and shouted and demanded, 'Answer me. Answer me! Why didn't you come and get me when you could have? I want to know!'

Isobelle's eyes filled with tears and she said that her husband wouldn't accept me because I was another man's child and not his.

I nearly fell on the floor in hysterical laughter. I reminded her that she was, in fact, raising not one, but six children that weren't hers. What was wrong with taking me, her real one? If she could take on his half-dozen, why couldn't he take on one?

Her answer was that she loved her husband and that she didn't want to spoil her life with him. I quickly retorted, 'So, in that case, you didn't love your own child enough.'

She tried to tell me that it wasn't like that, but that is how it came over to me, loud and clear. I looked at her and told her she had no idea what I had been through and what she had done to my life. She said, 'What happened? What are you talking about?' I just looked at her and told her not to worry, that I would sort my own life out.

In my mind I blamed her for what happened with Steve. Had I been with her, he would never have had the chance to touch me. I hated her so much at that moment. I asked her about John and Steven, the two children she had had with her husband. I wanted to know if they realised I was their half-sister. She said, 'Oh my God, they must never know, ever!' She asked me to leave before the two boys returned from school. She was obviously frightened that I might tell them. My parting words were that if she refused to tell me about my father, at least she should have the common decency to tell me what my surname should have been. At the door she told me that his name was Edward Buchanan and he knew I existed.

I looked at her nastily and said, 'Thanks a lot for nothing.' Then I turned on my heel and left without looking back.

I decided not to let on to the Donaldsons about my visit to Isobelle or my real father. I had reservations about hunting for him and decided to leave it until I was old enough to gather the facts together and understand the situation more clearly. I realised straight away that if he had had any interest in me at all he would surely have made contact with me by now. He, like Isobelle, probably had a family of his own.

I didn't want to approach anyone else who might know about my background at this point. It was time to let it all rest for a while. I still didn't accept Isobelle's explanation of why she didn't claim me back when she could have. That, too, I would deal with another day.

I didn't go straight home after my visit to Isobelle's. I had decided to investigate the slaughterhouse near my home. When I got there it seemed quiet and eerie. I looked around the outer area of the building. A sign said that it was out of bounds to anyone but staff. I poked around and no one questioned me. I suppose everyone assumed I was a staff member's child.

I walked around the building, trying to peer through

windows, until I came across a door that was slightly ajar. I pushed it open and the room was full of horns and hoofs. I picked up a couple of each and stashed them in my school bag. I thought I would give them a good cleaning and take them to school. Then I heard a horrendous noise and nearly leapt in the air. It was coming from a building directly behind me. I was very curious and walked in the direction of the noise.

I came upon two massive doors which were closed but, as they were on runners I found it easy to slide them back. Inside I saw a large number of cattle in individual pens. I assumed they were awaiting slaughter. I had climbed up on the bars of a pen to stroke a cow when a voice suddenly bellowed at me and I was so startled that I nearly fell head first into the cattle enclosure. An aggressive-looking man announced nastily that I was trespassing and had no right to be in the building.

I told him I lived locally and that the smell had led me here. I wanted to know what caused the smell. He said it would be best if I left or he would call the police. I got out of there as quickly as possible and toddled back to the flat with my school bag full of horns and hoofs.

I got home just before Mum arrived. In the moments when I was alone, before her arrival, my thoughts turned to Steve. I wondered what I would do during the Christmas holidays when Mum and Dad were at work. I had hoped I would be able to find refuge at the slaughterhouse but that was now out of the question.

I would be alone and easy prey for Steve. I decided to go out and about and find out what activities were going on for children in the area during the Christmas break. There was a local park called Baxter Park which had swings and seesaws. I decided I would spent most of my days there. Not far away was another place called Swanny Ponds. These were two large ponds that were likely to be iced over in December. Perhaps I could skate my days away until the Donaldsons got home from work.

Christmas arrived and everyone celebrated in their respective homes. It was a quiet Christmas for us. In my mind it seemed like just another day. I couldn't get into the spirit of the season. I noticed that this particular year there were very few presents for me and, for the first time, nothing from Isobelle. It was the last time I would receive Christmas cards from aunts, uncles and family members.

Christmas made me think more deeply about Isobelle. I came to the conclusion that, in fact, I really did love her and couldn't bear to lose her completely. She was, after all, my real mother and the only person who had seemed really to like me over the years. I also felt I had to get away from Steve. I was panic-stricken that I might get accosted by him again during the Christmas holiday.

I thought of my cousin Margaret whom I barely knew or saw. Margaret was Isobelle's niece. I had heard the Donaldsons say over the years that Margaret was a loner because her parents were alcoholics. I thought we had something in common, being loners, and that she might be able to relate to my problems. I thought she might have some wisdom to offer as she was five years older than me.

I decided to find her and learned that she was living in a women's hostel. She had left home at the age of fifteen because her father was an alcoholic who was always landing up in jail and her mother was a heavy drinker as well.

She couldn't tolerate being around them and had left with their blessing.

I went to the hostel, which was like a YWCA, and asked for her. It was bizarre. As soon as we saw each other, we both burst into tears and ran into each other's arms. I told her I knew the truth about Isobelle being my mother and I told her about Steve. I discovered that she knew about Isobelle being my real mother but had been instructed to keep her mouth shut. She cursed Steve openly and told me it was not safe to live near him but she advised me not to tell the Donaldsons about him because they would never believe me. She said that Isobelle was a good woman and that I hadn't been told the truth of what really happened when I was born.

The truth was as follows. When I was born, Isobelle had to go to work and the Donaldsons offered to babysit, providing she paid for my keep. The problems arose when Isobelle came to collect me each evening. The Donaldsons gave her a hard time about taking me away every night and suggested I stay overnight. This eventually led to me staying from Monday to Friday.

When I was about six months old, the Donaldsons threatened to inform the social services that Isobelle wasn't a fit mother. They said they would keep me on a permanent basis and not tell the social services, providing Isobelle maintained me financially.

I asked Margaret how she knew all this. She explained that she had often heard Isobelle and her own mother talking about the situation. Isobelle would be in tears over it. She wanted me back but felt that her aunt, Alexzina Donaldson, was blackmailing her.

The Donaldsons had put pressure on Isobelle by saying that she couldn't possibly work and look after me properly and that it would be wrong to leave me with strangers. Naturally, Isobelle dated occasionally but the Donaldsons made her feel that it would be a threat to my safety and also unsettling for me if I had lots of different babysitters or strange men around. Isobelle felt that leaving me with the Donaldsons was the only way not to lose me altogether. The Donaldsons had convinced her that she wasn't capable of looking after me properly. Isobelle was about thirty when I was born. She had never denied, not even to her husband, that she had a daughter.

My anger towards Isobelle subsided and left a clear space in my head to work out how to get away from the proximity of Steve. Margaret said she would help me to devise a plan. I did not go home that night. I stayed in the young women's hostel with Margaret. The wardens checked the rooms at ten each night, so she hid me under the bed when they were due. The room was cosy, with a lovely, warm coal fire and tidy, old-fashioned furniture. I wanted to stay with Margaret for ever.

It was decided that Margaret would take me to a friend's home the following morning. The plan was that I would stay at the friend's while she was at work and return to the hostel in the evening. I went to her friend's house but, as the day wore on, I started to get cold feet, then I panicked and headed home just after noon.

The police had already been called and the Donaldsons had not gone to work that day. I refused to reveal to the police or the Donaldsons where I had been. I had found a new haven and I had no intention of letting them know about it. I had also found a way of escaping from Steve. I would simply run away every time he harassed me. Margaret told me that if I continued running away, the social services would have to be called in to deal with me. That would suit our plans perfectly, for it would get me away from Steve permanently.

Steve continued to make sexual remarks to me and glare at me with a sick lust. I knew my luck couldn't hold out much longer and it was only a question of time before he got his hands on me again. He was just waiting for the moment. Rather than tell my parents what was really going on, I made myself out to be a horrible child, one that was totally out of control. I needed the protection of the social services.

Back then the social services weren't as aware as they are today about child abuse. I really needed to be taken into care, so I caused as much trouble as I could to provoke the social services to take action.

Margaret said the Donaldsons would break soon and have me taken away. I had run away steadily for four solid months. The police were being called in the whole time. I wondered why they didn't take it upon themselves to contact the social services, especially as I firmly refused to give any explanation for my actions. I didn't want to tell the policemen about Steve because I was too embarrassed to reveal these things to a man. I had started feeling dirty because Steven had touched me with his ugly penis and I was developing a mistrust of all men, even the police.

I felt that Margaret was the only person I could trust and I was right. Margaret was surprised that the Donaldsons still hadn't called the social services to take me away.

The final straw came when dirty Steve whispered in my ear that my budding breasts were beginning to look so attractive through my school blouse. He said he couldn't wait to get a better look. I nearly threw up. I told Margaret. She was so incensed that she came up with the ultimate plan to force the Donaldsons to call in the social services.

It didn't take much for her to convince me to run away to London. Margaret would accompany me, to make sure I was safe, which made the idea seem much more attractive. She went to the post office to collect her savings. She had about £15, which is worth roughly £45 in today's money. She said I should stay at home that evening and pretend I was going to school the following morning. I was to go to the hostel instead and we would leave from there. I had to get a good night's sleep because the following day would mark a new beginning for me. I was going on an adventure that would set me free.

I lay in bed that night thinking about London. I had heard that the streets were paved with gold. It was a wonder I fell asleep at all. I carried on as normal the following morning and left the flat and went to Margaret's as planned. She was waiting. I took off my school uniform and put on a pair of her jeans and a jumper.

Margaret thought it best to wait until nightfall to hitch-hike out of Scotland. I was excited beyond belief. The day dragged on as Margaret spoke of her plans. She said she would find a job in London that might enable us to stay there permanently. She had all her school qualifications and had been top of her class. She was confident that she could easily find work. Although she was not quite seven-teen, she looked older and felt that would work in her favour. She packed a couple of jumpers, toothpaste, brushes and a flannel and soap. Incredibly, we both forgot to pack knickers or fresh socks.

It was very dark by 8.30 p.m. Margaret decided it was safe enough to take me out into the streets. We got a bus to a main motorway heading south. We got off at the main entrance of the motorway and thumbed for a lift. I found it all very amusing. I was laughing so hard that Margaret had to clip me on the ear to shut me up. She said it was no laughing matter. About ten minutes later a big lorry approached. It passed and then slowed down. We ran up to the door and told the driver we were heading for London. He said he was going as far as Darlington. At least it was in the right direction. We jumped in the cab.

Margaret sat next to the driver and I sat by the passenger door. For the first half hour, we hardly spoke. Then the driver asked us what business we had in London. Margaret said she was going for a job interview. She claimed that I was her kid sister and was going with her for safety reasons. I was amazed at the speed of her invention. She certainly could lie when she had to. We were in the lorry for about four and a half hours before the driver reached his destination and were happy to get out because he asked far too many questions for comfort. He said he would give us an address of a relative to use if we got stuck in London and that we would be put up there for a few days. He said he would call his relative and explain about us. I thought that was very nice of him.

He dropped us by the entrance to a motorway leading to London. We were back to hitching again. It was gone midnight and it took us twenty minutes to find our next ride with another truck driver. He was travelling into the centre of London, which suited us perfectly. We said we wanted to go to Piccadilly and as luck would have it, he was passing through there.

About 3.30 in the morning, he asked if we wanted tea and sandwiches. I was quick to say yes. We went into a transport cafe full of truck drivers. They all stared at us. After we had hungrily devoured our sandwiches and tea, we headed on, non-stop, into London.

The driver let us out in Piccadilly Circus at 5.30 in the morning. I said to Margaret 'What now?' She snapped at me to shut up. She looked at the names of the shops in Piccadilly and waited an hour before phoning the first lorry driver's relative. The lady who answered said, 'Oh yes, Tommy rang me.' She gave us directions to her house at Bank. I thought she meant she lived in a bank where people kept their savings and that she must be very rich. Margaret told me I was a twit and that Bank was a part of London.

We took a tube train to Bank, then took a taxi to her house as we didn't know London at all. We knocked on her door but she was out of bed waiting for us. As soon as she opened her front door, we could smell sausages and bacon cooking.

I told Margaret that people in Scotland weren't as kind as this woman. It then dawned on me why Margaret took the name of the stores in Piccadilly. It was to name a place where her alleged job interview was to be, should she be asked. The lady, named Betty, did ask about Margaret's prospective work and Margaret rattled off the name of a shop she had spotted earlier. Betty said that she would feel better if we stayed at her house that evening, as it wasn't safe for two young girls to be wandering the streets of London.

She fed us a lovely breakfast of eggs, sausage, bacon, tomatoes, beans and mushrooms with buttered bread and offered to take us out that afternoon to show us parts of London but we explained that we didn't have much money to spare. She said that wasn't a problem and we didn't need to spend anything at all. Betty explained that the lorry driver was her brother. Margaret asked her if she had any children of her own. She said she was a widow with a grown-up son and daughter and that we would meet them later that evening.

When we returned to her place later, she started preparing dinner. I noticed that she laid the table for five as her son and daughter would be joining us for a meal. While Betty was busy cooking, I told Margaret that I thought Betty was a kind and generous woman. Margaret agreed and said she wondered if her children were just as nice.

At 7.30 sharp, the doorbell rang. We heard Betty answer it and could hear her greeting her children. When they walked into the room Margaret and I nearly fell through the floor. It turned out that her grown-up children were a policeman and policewoman. They were in full uniform and would be working the night shift in Hendon. I wondered if my face was as much of a picture as Margaret's. We were both clearly thinking the same thing. Our faces registered shock and horror. The daughter was very inquisitive and said I looked rather young to be in London.

Margaret explained that she was fully responsible for

me and I was there to keep her company. I got the horrible feeling that neither of them believed us and we were relieved when the two constables left.

I was very tired and wanted to go to bed. I hoped Margaret would take the hint and come as well. Fifteen minutes later she appeared. As she walked in, we looked at each other and fell apart laughing. I said to Margaret, 'Who would ever think of looking for us in a policeman's mother's house?' Margaret said it was too close for comfort and we should leave first thing in the morning. She set a small alarm clock, which stood by the bedside, for 5 a.m.

At 5 a.m., we crept down the stairs fully dressed and prepared to depart. I asked Margaret where we were heading but she didn't have a clue. She felt the most important thing for her to do was to find work. At least then we would be able to support ourselves.

We left Betty a note thanking her for her kindness and hospitality. We also confessed that I was a runaway and that we were worried because her son and daughter worked for the police force. We walked from Betty's to a tube station and went back to Piccadilly. Margaret thought it was a good central starting point. We wandered around and ended up in Trafalgar Square where we sat for four hours.

I wasn't happy about leaving Betty's as I had felt comfortable and safe there. I didn't like the idea of wandering the streets and having no roof over our heads. Margaret went into every cafe to see if they needed help. Twenty cafes later it was the same old story, no jobs. I started getting irritable. All the excitement, adventure and glamour of running away disappeared rapidly and was replaced by a fear of the unknown. Margaret told me to stop whining because everything would work out. She felt certain that we would soon be settled. I felt certain it was all a big mistake. She criticised me for not giving it a chance.

We ended up in Kings Cross station where we hid in a loo and that is where we spent the night. It was cold and miserable. We huddled up together on the concrete floor and tried desperately to keep warm. We had our bags, containing our few belongings, next to us. It was a wonder we fell asleep at all. Thankfully, we were physically exhausted from walking all day, which helped us to doze off.

At 2 a.m. we were woken by a man, all of eighteen years old. He shook us until we stirred. We opened our eyes to see him peering down at us. The first words from his mouth were, 'Do you want a fix?'

I thought he said did we want a box of tricks. He laughed at me and said, 'Not tricks, a fix.' We didn't have a clue what he was talking about.

He said his name was Jackal and he was selling drugs that make you happy. I was feeling miserable all right, but not enough to touch drugs. Margaret said we had no money, just in case he was thinking of robbing us. He said he knew of an easy way for us to get money and that I, being younger, would have no problem. He said he had a rich uncle who helped homeless people like us. I thought that sounded wonderful. Another kind Londoner, like Betty, ready to help those who needed it.

Margaret, being older and much wiser, knew Jackal was up to no good. They had a discussion which went right over my head as all I could think of was a nice warm bed and somewhere to wash. Margaret told Jackal to leave us alone and that we would find our own way. He said we were in for a hard time; London was a lonely place for strangers. Then he pulled a wad of money from his pocket. I was wildly impressed.

He offered to buy us breakfast but Margaret told me not to go with him. I thought he was being nice but Margaret only said that I had a lot to learn. Once more, she politely asked Jackal to leave. He said, 'Fine, if that is what you want,' and left.

Margaret explained that his suggestions of taking us to breakfast and meeting his uncle were to get us into prostitution. I didn't understand what prostitution was. Margaret explained that it was when women were paid money in exchange for having sex with men. The thought made me feel sick and I started thinking of Steve and why I had left Dundee in the first place. She told me not to worry and said she would look after me. We couldn't get back to sleep because we were too frightened that Jackal might return. I was rapidly learning that the streets of London weren't paved with gold.

Around 6 a.m. we had a freezing wash in a basin. We went out into the streets hunting for a cheap place to eat breakfast. I started complaining about everything and wanted to head for home. Margaret said that the police must be looking for me by now and that I should give it a chance. I told her that she had got me into more trouble than I had ever been in before. She smiled proudly and said, 'That was the idea, wasn't it?'

I had made up my mind that if we slept rough one more night I would go to a police station and hand myself in. At least they would provide me with a warm bed. I had thought running away to London was my big break to happiness but it wasn't as easy as I had imagined. I kept insisting that we should have accepted Jackal's help as he seemed to be such a nice guy. Margaret made it clear that he was nothing but a bad apple. In my innocence and inexperience, I just couldn't see things the way she did.

In fact, London was a really dangerous place for runaways. Margaret lectured me endlessly about it but I just thought she was being silly. I began thinking that my problems back home were a lot easier than the ones facing me here. At least in Scotland I had a warm bed and food.

We wandered around London and ended up in Soho. It had a terrible reputation according to Margaret and was a prostitutes' haven at all times of the day and night. Women were dressed in tarty clothes, thick make-up and fake jewels. They were openly offering their bodies for sex in exchange for cash.

It was growing dark and I became cold and agitated. We hadn't eaten anything since breakfast because we had to make our little bit of money last. We saw a small building surrounded by lights and went in to see what was going on. The woman at the counter nearly had a fit when she laid eyes on me. She said we had to leave because we were under-age.

Margaret said we were desperate for work. The woman said the kind of work she had going wasn't what we would be looking for. She said she could be imprisoned just for us being on the premises. We then realised it was a sex shop. As we turned to leave, the woman called Margaret back. She told Margaret to go to Kings Cross station and look for a fellow named Jackal. He would be able to sort Margaret out with a bit of grown-up girl's work. I knew then that

Margaret had been right about Jackal. He got young, penniless people into prostitution. I was truly fed up and was on the verge of walking into the first police station I could find.

Margaret begged me to give it a couple of days more. Things would get better. I didn't share her optimism. I wondered where we would sleep that night. We made our way to the Embankment by the Thames. I liked the lights on the bridges. My legs were so tired that I couldn't go any further and had to sit down. As soon as I sat down I collapsed in tears. I begged Margaret to do something. She held me close and tried to reassure me. I was lost for words.

A man approached us as I wept. He was a tramp and he wanted a cigarette. At that time, neither of us smoked. We weren't frightened of him as he didn't seem to have a threatening bone in his body. I asked if he knew where we could find accommodation as we didn't want to sleep rough another night. He said he had seen it all before with runaways like us. Margaret tried to deny that we were runaways but we must have had it written all over our faces.

It was true that Margaret wasn't a runaway but I certainly was. The tramp told us about the YWCA but, in the next breath, reminded us that if one, or both, of us was a runaway, they would take us in and call the police. He then told us of a place where people sleep rough and live like one big family. He took us along the Embankment until we reached Cardboard City. There were people sleeping there in boxes with plastic sheet covers.

He said it wasn't much but at least we would be safe

from people who would try to lure us into drugs and prostitution. I was miserable over everything that had happened so far. It wasn't meant to turn out this way.

At least we now had a place to sleep but I wondered what we would use for a toilet or to wash. I wanted to go back to Betty's. It didn't matter to me if she did phone the police. I welcomed the idea as I was sure things would only get worse. However, Margaret was eternally optimistic and thought I was being ridiculous. I put my head down for the evening in a cardboard box. A tramp loaned us a plastic sheet. It was smelly and awful. I thought we might catch a horrible disease or get bitten by a rat during the night. I couldn't go through this another day. My instincts were correct. Nothing improved.

We spent the following day arguing from the minute we opened our eyes. We made spectacles of ourselves by rowing in the streets. Margaret was on the verge of hitting me. We didn't speak for a couple of hours and walked aimlessly for miles. The sole of my shoe fell apart. It was the only pair of shoes I had. By now we were both dirty and smelly.

I saw a policeman and asked him where his station was. He enquired as to why I needed to visit the police station. Margaret looked daggers at me when I told him I was a runaway from Scotland and had been sleeping rough. He escorted us to the station and we were questioned for an hour but declined to answer most of the questions. I just couldn't bring myself to talk about Steve. I told Margaret not to say anything either. The social services were called in and they explained that, as it was the weekend, we would have to stay in a remand centre until Monday. I was delighted. Our room had a clean bed and a bath and we were supplied with clean clothes.

What I didn't expect was that the room would be kept locked at all times by a warden and there was no television or radio. There was one window with metal bars over it. The only person we saw during the whole weekend was the lady who delivered our meals to the room. We weren't allowed out, not even into the hallways.

Margaret and I argued constantly, apart from when we slept. We even had to share the same single bed which drove me crazy as she was a restless sleeper who tossed and turned all night. I couldn't avoid getting knocked around.

On Monday morning a social worker arrived and explained that we would be leaving in the afternoon for Scotland, by air. I was excited as I had never been on an aeroplane before.

A car collected us that afternoon. Two social workers escorted us from the moment we left the room. I took an instant dislike to them. They weren't interested in conversation and treated us as if we were criminals. When we arrived at the airport we were escorted to the waiting lounge where another social worker was on hand. Margaret thought it was getting all too ridiculous. The social worker said that they weren't taking chances that we might run off again. When we got on the plane I was relieved that at least the air hostesses were nice.

It was an outrageously funny scene. The only available seats were in the first-class cabin and there were Margaret and me looking like a couple of scruffy tramps, among a bunch of booted and suited business people.

The flight took just over an hour. I joked with Margaret that had I known it would take such a short time we could have saved up for a flight to London rather than hitch-hike. The stewardess found this rather amusing but the social worker did not.

We were about to land and I wondered about the reception awaiting us. I knew we would go our separate ways as soon as we got to Dundee but I realised that I really didn't want to be without Margaret. I had come to depend on her and I could certainly use her moral support as I knew I would be in a load of trouble. I was scared out of my wits. The plane was taxiing along the runway after landing when I noticed a police car waiting on the tarmac. We both wondered who the criminal on board was. Little did we realise that the police car was waiting for us.

The air hostess reminded us not to leave the aeroplane until everyone else had disembarked. At that point I wished we had never given ourselves up. Margaret said it was a bit late to think of that now so I thought instead of running as soon as we got to the bottom of the steps. As the police drew near, I took off but they were fitter than I had imagined and caught up with me within the airport itself. The policeman said he now understood why they had been sent to meet the plane.

I felt like a criminal. People stared at us and I wondered what was going through their heads. The officer asked me my age and I told him. He said he had a daughter my age. I replied that I was sure she didn't have half the problems I had. He said that in all his years as a policeman, he had never met a child who hadn't run away from home without a good reason. I took a liking to him instantly. He was understanding. He asked if I had anyone I could share my problems with. I told him I only trusted Margaret. I explained that if he knew the reasons why I ran away, the police wouldn't be so harsh on her for helping me.

It was a one-and-a-half-hour drive to Dundee. Margaret and I said little during the journey. The social worker spoke to the policeman as if I wasn't present. I resented it and told him so. I was told to be quiet. When I ran away, I thought I would get sympathy from social workers and some sort of understanding. I was wrong. I began to regret my little jaunt to London.

I thought I would automatically be put into care upon my return to Dundee. I wasn't. I was returned straight to the Donaldsons. A very long screaming match ensued. Where had I been? Where did I go? I was asked every question except *why*.

The twins accused me of making their lives a misery. In a weird way, I got a small thrill from that. After all, isn't that what they did to me for so many years? I now knew that it was easy to run away and, yes, I thought I would do it again, only next time, I would plan it much more carefully.

I kept a low profile for a while and continued my routine of going to school and having adventures exploring new areas. Things were never the same with Lala after we had our fight at school and we drifted apart.

I also continued to run away on a regular basis. The first place they always looked for me was at Margaret's so I couldn't use that as a runaway haven any more. I slept on tower block landings and sometimes at squatters' houses.

By my twelfth birthday, I was a skilled, professional runaway.

17

KARL AND KANDY – ADVICE AGED 11

Well, darlings, you have reached the grand old age of eleven. It will soon be time for secondary school. Some of your school friends from the present will move on with you. You will also meet new friends at your new school. The rules and routines will be more or less the same as at your present school but your studies will become more intense and interesting. You will find that the subjects and topics cover a wide area. You will be given a choice of taking certain subjects that may appeal to you or be useful towards your future aspirations.

I assume, at this age, that you may have a definite interest in a single topic. Maybe it will be computers, science, health or even drama. You will be given a chance to concentrate on what you are actually interested in.

At secondary school you may find many of the children don't eat school lunches and take the option of packed lunch or nipping out to a local takeaway. I have no objections as long as you do eat at lunchtime and return to your studies punctually. This is a normal part of developing your independence and self-discipline.

You will find your social habits changing. You may want to go out to the cinema with your friends or to go shopping. Daddy or your guardians may want to drop you off and collect you. This is not spying on you or treating you like a child. It is for your own safety as a lot of things can happen to youngsters on their own, especially after dark. I'm particularly concerned in the winter months, when dark falls well before bedtime. It is safer to be collected at this age rather than making your way home on your own.

At this age, you may be experiencing changes in your own body. You may develop body odour, probably under your arms. This is nothing to be alarmed about. It's just one of the signals that your body is preparing for puberty, as it is known.

At this stage you may also notice other changes. Karl, your voice may break and become deeper. Kandy, you may be developing a waistline and hips or your breasts may begin to grow. Around this time, if you haven't already done so, you will begin your menstrual cycle. You will have learned about this at school already and will have had guidance from Daddy or a guardian. This is also a normal part of life. Both of you will have to wash more frequently and use deodorants.

All I can suggest at this time is that you take care of your personal hygiene. By now you will be well into the routine of cleaning your teeth regularly. You learned that and practised it at home from a very early age. You were both dab hands with a toothbrush. You used them so much, I had to replace them every three weeks. So keep smiling and look upon your physical changes as a great adventure into adulthood. Life becomes even more interesting from this point on. There is a great deal to look forward to.

It is very unlikely that you will encounter the problems of child abuse that I did at your age. If anything occurs with an adult, that you instinctively know is wrong or feels uncomfortable, I beg you to seek help immediately. Don't feel embarrassed or ashamed like I did. Things were different in my day and there wasn't as much public awareness of child abuse. In today's society there are many help lines and charities to contact who will aid you. I hope you will never need to seek help for such problems but, if you do, turn to Daddy, your guardians, the police, your teacher, best friend or their parents but do – and I mean do – inform someone. Don't ignore child abuse or hope it will go away. There are many people ready to protect children today, like those mentioned above. Don't let an abuser make you believe it is hopeless to try to get help or that no one will believe you or that they would think it was your fault. It is not true. Almost every adult, like Daddy, or a teacher or the police, will listen. Child abuse affects a person for the rest of their life. Seek help instantly if something happens to you.

These things can happen in all walks of society, to the privileged as well as to the less privileged. It is unlikely to occur, so don't let the idea frighten you. However, should it happen, you know you can get help and protection. I put into you the trust that you will keep an eye on each other and that if either of you ever shows signs that something may not be right, you will get to the root of the problem and deal with it, whether it has to do with this matter or anything else.

You must never run away from problems like Mummy did. I ran away from home to escape my problems and it only made life more difficult in the long run. I had no choice, really, but in today's society, help is always available for children. Deal with your problems, no matter what they may be. If you run away from any problem, it will still be there when you come back. Problems only go away when they are dealt with. I hope you carry this conviction throughout life.

Chin up, my angels, there are worse things in life, most of which you will never experience because you have the benefit of loving parents. I had to let you know about these things for your own good and protection.

Most advice sounds filled with doom and gloom but I must emphasise that, on the whole, life is absolutely wonderful. Everybody encounters snags and problems throughout life but, at the end of the day, everyone wants to live. The reason for this is that life is filled with much more joy than sorrow and every cloud has a silver lining. Things may seem bad at times but those moments are always replaced with something marvellous that makes you pleased to be alive.

I imagine all caring parents wish their children didn't have to experience disappointments in life but that is the only way to learn and grow. I can only say that anything that goes wrong pales against the things that go right. I promise. Life is so wonderful. You'll see.

18

MUMMY – AGED 12

I had become a routine runaway. You could set a clock as to when I would take off. At this point, I was only disappearing overnight. Rather than react, the Donaldsons chose to pretend that everything was normal and didn't even bother contacting the authorities when I didn't come home. By a couple of months into my twelfth year, they acted as if I didn't exist. They had completely lost interest in me.

The only person who showed any form of interest in me was Filthy Steve. Sadly, it was an unhealthy interest. I had developed a waistline and my breasts were growing. The more my body changed, the more he lusted after me. I was desperate to be put into a home so that I could get away from Steve. I knew my days were numbered. He continually tried to create situations in which he could be left alone with me. I was scared of what might happen so I ran away whenever his plans looked as if they might become reality.

I hadn't seen Isobelle since I ran off to London because I didn't want another person preaching to me about my behaviour, especially as she didn't understand the reasons behind my actions. I was wandering the streets aimlessly one day in a state of utter despair when I became attracted to a gospel church, drawn to it by the vibrant, energetic voices of the choir. I couldn't resist wandering in. I stayed and watched the peaceful, happy faces of the congregation.

I felt so safe in there. I started going every Wednesday night and again on Sundays. I had never been baptised and asked the pastor to do this. I felt a strong need to belong somewhere. I had never known the sort of peace I experienced in that church and I wanted to become a part of the large congregation.

A few months later, the pastor felt I was ready to be baptised. I invited Isobelle and all the Donaldsons but, incredibly, not one of them attended my baptism. Many of the congregation were present for the happy event but it didn't compensate for the absence of my family.

I dressed in white for the occasion. By the altar, the floor opened to reveal a little pond of water. I was baptised in that pond. I continued attending for some time and became involved in most of the church events, such as day trips, Bible lessons and Sunday School. I no longer felt like a loner. All the members of the congregation genuinely cared for one another. I loved Sunday morning and looked forward to it each week. I joined in all the songs and sang with all my might. I developed a passion for singing.

It was leading up to Christmas and I sang 'Silent Night' on my own, by the altar. Even today I cannot listen to 'Silent Night' without my eyes watering. There was something about the hymn that touched me. The song reminded me of a close, happy family, the very thing I had wished for all my life. By this time the congregation knew of my background and they called me Orphan Annie. I saw a lot of wet eyes when I sang 'Silent Night' that day. My own family weren't present but the congregation had become like one large family to me. Even so, nothing really compensated for the real thing.

I was now at Stubs Well Secondary School, which took me into a new neck of the woods. I enjoyed exploring the area, although I didn't like the school itself and dodged lessons. I went to registration in the morning and immediately left the building afterwards. I would go to Margaret's friend's house and play cards for hours, then go home in the afternoon as if I had been to school.

At school I would produce letters which I had written myself, to explain my absence. I always signed them Alexzina Donaldson. I was finally caught when a letter of complaint about absenteeism was sent from the school to my parents. Mum Donaldson was outraged when she was summoned to the school to explain my lack of attendance. This erupted into new problems at home, which resulted in me running away again, this time for three days. I stayed at a squatters' house.

They said I should cut my hair short, like a boy's, so that the police wouldn't recognise me because they would be looking for someone with a different description. It made a lot of sense so I cut off my long brown locks. My new hairstyle made me look like a skinhead. The squatters gave me boys' clothes and I stayed indoors during the day and only went out when it fell dark. Ironically, I was virtually on Mum Donaldson's doorstep as I was only around the corner from our flat.

One of the squatters kept pressuring me to tell him why I continually ran away from home, but I refused. He was worried that the members of the household would get into trouble for hiding a minor so I left after three days and returned to the Donaldsons.

When I got home, Mum Donaldson said she no longer

wanted me in her home. I had finally achieved what I had hoped for. I was greatly relieved. My battle was over.

That very same day I was taken by the social services to Burnside Remand Home, where I met a woman called Ziggy who was appointed as my social worker. I took an instant liking to her. Ziggy was from Norway. She was tall with blue eyes and long, blonde hair. She spoke perfect English. The remand centre was for young offenders or children who were beyond their parents' control. There was one section for fifteen boys and another for five girls. The offenders and runaways shared the same quarters.

My first interview was with the headmaster of the home, Joe Miller. I became very fond of him and grew to trust him. He was a fine, upstanding man with sound values and character. I respected him. He was, in fact, the first person I had ever respected. He was fair to all the children in the home and extremely dedicated to his work. Somehow, he always found time for every single child. He believed that all children are individual and special and felt they had to be treated accordingly. He made sure that he knew us all very well and developed a caring and loving bond with everyone under his roof. He called me Annie Anderson. I used to hate being called Annie but it sounded like music coming from him.

We had our very own billy goat, chickens and geese. We all had appointed chores which were carried out like clockwork. On wash day, the girls were assigned to wash all the boys' uniforms as well as our own.

I loved feeding the goat all our scraps after mealtimes. The only thing I missed was freedom to wander and explore. We weren't allowed out of the grounds and received our education within the boundaries of the remand centre.

No child stayed at Burnside for more than three weeks before a panel decided the youngster's future. The child was then returned to Burnside until the appointed time when they were sent to begin their new lives. That usually took a further two months.

I enjoyed my stay at Burnside. In fact, I loved it there, although I was sorry not to be able to attend church. I must add that I didn't miss the Donaldsons at all. Isobelle rarely entered my thoughts, although, occasionally, I wondered what Margaret was up to.

Parents were permitted to visit their children one day a week. I was the only one who never had any visitors. Then, one afternoon, Mr Miller told me that someone had arrived to see me. I was absolutely stunned. At first I thought it must be Mum Donaldson. Then Mr Miller said it was my natural mother but I didn't have to see her if I didn't want to. There were a few things I wanted to say to her, however, and I thought now was as good a time as any.

She was waiting at the bottom of the stairs with bags full of goodies. Anger rose within me as soon as I set eyes on her. She was all smiles. I wondered what she found so amusing. I still resented the fact that she hadn't come to claim me once she knew she could. She said she wasn't there to argue and had come to see if I was all right. I said it was a bit late for that. She offered to leave if I wished but I didn't feel it was necessary. I was very bitter about her children, most of whom weren't hers while I, her own flesh and blood, had had to manoeuvre myself into the situation I was in for my own protection.

Isobelle expressed her guilt over what she had done but made it clear that it was too late to turn the clock back. I didn't feel in the least bit sorry for her. I had got to the stage where I didn't trust her. After all, it was Margaret who had told me the truth. I wondered if Isobelle would ever be honest with me. I didn't have much faith in her. All I wanted was the simplest, most natural things in life; the gifts that most children are born with. I wanted to be part of a proper family and belong to someone. I wanted someone who belonged to me. I couldn't concentrate on what Isobelle was saying. My mind kept drifting to my own thoughts.

I marvelled at how lucky my two half-brothers were and how I had been dealt a rotten blow. Just as those thoughts circulated through my mind, Isobelle said something that shocked me back to the present. She informed me that I had another brother. I stared at her in complete bewilderment. I wanted to know where he was and who he was. What happened to him? When was he born? What did she do with him?

She explained that he was born after me but before she met John. He was given up straight away at birth for adoption – or so she said. She wouldn't tell me who his father was. I wondered if we shared the same father. She wouldn't even tell me his age but she did say his name was Stewart. No surname. He had been adopted by a Mr and Mrs Cookson or Cootson from Dundee. I have never seen him and I have tried over the years to trace him without success. Even as I write this, I am desperate to know who he is and where he is. All I know is that he's my brother.

At the time Isobelle said it was best to let sleeping dogs lie. That seemed to be the story of my life. I dimly remembered having heard that she had given birth to a boy when I was little, but I had forgotten all about it. I wondered why she had bothered to tell me at all. Why did she reveal some things but not everything? I had had enough. Not only had she abandoned me, she had also done it to another poor child as well. I only hope he went to a better home than I.

I was sickened and disgusted at this new piece of information. I was also outraged that Isobelle chose yet again to tell me only one-quarter of the facts and that I had to guess whether she had mingled lies with the small offering as well. I looked at her and suddenly realised how easily Isobelle disposed of her children. Did she not have any feeling for human life, for the children or their fathers? It made me realise that I didn't know the woman at all. I was relieved when the visiting hour was over. I needed time on my own to collect my thoughts. That was the only moment I regretted being in Burnside because I couldn't walk out of doors and into open spaces. I needed to be by water. I needed to think.

As I climbed the stairs to my room, I caught sight of Mr Miller. He knew I had been unnerved by Isobelle's visit. He asked me to come downstairs and see him in his office. I was so enraged by what I had learned from Isobelle that I responded to Mr Miller's request by cursing and swearing. I kept saying, 'Why is everyone doing this to me?' He tried to comfort and calm me but I was beyond that.

He marched me upstairs and put me in an isolated room.

He said he would talk to me when I had calmed down; it was pointless trying to communicate with an hysterical person.

I sat in solitude and sang songs to comfort myself. The one that fell from my lips over and over was the song Daddy Donaldson sang to me for years, 'I'm Nobody's Child'. I wallowed in self-pity. I slid down the wall in the corner of the room and sat crumpled in a loose heap for I had no strength left even to sit up straight. The intolerable frustration had drained me.

I thought of kind Mr Miller and how horrible I had been to him. He was the only person who had ever shown any faith in me and I had abused him with my angry words. Somehow, I knew he understood my actions. I'm sure I wasn't the only emotionally confused child he had under his roof.

A few hours passed and I could hear his distinctive footsteps and jolly whistle as he approached the isolation room. He unlocked the door and let himself in. I was still a crumpled heap in the corner. He asked me to stand and I did and instantly apologised for my behaviour, adding that I couldn't take any more of life.

He said I clearly had problems and I should share them with him. I said I'd rather keep certain things to myself. He chose his words very carefully and asked me in a roundabout way if I had ever been put in an uncomfortable or unnatural situation with a man. He said it was clear, from his experience, that something was desperately wrong with me. I was a damaged child. I could feel my face turn red. I can't really explain it but I felt so ashamed that I had been tampered with by Steve that I couldn't get a word out. I guess he already knew. The details were unnecessary.

He offered to let me out of isolation if I stayed calm and returned to my unit. I joined the rest of the boys and girls for tea and ended up in fisticuffs with a fifteen-year-old boy who said something to me that reminded me of the nasty things Steve used to whisper in my ear. I lost my temper and threw a cup of tea at the boy. A male teacher summoned Mr Miller and I was marched up to the isolation room for the second time that day. I didn't go easily. I kicked and screamed like mad. Shortly afterwards a house-mother arrived with my meal on a tray. I told her to take it away.

Within minutes Mr Miller's determined footsteps neared my door. He was not whistling this time. He stormed in and told me I would remain there until I learned to control my temper. I sobbed and he came closer and took me in his arms like a caring father. I felt so safe and protected. He took a white hanky out of his pocket and wiped my tears away. He pleaded with me to talk to him. I just said, 'Please don't ask me about these things.'

I stayed in isolation until the next morning as he felt I needed time to myself without distractions from the other children. The full day had been too much for me. I was so exhausted, physically and mentally, that I fell into a deep sleep.

Mr Miller started work at 8.30 in the morning. I had hoped he would be the first to open my door and, indeed, he was. He was about five feet nine inches tall with broad shoulders and a big tummy, which seemed to say that he was well looked after at home. He had a moustache like the upturned handlebars of a bicycle, warm blue eyes and a balding head. His aftershave always lingered long after he was gone. When he entered my room, he asked in a fatherly tone if I had slept well. I inhaled his familiar scent, smiled and replied, 'Very well indeed.'

He invited me to join the rest of the children. I was more than eager but I didn't want to go without apologising. I asked about the boy I had thrown the tea at and was relieved to hear that he was fine.

The following few days were happy and I settled down once again. I had the task of setting the staff's dining table for lunch and dinner. I enjoyed this as it was next door to Mr Miller's office. I liked being nearby and would find little excuses to pop in for a chat.

Mrs Miller was petite with a large, warm heart. I respected her as well but preferred to be near Mr Miller. He called me a cheeky little monkey. I dreaded the day I would have to leave Burnside but it was inevitable.

The day was fixed for the children's panel to decide my future. I asked Mr Miller if he knew where they would send me. He had no idea. I was accompanied to the panel by a social worker. All those supposedly skilled people discussed my future as if I wasn't even there and I resented it.

One woman sniffed at me, 'And what do you have to say for yourself, young lady?'

I demanded to know what gave them the right to make judgements about my future without knowing what they were actually dealing with. I felt futures shouldn't be decided upon on the strength of notes in a file. I enquired as to whether they had already made their minds up as to where they were sending me. When they confirmed they had, I simply replied, 'Then there is no need for me to tell you what I have to say for myself as it will have no bearing on decisions you have already made. It can only serve to feed your curiosity.'

I was asked to wait outside. I bit my fingernails in the waiting room and fumed that I had no say in my own future.

Fifteen minutes later I was summoned to the room and told to be seated. I felt as if I had been betrayed by the system itself. I wanted my feelings to be taken into consideration but I had no say in the matter. I hadn't bargained on that when I set out to be taken into care.

I was told I was to be transferred to Balnacraig School in Perth. It was a school for uncontrollable or abused children. I was to be boarded there. In other words, that was my new home. I wouldn't be able to leave the grounds unless I was escorted by a housemother. An available place was coming up soon and I was to stay at Burnside until that time arrived. Later that afternoon Mr Miller wanted to know how I had got on. Before I had a chance to answer, the social worker took it upon herself to answer on my behalf. I was not amused.

I told the other girls that I would be leaving soon. I was worried about moving away from Mr Miller. I would be entering the unknown. I liked the comfort and support Mr and Mrs Miller provided and knew I would sorely miss them. The only decent thing to be said of the outcome was that I would be far away from Steve.

The following week a vacancy came up at Balnacraig. I was dismayed. I had never expected things to happen so fast. I had only two days to prepare for my new move.

I left with all my worldly belongings – the clothes and undergarments that I stood up in. I left all the toiletries Isobelle brought for me at Burnside for the girls to share out among themselves.

The social worker explained that I would be wearing a school uniform at all times. The school provided soap, toothpaste, toothbrush and all the bare necessities. I wasn't allowed any contact with outsiders apart from my parents, so I was unable to inform Margaret of my move. We were allowed to write and receive letters but all outgoing and incoming post was read. Those in power decided what would be sent and received.

A social worker collected me by car. After long goodbyes with Mr and Mrs Miller, I was escorted to Balnacraig School. As the car pulled away, I instinctively knew that I would see Mr Miller again. The thought warmed me.

Perth was 23 miles away from Dundee. I never uttered a word during the entire trip as I was so scared of what lay ahead. I wondered what the other girls would be like and if they would give me a hard time. There were no boys at this school.

As we turned into the drive I saw an enormous, attractive house with big, arched windows. It was surrounded by beautiful, green, well-kept grounds. A housemother answered the door and introduced herself. I was taken to an office where I was informed of the rules and regulations of the house. I knew from that moment that I wouldn't enjoy my stay. There was no smoking, no leaving the grounds, no phone calls. Everything was regimented, right down to the time they expected you to close your eyes and fall asleep. There was a book of rules to be obeyed or else privileges, such as watching television, would be taken away.

Janet, who had started as a cleaner and had been promoted to housemother, escorted me to a little room where I was given pants, socks, a towel, a toothbrush, toothpaste, soap and talcum powder. That was the room where we would do our ironing and mend our clothes.

Then she took me on a tour of the house which was packed with bedrooms. Each room bore the name of a mountain or loch in Scotland. The dining and recreation rooms were huge. There were stunning leaded windows which revealed a beautiful lawn and the gardener's house beyond. There was a tiny piano room and a scullery set at the back of the house. Leading from the kitchen was a row of toilets. Some of the girls who were allowed off the grounds would sneak cigarettes back and smoke them in the loos.

There were stairs leading from the back of the house up to the bedrooms. A magnificent hallway led to more stairs and dormitories. I never believed I would learn my way around. In reality, it didn't take long. I took an instant liking to Janet. She constantly chewed gum to hide the smell of the cigarettes she smoked, strictly against house rules. She had had a humble and troubled background and I imagine that is why she understood the girls at Balnacraig better than the trained staff did. If girls had problems, they went to Janet rather than approach other members of staff.

I made up my mind early on that I wouldn't get up to any tricks to draw attention or impress anyone at Balnacraig.

I shared a bedroom with three other girls. We had the freedom to arrange our room the way we saw fit. I pushed my bed over so that it was under a window and built a partition with my dressing table and bedside locker. It became my little domain. Over the next few months, I watched rows, cat fights and petty jealousies flare up the whole time among the girls. I suppose that is only to be expected in a closed environment full of young women.

After a few months, I started experiencing stomach pains. The nurses thought I was starting my period, then, one evening, I collapsed in the recreation room and was rushed to hospital in an ambulance with blue flashing lights. I was taken into Casualty and prepared for the operating theatre straight away. My appendix, which was on the brink of bursting, was removed.

In those days this was a big operation which left a tremendous scar. I convalesced in hospital for a further ten days after the operation and I was excused from house chores for a further two weeks.

There was only one teacher assigned to educate the girls between the ages of twelve and fifteen. All the girls, despite their difference in ages, were put in one single class. It seemed highly unlikely that I would learn anything at all.

Although the house was beautiful and Janet was as sweet as could be, I felt there was more to life and I wanted to move on. I was nearing my thirteenth birthday when I decided to run away, hoping I would be sent back to Mr and Mrs Miller. I missed them and wanted to be under their roof once more. I took off one day when everyone else was preoccupied and headed back to Dundee. I hitch-hiked because I didn't have a single penny to call my own and I was given a lift by a married couple who didn't question my age or my actions.

As soon as I arrived in Dundee I went looking for Margaret at the YWCA. She was delighted to see me as we hadn't seen each other for half a year. I told her the police would soon be looking for me and I assumed Margaret would be their first stop.

She took me to a friend's house and told them about my situation. They tried to help me as best they could. Over a period of three weeks, I stayed at several different addresses, all belonging to Margaret's friends. They kept me in food and spending money.

One evening I couldn't get back to where I was staying so I found a landing on a tower block and made a bed out of assorted doormats which I borrowed from tenants' doorsteps. A milkman saw me snoozing early in the morning and called the police. I was taken to the local police station and Balnacraig was notified of my whereabouts.

Margaret guessed that the police had picked me up when I didn't return to her friend's flat. I was put into a cell at the police station and informed that I would be collected by a staff member from Balnacraig. Fortunately, it was Janet. I didn't want to return to Balnacraig but had little choice. I spent the whole ride back to school telling Janet of my adventures. She couldn't get a word in edgeways.

I was asked hundreds of questions by the headmaster but I refused to tell him where I had been. I didn't want to get those who had helped me into trouble. All the girls were very inquisitive but I didn't share my adventure with them because I thought they were untrustworthy.

I started looking forward to my thirteenth birthday because then I would officially become a teenager. I was told by the headmaster that Mum Donaldson would be visiting me on my birthday. She would be accompanied by Mr Donaldson and their son. I had mixed feelings about seeing them after all this time as I hadn't seen or spoken to them for nearly a year. I was apprehensive and felt that, had they been more honest or understanding, my life wouldn't be in such a mess. They were happy people. Wasn't I entitled to happiness as well? The Donaldsons were in my last thoughts before falling asleep and in the first when I awoke. They occupied more space in my mind during the day than I felt comfortable with. I began dreading my birthday but, finally, the day arrived.

19

KARL AND KANDY – ADVICE AGED 12

I think you will notice at this age, more than at any other time to date, the genetic traits you have inherited from your parents. You may notice physical or intellectual similarities between yourselves and us. I would not suggest, however, that your life is in any way parallel to mine and have endeavoured to make sure that it certainly will not be.

At this age, much about life will already have become obvious to you and many senses will have developed. I have now come to the point where I feel it is time to talk about disappointments.

Life is what we make it. There will be things you won't approve of and things that you will. You must try to take the good with the bad and make things work for yourself. There won't always be a role model to motivate you. Search within your own heart and consider very carefully the conclusions you come to. Balance the advice given to you by Daddy and your guardians. At the age of twelve you will have the ability to exercise a great deal of reasoning.

There will be times when you won't know which way to go or what choices to make but instincts often help to overcome uncertainty. Fear, panic and indecision are terrible things but life would be dreadfully boring without having to make any choices. Life is like a shell on the beach, which has a variety of different patterns and colours running through it.

Around this age you will be taking on more responsibilities. You may feel a strong desire to care for and protect the people you love and you will become more aware of their feelings too. You will want to share your good or triumphant moments with those who mean the most to you. Wherever you two go in life, you will meet people who will be delighted to see you do well and also maybe some who will be jealous and try to interfere with your progress. Again, I will remind you to believe in yourself, hold strong to your moral code and always be positive. Look on the bright side of everything because life is filled with goodness and joy, although sometimes it takes a while to see these things.

You only have to look at someone less loved, less healthy or less privileged than yourself to realise how lucky you are. That is when you will appreciate all you have and all you have to look forward to.

Life is a precious gift that we have been given to make as good or difficult for ourselves as we choose. Make the best of it. By your thirteenth year more will be expected of you, from teachers, Daddy, guardians and society in general. Be a good example to each other. I trust and hope that, when you reflect on my life, certain things will become clear.

I hope you will be a credit to me and to yourselves, not forgetting Daddy, of course. God bless. Enjoy the bright side of life and I hope you make more right decisions than wrong ones. I've been there too. Whatever happens, I can guarantee that you will learn from most of your experiences. Life itself is a never-ending education. I can only pray that most of your experiences will be good.

In many respects, life gets easier as you go along, knowing that something new and different is always right around the corner. That's what makes everything so exciting. Somehow, you always know that there is a great deal to look forward to. Enjoy!

20

MUMMY – AGED 13

I spent a restless night on the eve of my thirteenth birthday. I had mixed feelings about seeing the Donaldsons. The morning seemed to drag on. By the time I was informed that they had arrived and were waiting for me in the drawing room, I was understandably nervous and tense.

They were quite obviously shocked at the sight of me. My hair was cut to a quarter of an inch from my head. I liked my haircut as it was very trendy at that time. I liked it even more when I saw the appalled look on their faces.

We didn't run into each other's arms as most caring families would. I hadn't spoken to them on the phone nor corresponded since I had arrived at Balnacraig. The atmosphere was awkward. I felt as if we were strangers. I didn't think I had much to say to them.

They hadn't changed much during the year, although Dad Donaldson seemed to have a little more grey hair. They were now in their fifties and looked well for their ages. My brother was quiet. We didn't really know each other because he had moved away from home while I was still tiny.

Very formally Mum Donaldson enquired about my health. I said I felt fine and I was coping well. I didn't want to give them the pleasure of thinking that I was suffering in any way. She handed me a gift and a couple of cards. I was thrilled with the present. It was a red Fidelity AM/FM radio which was battery-operated. It didn't mean a thing to me that it came from the Donaldsons. I would have been just as happy with the gift if it had come from strangers. I hadn't actually expected anything from them and was very surprised when they actually handed me the perfect present. I loved music and was delighted to have the radio.

I thanked them and really meant it. I invited them to tour the school and grounds. We took a leisurely stroll and didn't talk much for fear of saying the wrong thing. They stayed a couple of hours. During that time I asked after Isobelle but all they said was that they hadn't seen much of her.

I was relieved when they said they had to be on their way. I saw them to the door, then ran straight to my room. I was surprised to find tears rolling down my cheeks. I wondered what the tears meant.

One of the other girls asked who my visitors had been. I told her that I wanted to be left on my own. I felt confused. I hated what they had done to me and I hated myself for what I had done to them in return. My room-mates told me to put it all behind me before I drove myself mad. They said I would end up with a nervous breakdown. I didn't even know what that was. I stayed in my room when everyone gathered in the dining room for their evening meal.

I had shut myself away to think about the mother who had left me behind and the Donaldsons who fell out of love with me when I was no longer a cute little toddler. I lay in my bed and longed for Mr and Mrs Miller and their love and warmth. Whenever things went wrong I would think of them and somehow it would ease my torment. Isobelle and the Donaldsons didn't have an inkling what their denial and rejection had done to me.

Sparrow, a tiny girl whom I had befriended, came to the room and asked what was troubling me. I don't know why, perhaps I was very vulnerable at that moment, but I actually told her in detail what was upsetting me. As young as she was, she too, had been through a great deal and she told me very firmly that I was green around the gills. She said if adults treat us badly we tend to rebel. It is a natural reaction. Then we are tagged as problem children and are always in the wrong. When we are good and merit praise, some adults never notice, but when we do something wrong they are sure to criticise us for going off the rails. They never take any form of blame for the things we are pushed into doing. Often we do things for attention. It is our way of crying for help but adults never see themselves as the catalyst. It all made sense to me but it didn't change the situation I was in.

Sparrow was twelve but looked younger and acted a lot older. She was very wise. I told her I couldn't wait until I was sixteen so that I could do what I wanted with my life. She said I was foolish to wish my life away. She pointed out that we weren't the only young people with problems; there were a lot more just like us.

I told her I had plotted to be taken into care for my own safety although I didn't go into the gory details. I learned about the circumstances that had bought her to Balnacraig.

Her mother had died when she was nine and she had

spent long, lonely nights missing the mother she had been so close to. She said nothing about her father. She had continually run away, looking for the love that had died with her mother. I already knew there was no substitute for a mother's love but it is so strange how people never give up looking for it. We both burst into tears. I told her how sorry I felt for her. She had taken a burden off her shoulders just by talking about it.

I suggested that, one day, when we were older, perhaps we would sort our lives out and give our own children the love and support we had been denied. We would then have a chance to experience what we had lost through our own offspring – as I did with you two babies.

Sparrow and I wiped away our tears and joined the others in the recreation room. We sat in our chairs staring at the television but we neither heard nor saw what was on the screen, for our thoughts were elsewhere.

I suddenly felt nauseous and went to the kitchen for a glass of water. My hands were clenched into tense, tight fists. My knuckles had gone white. How I hated everyone who had hurt me. I was a person, a human being with needs that continued to go unnoticed. I felt I couldn't take it any more and so I ran away that evening.

I hitch-hiked back to Dundee and wandered the streets all night, then contacted Margaret the following day and told her I didn't know what to do with my empty life. She didn't know what to say to me. I left the town centre and wandered to the Broughty Ferry pier. The tide was in and the water was high and raging. I stood at the edge and watched the rough waves crashing on the rocks. I thought of Isobelle, the Donaldsons and Steve. I went to take a step forward so that I could be devoured by the angry sea. It seemed only right that something so like myself should claim my life. My body was just about to fall into the water when a pair of strong hands grabbed me and pulled me to safety.

My rescuer was a large man with a full beard and very wise, piercing blue eyes. He gently and silently guided me away from the water's edge. I sobbed in desperation. Why had he stopped me?

When we were a safe distance from the water he stopped and looked at me. His voice was kind and soothing. His first words were, 'Are your problems so big? Have you no parents?'

I didn't reply. He was about to phone the police and I pleaded with him not to. He thought about it for a few minutes and took me to his house instead, where he made a mug of hot chocolate for me. He enquired as to the whereabouts of my parents. I told him I was an orphan but I knew he didn't believe me. He asked if I was a runaway. The heat rushed to my face, turning me scarlet. 'Ah,' he said, 'so you are.' At that point I told him I was leaving. 'Where will you go?' he asked, gently.

I replied, rather grandly, that I would sail the seven seas, never to be found. He let out a hearty laugh. He told me it was a criminal offence to hide a runaway but he would feel very guilty if I returned to the waterfront and took my own life. I hoped he was implying that he would let me stay. He told me his name was Jack and that he was a fisherman. He said he would help me as long as I was truthful. He wanted to know who I was, where I came from and why I was going to kill myself.

I told him everything about myself, Isobelle and the Donaldsons. The only thing I left out was Steve. He said he would let me stay providing I did not wander out during the day as he could get into serious trouble if I were found and traced back to his house.

Jack lived alone and his house was immaculate. I couldn't help but wonder for a moment if he was like Steve. I hoped he was just a warm-hearted person who was willing to help a lost child to find some sort of direction. He showed me to a spare room. It was a child's room, suitably decorated for a girl. It was very clean and I wondered why there was such a room in his house. He told me he was divorced and had three daughters. He said he always kept the room ready in case they returned. He lived in hope. I thought he was kind to think so much of his children.

Jack showed me the bathroom and gave me some towels. He told me he would shop the following morning and buy me a change of clothes. I awoke to find a pair of trousers, a T-shirt, underwear and socks outside my bedroom door. There was also the smell of sausages and the sound of Jack whistling a merry tune which carried right through the house. He cheerfully wished me good morning and asked if I had slept well although he already knew I had because he told me he had checked on me during the night to make sure I was all right. I couldn't believe my luck!

The only thing I wasn't happy about was having to stay indoors. I was desperate to explore the seafront but I didn't want Jack to get into trouble over his kindness so I thought it best to follow his rules. I was asked not to answer the phone or the door as people might question my presence. I amused myself by watching television.

We got along very well and truly enjoyed each other's company. Jack cooked breakfast every morning and I kept the house spotless. I would prepare the vegetables for our evening meal and Jack would come home and cook again. He thought it was wonderful to have company and said I livened the house up. He liked coming home to the sound of human activity and a crackling, warm fire.

Two weeks later I told him I was going crazy and couldn't stay closed up indoors a minute longer, so he started taking me for walks in the evening. We walked along the beach and I looked at the water which was no longer crashing violently. The sea was as calm as I was. I was so content with Jack. He made me feel that life was worth living. He treated me as I deserved to be treated, like a human being.

He suggested that he should contact a social worker and arrange to look after me. He said he felt fatherly toward me and didn't want me to go if I was happy. I explained that the authorities would not allow him to care for me as he was unmarried and was basically a stranger. I told him I would rather keep him to myself so that, if I had problems, I would always know there was a safe and caring person behind me. He agreed to this. I had become very fond of Jack and started to worry about the serious trouble there would be for him if I was caught at his house.

That is when I told him I felt it was best for me to move on. He took me for a walk and sat me on a rock by the waterfront. It was the same rock I had nearly stepped off on the night that I met him. He said he had a favour to ask of me. He requested that when I chose to go, I would do it when he was not at home. He said he couldn't bear to say goodbye to me. I told him that I had already made up my mind to do that anyway. I would leave within the next few days. I said how grateful I was for all he had done and wished I could stay longer. I knew he must have been a good father to his daughters and I pitied them for being denied his company.

Three days later, I waited until Jack had gone fishing then packed a bag that he had given me. As I was filling the bag I found an envelope in it and I opened it to see £50 (worth £150 in today's money) and a letter from Jack. It read, 'I don't know when you will go but you will surely have to pack this bag. I hope the money will help you on your travels. Wherever your path leads you, I hope it will lead back to me someday. I don't know where you will go or what will happen to you. Make sure you take my phone number and call me if you need me any time of the day or night. I will always be here.' 'Yours Sincerely' was scrubbed out and replaced with 'Lots of love, Jack.'

I was overwhelmed. I put my bag down and thought about staying but I knew it would be best for Jack if I left. I wouldn't be able to live with myself if he got into trouble because of me. I looked through the house one final time before parting and I inhaled all the familiar scents. Even today, as I write this, I can almost smell Jack's house.

As I made my way to the bus station, I thought about what I was leaving behind. The clear image of Jack walking through his front gate and in at the wooden door was so vivid. I could see him sitting on the floral sofa in front of the fire. Tears filled my eyes.

I stood at the bus station not wanting to go anywhere except back to Jack's. I didn't board the first two buses that came because I was still trying to reach a decision as to whether I should go or stay. I finally jumped on the third bus and headed for Glasgow. I didn't feel ashamed about being on the run. The only thing I was unsure of was my destiny. I wondered what would happen when the police found me. I was on my own again. I got off the bus in Glasgow and boarded the next one straight back to Dundee. Three hours later I was on Jack's doorstep. It was 8 p.m. and I knew he wouldn't be in yet because I knew his routine so well. I strolled along the beach to pass the time, knowing he would be home around 10.30. I sat on my rock and stared at the sea for ages. I had no shadow of a doubt that he would be pleased to see me. I was right.

As I neared Jack's, I could see that the sitting-room light was on. I quietly opened the gate and hesitated before knocking. He opened the door and swung me up into the air. He was so glad I had come home. I asked if I could stay one more week and then turn myself in to the authorities. Jack agreed with this because he wanted the assurance of knowing I was safe.

It was such an enjoyable week. Jack gave up his fishing to take me out during the day. We went sailing in his boat and picnicked several times. We went to the cinema to see *Pinocchio*. I had more fun in one single week with Jack than I had had in all my thirteen years with anyone else. I told him that the only other thing I had really enjoyed was when I rode at the stables. He told me he had heard of Mr Conky. The only thing I continued to hide from Jack was the story of Dirty Steve.

The week went too fast. I dreaded Monday, which was when I had promised to hand myself over to the police.

When I awoke that day I didn't want to go but I kept my word. I owed that much to Jack.

He left the house as usual that Monday morning. I couldn't eat the breakfast he had prepared. I left soon after and went straight to the police station in Dundee. The officer laughed at my attempt to give myself up. He said, 'Oh, no. Not another one.' I was collected and taken back to Balnacraig.

Sparrow was very excited by my return. She wanted to know every detail of what had happened but I never told her a thing about Jack. As I had promised, I kept him a secret. I found it impossible to settle back into the routine of the home now that I knew there were greater things beyond Balnacraig's gates. A few of the girls were allowed out of the school grounds and I depended on them to post letters secretly for me. I wrote several times to Jack. He couldn't reply because he knew his letters to me would be read by a school warden. On Sundays I would slip away from church for a few minutes without being noticed. I used those stolen minutes to phone Jack.

I decided that the next time I ran away, it would be for good and I knew where I would go. Christmas arrived and I spent it at Balnacraig. The only card I sent was to Jack. I received only one card. It bore a Broughty Ferry post code and had been opened by a warden. It was signed, 'Love from father Donaldson.' I knew it was from Jack and I kept it under my pillow for years. Whenever I felt down I would look at the card. Just knowing Jack cared was enough to put me in good spirits again.

Shortly after Christmas, I ran away again. This time I went to see Margaret because Jack's milkman had informed me that he had gone on holiday for three weeks. I stayed at Margaret's friend's house for two weeks and when I marched into the police station to give myself up once again, I discovered, much to my delight, that Balnacraig had refused to have me back.

It was like a dream come true because now I was sent back to Burnside and into Mr and Mrs Miller's fold. Mr Miller sent me to a school called Kirton High, where I ended up in the same class as their daughter. I did remarkably well at that school because, for once, I was happy. Mr Miller had given me an opportunity to prove myself and I didn't let him down for many months. My fourteenth birthday was just around the corner and I couldn't have been happier because I was in a place I loved.

There were no phone boxes between the school and Burnside as it was a very isolated area. I had no way of letting Jack know where I was until, finally, I persuaded someone to post a letter for me. I hadn't spoken to the Donaldsons since my last birthday and hadn't heard from Isobelle in nearly two years. They didn't matter to me any longer.

My hair was growing beautifully and I had started experimenting with make-up. I was blossoming in all the right places and noticed that I was turning into a young woman. I went to bed thinking girly thoughts. It was nice not to be dwelling on unhappy things for once in my life. I dozed off thinking about how I should wear my make-up and do my hair to celebrate my birthday the following day.

21

KARL AND KANDY – ADVICE AGED 13

Congratulations! You are now teenagers! This is a difficult phase, in which you will hover somewhere between being a child and an adolescent. It may seem a bit unnerving for you both but go with the flow. There is a lot of fun to look forward to from this point on.

Don't blush when Mummy says this, but it is now time to have a chat about sex. At this age, Karl, or perhaps a little before this age, depending on your physical development, it is actually possible for you to father a child.

Don't giggle, Kandy, because it is also possible for you to become a mother!

I have no doubt that, by this stage of your life, you will have been told at school about AIDS, sexual relationships and sexual bodily functions. Without being too heavy and clinical about it, I want to make a point to both of you about protection from sexually transmitted diseases and about getting a girl pregnant, or in your case, Kandy, getting pregnant. Many would agree that it is better to be safe than sorry.

If you haven't done so already, you are soon likely to have thoughts about kissing or having other physical experiences with a person of the opposite sex. I would like to point out that at the time when I am writing this, the law states that it is illegal for people to have sexual intercourse under the age of sixteen. Of course, that doesn't stop people from doing so. I feel I must give you advice in case you are tempted into sexual experimentation at an early age but I pray to God, especially with you, Kandy, that this doesn't happen for some years to come. None the less, this is as good a time as any to talk about it, although it is going to be a one-sided conversation as I am likely to be doing all the talking and none of the listening.

I would prefer you to experiment with kissing, cuddling, touching or sex at a later age but one can't possibly dictate that side of nature's progress to another person. First experiences can be very pleasurable but can also prove to be a dangerous voyage into the unknown. I would like them to be only pleasurable for you two as the danger is avoidable if you heed certain precautions and begin at a suitable age, like nearer to twenty. I must say, in all honesty, that I have almost lost my nerve about advising you on sexual activities. If only you could see the colour of my face right now! I would like to cut this short but I know I mustn't.

Karl, I assume that by now you may have experienced what are known as wet dreams. This is nothing to be ashamed of or embarrassed about. It happens to practically every boy at your age, so you are not the first nor the last. My advice to you is that if, and when, it happens, when you wake in the morning, take your bed linen off the bed and pop it into the laundry basket. Both Daddy and your guardian will be very understanding about this topic.

Kandy, it is likely that, within the next two years, you may give a boy a proper kiss. When this happens, you might feel strong physical reactions that will make you want to go further. Please don't. It might be better if you simply don't kiss until you are at least sixteen or seventeen.

Whatever happens to you two in the years to come, I'd like to emphasise that the use of a condom will protect you from diseases or pregnancy.

Phew, I'm glad that's over. I am now standing here with sweat dripping from my forehead.

So there you are, darlings, that was my offering on the birds and the bees. I will talk to you soon, around the age of sixteen, about falling in love, falling in lust, and infatuation. There is a difference between them all although they may, in the beginning, feel the same.

Talk to you next year. This is the first time I'm glad to sign out. What a relief!

22

MUMMY – AGED 14

The Donaldsons had been informed that I was back at Burnside but there was no indication that they would visit me on my birthday. I was relieved. I woke up with a feeling of great optimism. That feeling fizzled out within hours.

It was the strangest birthday I had had to date. It didn't feel like a birthday at all. I sat back and realised that my enthusiasm for birthdays had lessened with each passing year. I wondered if it was an indication that I was growing up. For a moment it saddened me to think this might be what growing up is all about.

The other kids in the remand centre, whom I barely knew at all, simply mumbled happy birthday without any real emotion behind the words. Mr and Mrs Miller gave me a card. There were no gifts at all. By 10.30 a.m. it felt like just another day. By noon I was rather depressed. It was the school holidays and I was bored. Mr Miller and a social worker said that I could go hiking for two weeks with an experienced school friend called Lizzie. It was agreed that the break would do me good.

Lizzie and I hitch-hiked all over Scotland, England and Wales. We stayed at assorted Youth Hostels along the way. I paid my way with the pocket money I had accumulated from the social services. We took tins of corned beef and baked beans with us to reduce expenses.

Our first stop was at a Youth Hostel in Piccadilly, London. We did the touristy thing and went sightseeing. We visited Buckingham Palace, the Tower of London and other places of historical importance. It was well organised and I enjoyed every minute of it. What a stark contrast to my first visit to London! This time round I didn't fear being seen by the police as everything was legal and above board. I enjoyed travelling under those circumstances and liked the comfort of knowing I would be clean and warm and had a bed to sleep in at night.

We decided London was a bit expensive and headed for Pontypridd in Wales but it seemed too quiet after the exciting hustle and bustle of London so we stayed just one night before moving on. I suggested that we work our way back up to Scotland. We ended in a place called Crianlarich, a small village in the glens. The scenery was absolutely stunning.

Wise Mr Miller had made a good decision for I now felt quite grown up and independent. We checked into the local Youth Hostel and had a quick look around the village as darkness was about to fall. Lizzie and I agreed to stay there for a while.

We woke at the crack of dawn and didn't bother about breakfast. We walked though forests and climbed a mountain called Ben Lawers. We reached the summit at 2 p.m. and stood and marvelled at the breathtaking view. For a moment I pitied people who would never see such a sight. The clouds seemed so near that I thought if I could jump high enough I would be able to touch them with my bare hands. I stood with my hands above my head and yelled at the top of my voice 'I'm free, I'm free!'

Lizzie looked at me in bewilderment. I explained that it was just a great sensation to stand there and feel free of the pressures of my childhood. I didn't have a worry in the world standing on Ben Lawers. It was my moment. I felt very proud of having reached the summit.

Lizzie laughed and said it wasn't such a great accomplishment as we had taken a footpath straight up rather than climb it. That would have been more difficult and complicated. It didn't matter to me, though. As far as I was concerned, I had reached the top and that was all that mattered.

We had to carry our belongings with us each day as we weren't allowed to leave anything in the hostel. We were only allowed to book in on a daily basis and couldn't check in for the week, so we had to return every afternoon or evening to book ourselves in once again. Basically, it was just a place to put your head down and have a wash and something to eat.

We unloaded our backpacks and sat there for some time, just munching on chocolate bars and taking in the view. Then Lizzie started asking questions about my childhood. She said she had seen people like me before, and that we wear a happy exterior which served to camouflage a troubled past. I told her that one day it would all come out and everyone would know about me. I made light of it. I hadn't worn myself out reaching the top of the mountain just to talk about my past. We made our way back down before it grew dark.

When we reached the bottom, I told Lizzie I remembered seeing a small body of water and that I wanted to soak my throbbing feet before returning to the hostel. We took our shoes off and gratefully placed our aching feet in the water. I could have sat there for ever. Lizzie wanted to go back to the Youth Hostel but I wanted to stay put. I told her to go back and that I would catch up with her later. She thought I was mad because all I wanted was to sit by the loch. She didn't understand the tranquil effect water has on me. I sat mesmerised by the gentle ripples and watched the water rush between my toes. My thoughts turned to Jack. I wondered what he was doing and if he was thinking of me. Then I looked at my watch and knew exactly what he was doing at that moment. He was such a creature of habit. I adored him for that because it made him very dependable.

I didn't have any urge whatsoever to return to the Youth Hostel, preferring the company of my own thoughts. If only Jack had been by my side. I could have showed him this beautiful place. He had enriched my life in so many ways; I wanted to do the same for him. I thought about the bond I had with him. He could easily have been my father and I wished that he was. I really felt I belonged to Jack. I hoped that someday I would be able to let everyone know about him. He was warm, unselfish, loving, genuine and more importantly, he was mine. My secret, safe, guardian angel. I could feel a lump grow in my throat. My eyes burned with tears. I could have sat by the stream all night but I didn't want to dwell on things that made me feel sad any longer and it was time to head back to Lizzie.

I didn't bother putting my shoes back on but carried them in my hands as I walked the short distance back to the hostel. Lizzie had wondered what was taking me so long. She couldn't imagine how anyone could be so happy on their own. She said I was 'some strange flower'.

As darkness fell, the hostel started to fill up with other travellers from all walks of life. We chatted to two French boys, Rafael and Jos. They told us the entertaining tale of their journey from France. Rafael had a guitar and he suggested that we head for the hills and build a campfire. We would sing the night away. I immediately forgot about my swollen feet and couldn't wait to get going.

We reached our destination and built a warm little fire. We boiled some water to make coffee and Jos started strumming on his guitar. We burst out laughing at the first song, 'Frère Jacques'. I asked Rafael if he knew the song called 'The Banks of the Ohio', which Olivia Newton John sang. I started the tune and he picked up on it. By the end of the night we were all in harmony. They complimented me on my voice. We cut it rather fine getting back to the hostel and just made it through the doors before the 11 p.m. curfew.

We bade each other goodnight in the hallway, only to bump into each other again in the kitchen less than an hour later. We drank mugs of coffee and exchanged more stories about our travels. Jos thought I was very amusing and well adjusted. He said I must have had a wonderful childhood, which made Lizzie and me laugh.

When he started asking about my parents, I decided it was as good a time as any to go to sleep. After such a wonderful day, the last thing I wanted was to talk about my family, or rather my non-family. I thought it best that they kept their illusions.

I lay in my bunk bed and thought about my past. Jos's last statement was an irony in itself. It put paid to Lizzie's remark that I wore my past clearly. Somewhere in the few hours since Lizzie's comment, I had learned to hide my past quite well. I had great difficulty in falling asleep that evening, perhaps because of all the coffee I had drunk. I felt as if I was missing something. I had a sudden urge to phone Jack but I couldn't leave the hostel at that hour and there were no public phones indoors. At 3 a.m. I finally drifted off. When it was time to rise, I felt depressed and tired.

Lizzie was still snoring. I woke her and pointed out that we had a full day ahead of us. Over breakfast we discussed our plans for the day. We would hitch-hike to Fort William and Fort Augustus, roughly one and a half hours away by car. We collected our worldly belongings, exchanged addresses with Jos and Rafael, which were never used, and headed off.

We reached the town of Fort William, which was most unexciting, and decided to make our way back to the hostel later that afternoon. Lizzie washed her hair and I seized the opportunity to nip out to the small stream I had soaked my feet in the day before. I sat among the greenery and stared into the crystal-clear waters. Small fish swam lazily below. They didn't seemed at all threatened by the presence of my feet in their domain. Birds chirped and fluttered from tree to tree. It was as if the moment was meant for me. I hoped Lizzie would take a few hours to wash her hair. I felt the need to be alone with my thoughts. I loved the water. Each ripple was so different and varied. They formed, flowed, changed and disappeared, never to be repeated in the same way again, just like my past years.

I heard footsteps approaching. It was Lizzie with a broad smile on her face. She revealed that she had watched me from a distance for a good 25 minutes. She said she had never met anyone who could sit by water and look as content as I did. I told her that water was one of my great loves; it was something I needed in my life. She gave a hearty laugh and said that Robert Burns, the famous Scottish poet, and I would have made a great team. I laughed with her.

She wanted to join me but tactfully asked if I would rather be alone. I invited her to listen to the earth with me. We sat next to one another in silence. I wondered why some humans couldn't be as nice as nature itself.

The following week passed quickly although nothing spectacular occurred. We stayed in various hostels and discovered more beauty spots. We were due back in Dundee soon and should have started planning our journey home but I had found a sort of freedom and euphoria during that break and I wasn't ready to let go of it. I had to tell Lizzie I wouldn't be returning with her. I didn't know how I would survive but I needed a little more time on my own.

Lizzie went on her way and I wandered from hostel to hostel for another couple of days until I ran out of money. Then I started sleeping rough. Loyal Lizzie never uttered a word to anyone as to my whereabouts.

I really didn't like sleeping rough and I began to worry about abusing the trust Mr and Mrs Miller had placed in me. It was an act of pure selfishness on my part and I felt dreadfully guilty, so I set off home.

I made it back to Dundee around 2 a.m. and phoned my social worker, Ziggy. She collected me from the town centre and I slept on the sofa in her apartment. She told me that everyone was furious at my behaviour and I hung my head in shame. I tried to explain that I had needed some extra time on my own before I could come to terms with returning to a restricted life. Ziggy had bad news for me.

Because I hadn't returned to Burnside on the agreed date, I had lost my place there. She said that if I had even phoned to let everyone know I needed a few extra days to myself, they would have been able to keep my place. One little phone call would have made all the difference.

Ziggy said we would have to find a foster home that would take me. Most people wanted younger children and it wouldn't be easy. I was put into a temporary care centre. No foster parents were willing to take a teenager so the Donaldsons were contacted and asked to take me back. I hadn't heard from or seen them since my thirteenth birthday.

Ziggy took me to Mum Donaldson's place of work, where she laid down the law to me. She said I would be out at once if I didn't behave myself. I learned that the Donaldsons had moved into a one-bedroomed flat on Forest Park Road in Blackness, Dundee. I knew I would behave myself there, for the new flat was miles away from Steve.

She said that Dad Donaldson was unwell and would be pleased to see me. I had wondered why she had agreed to let me return. Dad Donaldson had always liked me and Mum Donaldson knew my presence would give him a bit of a lift.

I went to the Donaldsons that very evening. Dad was delighted to see me. I felt sorry for him when I realised how much he had missed me and regretted causing him heartache in the past. I hadn't set out to do that; I only wanted to get away from Steve.

He was full of questions about what it was like in Balnacraig and Burnside. I wondered why he hadn't tried to contact me but didn't bother asking. I knew Mum Donaldson ruled the roost and he probably led an easier life by giving in to her.

I learned that Harry and Sheena had split. Sheena was living on her own in a flat above us with her two children.

In the months that followed, I spent a lot of time with Sheena and the children. A good side of Sheena's nature seemed to have surfaced and for a while, we became close. I was older now and could relate to her on more of an adult level and she treated me like an equal. Mum Donaldson suggested that I go with her and Sheena on their fortnightly excursions to the bingo hall. This became a regular routine. Mum agreed to pay for my bingo books until I had saved up my own pocket money.

I attended a school called Logia, where I improved in leaps and bounds. I slept on the sofa again but felt quite content except for an occasional niggling feeling that Harry Brown might try to push his way back into Sheena's life. I wouldn't be able to bear him living so near, as there was always friction between us.

Sheena and her children spent a quiet Christmas with us. That was when I noticed that Dad had begun to pay regular visits to the hospital. At first I was told it was because he had a bad back, then Mum told me that Dad had to go into hospital to have a wart removed from his thigh. I wasn't alarmed as it seemed a very minor thing to me.

Dad had been coughing lately and the hospital decided to X-ray his chest and lungs while he was there. I only became alarmed when two weeks after going in to have the wart removed, he still hadn't returned home. When I saw him again his weight had plummeted and his whole body seemed to be shrinking. He looked like a different person, so frail and bone-thin. Seeing him gave me quite a fright.

I asked Mum what was wrong with him and she said she didn't know but he would be coming home from hospital within a few days. I was delighted and thought he must be improving if he was to be sent home. When he came back, I noticed that there was no improvement and that he seemed even weaker than the day I had visited him. He was bedridden now and someone had to be at home at all times to look after him.

The following week Dad had to return to hospital. I became very suspicious that something was drastically wrong and that I wasn't being told about it. By this time I was nearing my fifteenth birthday. One evening I went with Mum Donaldson to visit him in hospital. He reached into his bedside locker and gave me five pounds for my birthday. He told me to go and buy something with it. I noticed that he had deteriorated even more. All his bones seemed to show, even through the sheets. Mum pulled the blankets back and I was horrified at how thin he had become. I saw some marks on his back but made no comment to my mother. When we left the hospital that evening I was completely bewildered but no one would tell me what was going on so I stopped asking questions.

I gave no thought to my imminent birthday. I couldn't think of anything else but Dad Donaldson in hospital.

23

KARL AND KANDY – ADVICE AGED 14

At this age it is likely that the adventure in your soul will get the better of you and you will wish to take a holiday with your friends – i.e. without an adult in tow. This is very healthy, good fun and also possible if you have already proven that you are responsible teenagers.

Perhaps you have spent a few years in the Scouts or Guides or have displayed good self-discipline and common sense. That's all you need to have a safe, fun holiday, perhaps in France or on a school trip skiing or strawberry picking. If you do go on a school trip, you really won't notice the presence of your chaperones. They will try to make you feel very independent and adult at this stage.

If you remember my account of my life, I climbed Ben Lawers at fourteen. It is nothing like Everest but it was quite an achievement for me at the time. Maybe one day you two will be tempted to follow my footsteps up Ben Lawers and feel the magic I experienced. Maybe you will want to climb a mountain of your own.

Although my friend Lizzie and I went on a hitch-hiking expedition, it was actually safe to do that in those days if you travelled with a companion. I would never wish you two to attempt such a thing today. All you have to do is listen to the news or read the newspapers to know why. I'm sure you will understand that by now.

I would imagine that you are probably thinking quite

seriously about your futures and your careers. With the help of Daddy and your guardians, you may already have started making plans to reach your goal. If this is the case, I wish you well and I hope you succeed in everything you set out to do. You have my blessing.

I wonder if, by now, you have developed an interest in any particular girl or boy, beyond friendship. I wonder if your hearts are stirring. We shall discuss that next year.

Before I go, there is one more thing. I don't mind you having girlfriends or boyfriends. That is part of life. It does have a way of interfering with school work and careers, though, when your emotions start running wild. There is plenty of time for that later but no one can control when you will experience your first romantic interests. I just hope all goes smoothly.

Happy journeys and adventures.

24

MUMMY – AGED 15

My fifteenth birthday came and went in a haze. I wasn't in a festive mood, only filled with concern because Dad was so ill. I continued my visits to the hospital with the family. Then, one Sunday, my girlfriend Caroline persuaded me to go out with her for the evening. Just as I was about to leave, Mum called me back and said my brother John was waiting in the other room to have a word with me. I walked into the bedroom and he asked me to close the door. He asked if I knew what was wrong with Dad. I said he had a bad back. John asked if I knew what cancer was. I didn't.

He explained that my father had a life-threatening disease called cancer and that he was now at the end of his days. I froze. Goose pimples rose up all over my body. I had never been close to someone who had died and the thought terrified me. I sobbed, and John put his arms around me and told me it was for the best. Dad was in a great deal of pain and it would be better if his suffering came to an end. John explained that Dad had cancer of the lungs.

I asked Caroline to leave. My whole world was crumbling. I was sent to school the next day although I didn't want to go. During the lunch hour, I took the opportunity to nip over to the hospital. The ward sister asked what I was doing there and I said in a soft voice that my dad was dying and I wanted to sit with him. She kindly allowed me to see him on condition that I didn't tell him what was wrong with him. No one ever told him.

As I came face to face with Dad I just wanted to throw my arms around him but I did not dare because he looked so frail. There was so much I wanted to say. I wanted to apologise for hurting him in the past but the words just wouldn't come out. If they had I'm sure he would have realised he was dying. I knew it was best to say nothing. He asked what I was doing there. I told him I wanted some time with him on my own. Silently, I wondered if all the worry I had caused him as a child had led to his illness. He was very happy that I had popped in to see him. He enjoyed our private moment and said he would keep it our secret. In the days that followed, I continued to visit him during my lunch breaks.

During one of my visits, he did something that I felt was most odd and which made me believe he was aware that his life was coming to an end. He gave me a five-pound note from his bedside locker and said, 'Take that. It is the last thing you will ever get from me.' I was shocked by this remark. What could I say to console him? Nothing. It was so clear by his gesture that he knew he was dying.

I told him I had to get back to school. I didn't want to weaken and cry in front of him. As I left, I bumped into the ward sister. By this time my tears were flowing. She asked what the matter was and I explained what had happened. I begged her to do something to save him but I could tell by the sad look in her eyes that she was powerless to help him. By this time his bed had been moved closer to the ward door. Nowadays, I know this indicates that a patient is dying.

I didn't return to school. I headed straight for Broughty Ferry beach and sat on my rock, screaming at the top of my voice. I must have sounded demented. How could I go home and face the Donaldsons, knowing that Dad was aware that he was dying? I didn't want to go home.

The water soaked my shoes and socks. I thought it might be best to tell Mum Donaldson about what had happened then they would know I had slipped out of school to visit him. I thought I might get into trouble and should just let the incident pass.

I made my way back to the bus stop, which meant passing Jack's house. I hadn't seen Jack for two years. I was going to call in but hesitated. Just as I was about to turn away, his door opened. Tears were flooding down my face. He took me indoors and wiped my face.

I tried to tell him about my past two years but I didn't make a very good job of it. I explained that I was back at the Donaldsons'. Then I blurted out what was really on my mind. Dad Donaldson was dying of cancer. Jack's eyes filled with tears. He asked if there was anything he could do but I knew I would have to come to terms with it myself.

Jack made tea and sandwiches. I couldn't eat but I drank the tea. When I had calmed down, Jack said that everything in his home had come alive when I stayed with him two years ago and that, after I left, it all seemed to go to sleep again. He missed my company and had never stopped wondering where I was and if I was safe.

I said, 'I'm just like a bad penny. I will always come back.'

He said, 'Oh no, Anne. Not a bad penny. Just a lost ship in the night. You will always return to your favourite harbour.'

I could hear the hurt in his voice as he enquired why I hadn't contacted him for so long. I had no answer but assured him that he was often in my thoughts. I explained that I had nearly picked up the phone on several occasions. Perhaps I just needed to find my own way. He wanted to be assured that I would keep in touch. I promised faithfully that I would.

I couldn't bring myself to go back to the hospital and face my father again. That Saturday evening I made an excuse not to go with Mum Donaldson. Everyone returned from the hospital looking very happy. They said Dad was very chirpy and was sitting up in bed fluffing up his own pillows, almost as if he had a second lease of life. I wondered if a miracle had occurred. My hopes soared and I thought that perhaps he was going to make a recovery.

At six o'clock the following morning I was wakened by the phone ringing. It was the hospital. They informed me that Dad had passed away. We were all in tears. I went to the kitchen and put the kettle on. The fact that he was no longer with us just wouldn't sink in. He had died all alone. No one was with him at the moment he passed away. I don't think anyone expected him to go so suddenly, especially after he seemed to improve quite out of the blue. Apparently he had died in his sleep. I asked about the marks on his back that I had seen weeks before and learned that they were radiation treatment burns.

Even as I write this it is very difficult to think about Dad Donaldson passing away. I, too, have cancer and only hope and pray that, when my day comes, I won't be alone.

Mum Donaldson made many phone calls to inform other members of the family and our friends that Dad had died. At the time, it didn't seem real to me. I couldn't absorb the fact that he was gone. A few hours passed and I couldn't bear to be in the flat any longer where more and more distressed people arrived and crammed into the tiny sitting room.

I walked out for a breath of fresh air and found myself heading towards Jack's. I had no coat on, just trousers, a jumper and shoes. I don't remember the journey. Before I had a chance to ring the bell, Jack opened the door. I didn't have to say a word. He knew Dad had died. He took me into the front room and held me. He stroked my head and said that everything would be all right. I wept. There were so many things I had wanted to say to Dad and I never did get the chance. I regretted all the heartache I had caused him. I always thought Dad Donaldson would be a grandfather to my children and give me away when I married. I took it for granted that he would be around for all these things.

Jack said he thought roots were very important to me but, really, I didn't have any. He knew me better than I knew myself. He asked about the funeral but I didn't have any details at that time and I had watched Dad dwindle away to nothing. I told Jack that I hoped never to die of cancer. Dad Donaldson's death had a great impact on me. I was so young and had just found him again, only for him to be taken away.

Jack said I could stay as long as I wanted. He asked what

I planned for my future. I didn't have any answers. It was nearly 6.30 p.m. We talked for what seemed to be ages then I decided I should head home to see if there was anything I could do. I worried about Mum Donaldson. I knew how much she had loved her husband. Now she was alone. I knew what it was like to be alone and felt very sorry for her.

I told Jack that I would visit again after the funeral. He said his thoughts were with me. He wanted me to phone and let him know the day Dad was to be buried so that he could say a prayer for us all. My eyes filled with tears at Jack's kindness.

During the bus ride home, I wondered who would be waiting in the flat and what state everyone would be in. When I arrived I learned that my mother and brother had been to the hospital to collect Dad's personal belongings. Dad was to be delivered home on Tuesday to be buried on Wednesday. The thought of my father in the house in body, but not in spirit or soul, tortured me. I didn't want to see him that way. I wanted to remember him as he used to be, not in the state he was in when he died.

Dad's sister, Aunt Chatty, was in the flat. We all drank tea late into the night. Mum said she was bearing up well. I didn't know what to say to them, fearing the wrong words might come out of my mouth, so I remained in the background.

They asked where I had been and I said I had been sitting by the water collecting my thoughts because I needed to come to terms with what had happened. I waited for a sarcastic remark from someone but none was forthcoming.

I found it difficult to sleep that night. I lay on the couch thinking about the times when we went to the betting shop and the times I waited for him when he nipped into the pub. I thought about his sneezes and coughs and the time his false teeth flew out of his mouth.

I must have dozed off. The next thing I remember was Mum waking me. There was a lot to arrange that day. Flowers had to be ordered and the newspaper informed so that his death could be entered in the obituary column. Mum told me I had to go shopping for a black outfit and shoes for the funeral. I bought them at a local department store. When I got home the house was teeming with people I had never met before. I was introduced as 'wee Anne'. I didn't want to talk much, so I sat and listened to the adults reminiscing. They spoke about what Dad was like in his younger days and how proud he was when Mum gave birth to the twins. They spoke of the years before I ever came into their lives. Then one person said, 'I'll bet wee Anne will miss him.' I couldn't stand it. I had to leave the room.

I sat on my own, thinking about Dad's body being delivered to the house the following day and then fell asleep while everyone continued talking.

The following morning came far too quickly. When I woke up, Mum was already in the kitchen, making tea. I declined the offer of breakfast. I told her I was going out for the day as I didn't want to be there when Dad's body was delivered. She said she understood.

I washed and dressed and left straight away. I found a phone box and called Jack. I gave him the funeral details and explained that Dad would be in the house, in a coffin, all night. I told him I felt very mixed up. He invited me to spend the day with him and I arrived an hour later. He looked as if he had been up all night. He said he hadn't slept well. He was worried about me and wondered how I would cope with this latest blow in my life. He asked if I was frightened about Dad's lifeless body being in the house. I replied through my tears that Dad never did me any harm in life and that he certainly wouldn't in death.

Jack asked how long I would stay that day but I didn't know. He wanted to know if there was some way he could lessen my burden but only time could do that. I didn't have an appetite and wanted to sit quietly. He popped out to leave me on my own for a while. I hoped he didn't think I was being rude but I needed some breathing space. Somehow I felt I wasn't included in my father's death. Very little mention was made of me when the adults had their conversations. I didn't think I would find the peace of mind I was looking for among them.

I stayed on at Jack's until six in the evening and shared a light meal with him. He said he would be there for me if I needed him. He said it was a pity that they never knew I was in safe hands when I was with him. He didn't want Mum Donaldson to worry, so he put me on a bus home. I dreaded going back because I knew Dad Donaldson's body would be there. I broke out in a cold sweat and started trembling. I had never seen a dead body before, let alone the body of a person I loved.

He was lying at rest in his coffin in the bedroom. Apprehensive as I was, my brother took me to see his body. He said I mustn't worry. The second I laid eyes on the open coffin, I felt physically sick.

Dad lay there surrounded by satin and frills. There was a

small silk napkin over his face. My brother gently lifted it. He didn't look at all like my father; he looked twenty years younger. It was Dad – yet it wasn't.

I kissed him on the forehead. He was so cold; his skin so tight and pale. All I could see was his head. At least he looked peaceful, which was a saving grace. My brother gently replaced the napkin. In my mind I said my farewells to Dad and all the things I wished I had said before he died. Some minutes passed before I turned to leave the room. That was the last time I saw Dad's face.

As I entered the sitting room, Mum asked how I was and I began to cry and went and locked myself in the toilet. I sat there for a good fifteen minutes, pulling myself together. Everybody else seemed composed and I didn't want to reawaken their grief by showing mine. I returned like a new person. People came and went throughout the day to pay their last respects. The teapot and kettle had never been worked so hard.

My father had an identical twin brother, whom we called Doddie. His real name was George. I dreaded him coming to the funeral. It would be too strange to have a man who was the spitting image of Dad present while he was being laid to rest. I stared out of the window at the fullness of the moon. Its light fell directly on my father. I kept asking my brother if he felt comfortable in the room with Dad. He said he did. I couldn't sleep straight away. I wondered if Dad knew we were there.

Mum checked later to see if we were OK. When I said yes, I realised I really meant it. I knew then that I was lucky and very grateful for sharing one last night close to Dad. There had been no one there when he actually passed away and at least he had this one last chance to be surrounded by his family before going to his final resting place.

Before falling asleep, I wondered what life was going to be like without Dad and how it would affect each of us. My last thought was that if I had been given the opportunity to express my love, perhaps it would have helped to make Dad's life more complete. We cared so much for each other and it must have been frustrating for him not to be able to show it openly.

We all woke up early and took turns washing and dressing. Relatives and friends popped in and out throughout the morning before Dad's coffin was removed. I tried desperately to remember what he was like in his healthier days but kept seeing his face in the coffin. I didn't want that to be the memory of him that would stay with me but, even today, his face in the coffin is as clear as the chime of a bell.

The minister arrived and said he had come to console the mourners. He offered his deepest sympathy. Before the service in the flat had ended, he had everyone in tears. As prayers were said by the minister, the coffin was removed by the pall bearers. Isobelle was there. I hadn't seen her in years and I didn't have anything to say to her. My thoughts were all with Dad and it didn't occur to me to search her out in the crowd.

We went to our assigned cars. I travelled with the twins and John in the car behind my father. I don't remember much about the journey to the graveyard. All I can remember is that I sobbed endlessly. We all did.

As we neared the graveyard, the minister was waiting.

We surrounded the hollow space in the ground and watched my father slowly lowered. The minister was reciting his service but, for some reason, I couldn't hear it.

We returned to our respective cars and were driven back to Mum's. Mum had not been at the graveside and I wondered why. She later told me that she wanted to remember Dad as he was and couldn't bring herself to say that final farewell. Sometimes I wish I had done the same. Even as I write this now, the memory of the last few weeks of my father's life and that final goodbye is as fresh as the air I breathe.

Back at Mum's, everyone drank and reminisced. Some of the memories were very amusing and everyone seemed to be laughing and joking. I couldn't understand how everyone had grieved only hours before and became so jolly soon after.

There was a lovely buffet and plenty to drink. I couldn't make sense of the festive feeling that filled the room. It made me angry. I locked myself in the toilet and refused to be a part of it. My brother's wife was walking around with a bottle of rum. I asked if she thought she was at a Christmas party and was instantly reprimanded and told to hold my tongue. I felt so out of sorts. The flat was small and there was nowhere to be on my own so I stepped outside for fresh air.

I headed straight for a phone box and dialled Jack's number. I knew he would be waiting. When I heard his voice, a feeling of relief overwhelmed me. I told him it was all over. He offered to come and collect me. Half an hour later, his familiar little Austin car pulled up to the kerb. I got in but didn't want to go anywhere in particular. He said he knew the ideal place. I smiled and knew exactly where he was taking me.

When we arrived at the waterfront, I headed straight for my rock. When I think back, I wonder how it was that no one understood me, not even my parents, the way Jack did.

Jack said that, at my age, I might soon find myself planning my future. From that point on, my life would change dramatically. Jack said he would be my 'stand-in' parent and give me the guidance he felt I would need.

He asked whether I would stay for tea or return home to see if my mother needed help. I would have preferred to stay with him but felt I should return home. I knew there was little I could do to relieve Mum Donaldson's grief, but being there would be some sort of help in itself.

In the days, weeks and months that followed I rarely mentioned Dad. I didn't know how everyone else would react so I avoided the topic altogether. Mum became very close to Sheena and I felt like a bit of an outsider. There weren't any arguments or differences; it just seemed that I was always alone except for the evenings when I was invited to join them for a night out.

I started going to lots of parties. At this time, David Bowie, a famous pop star, was doing a concert in Cared Hall in Dundee. A friend called Sheila managed to get a couple of tickets.

I dressed myself up like my pop idol. In those days Bowie wore a lot of make-up. He had spiked hair and painted a lightning bolt across his face. I was the spitting image of him by the time I left for the concert. We got to the hall and the atmosphere was electric. The special effects were out of this world and I had never experienced anything like them before. I desperately wanted Bowie's autograph but there was no way to get it as thousands of other people were after the same thing.

I went on to a party after the concert. At three in the morning, Sheila and I decided to take a taxi to the Angus Hotel where Bowie was staying. I thought we stood a better chance of seeing him when there were no autograph hunters around.

A porter approached us and said we should be tucked up in bed instead of autograph hunting. We said we were willing to take the chance of getting into trouble with our families if he would just do one favour for us. He chuckled and marvelled at what some kids go through to meet superstars. He said he would see what he could do. Minutes later a burly bodyguard appeared. We told him what we were after and he laughed and asked if our parents knew we were there. We said: 'no way!' He told us to take a seat and said he would see what he could do.

We sat quivering with expectation and excitement. Then I looked round and nearly fell off my chair for there was the great star himself. He introduced himself and had a chuckle at my make-up. I wore bright yellow tights, black hotpants, a black and yellow top and knee-length leather boots. With my hair tinted orange and the thunderbolt across my face, I must have looked a picture. He enquired as to our ages and said if he had a daughter he would be furious if she was wandering the streets at such an hour.

His bodyguard produced a pen and some paper and David signed it 'With love and good wishes'. He kissed each side of my face and I couldn't bring myself to wash it for days.

Our friends were all stunned at our tale about meeting David Bowie and chose not to believe us, but they knew we were telling the truth when David did a radio chat show the following day and told a story about two little nighthawks, one dressed like himself, who had collected autographs from him at three in the morning. My popularity at school escalated.

I started finding my feet as the months rolled on. I made up my mind to leave school after Christmas. I wanted to be independent, live on my own and pick up my life. I had my own values, principles and morals and wanted to live by them, not by anyone else's. I felt that settling on my own was the only way to achieve this. I liked being around children and thought it best to find a job as an au pair. At least with that type of work I would have live-in accommodation and a wage.

Christmas arrived and it was strange to be at the Donaldsons, without Dad. Everyone was tense and we avoided talking about him. We carried on with traditional events like Christmas lunch as if we were well-rehearsed robots. It was a relief when the holiday came to an end.

As planned, I left school and answered numerous advertisements for au pair and nanny positions but none of my applications were successful because I was not yet sixteen. I took a job in a shoe shop to fill the gap, but I hated it and was even more determined to find a job looking after children.

Then another advertisement for nannying caught my eye and, fortunately, they were willing to see me. I was dazzled as I walked into their stunning farmhouse one hour's drive from Dundee. The entrance hall was lined with natural dark wood, with an enormous mirror adorning one wall. The lady who interviewed me had one three-year-old child and another on the way. She told me she was seeing other people and would let me know of her decision.

Anxiously I waited all week to hear from her. Then, out of the blue, my phone call came but it was not good news. She felt I was too young to take on the responsibilities of looking after a young child and a newborn baby. I was very disappointed but didn't show it.

I continued to be turned down for similar jobs because of my age but refused to give up. Mum Donaldson was very sympathetic and said that once I was sixteen I would find it much easier to find the job I was looking for. Holding on to that thought, I eagerly awaited my sixteenth birthday.

25

KARL AND KANDY – ADVICE AGED 15

Hello, my darlings. Another year passes. I guess you, Karl, are now starting to look rather manly and you, Kandy, like a young lady. You may both be tall and filling out and will certainly be attractive if the way you looked as children is anything to go on.

Your bodies are probably in the throes of taking on the shape and form of an adult's. You will have learned a great deal at school about your physical changes. We were taught about it in my day and I'm sure schools are even more thorough now. I expect that any advice I could offer you now will already have been taught to you. My advice would probably sound old-fashioned in comparison to your 'up-to-date' Daddy, guardian or school. However, I feel I must add my little bit.

You are probably under the pressure of exams at school and I hope you will take them very seriously as they are an indication of what your future holds. It is a very important stage of your life. You will probably have mixed emotions or feelings about your future. It is important to sit these exams and do well. Hopefully, you both plan to go on to university. It would give me great pleasure to know you have gone to university and pursued a career. Maybe with the help of the advice, experience and wisdom I've tried to pass on to you, you may one day stand proud, with self-respect and dignity, and say to yourselves, 'My mother may not be here in body, but, wherever she is, her spirit never left us.' I had always hoped that you would have all the chances in life that I did not and I provided many opportunities for your futures. I hope you made use of them wisely.

I would love to see you two stand back and say, 'If Mum could see me now, she would be the proudest person in the world.'

I told you in the past, and I want to remind you now, that some people will be pleased about all you achieve and some may envy your abilities and drive. Do not let anyone stand in the way of your dreams.

Relationships, education and trust are important all throughout life. You will meet disappointments along the way but, no matter what happens, press forward and never look back.

As you know by now, I've made many mistakes in my life, some of which I was ashamed of and some which brought no regrets. I realised that I had an opportunity to help you to avoid making the same mistakes and, through my honesty, I hope you have learned by my mishaps. I hope my life, as error-filled as it was, was not in vain. Even if I were still around, there is no guarantee that you'd heed a single word of my advice. It is human nature to make your own mistakes and learn by them. I just hope all this makes it somewhat less of a rocky road for you.

You may both have developed an infatuation with a person of the opposite sex. Try to keep your heads screwed on because those sorts of emotions invade every part of your being, especially the first time round.

Try to be sensible and don't let love, triumph or disaster

interfere with your school work or moods. It is a tall order and easier said than done. I hope you are able to draw on some reservoir of strength to help you through the emotional times. I can only say that when there are disappointments in love, there is always something better waiting to happen. It may not seem so at that moment, but this is true. We will talk about this a bit more next year as I am paranoid about it interfering with your studies.

Keep your spirits up, think positively and I believe in my heart and soul that you'll make it.

26

MUMMY – AGED 16

I welcomed in my sixteenth birthday by replying to a lot of new ads for live-in childminders. Mum Donaldson was adjusting to life without her husband and was very supportive of my ambition to find a job as an au pair.

We enjoyed a nice birthday tea and scoured the advertisements together. She seemed to enjoy the role of helping me into the adult world and gave me lots of useful advice about filling in employment applications. We spotted a notice that looked as if it had been written just for me. It read 'Child's help required for farmer's wife'.

Feeling rather confident, I answered the advertisement and spoke to the farmer's wife, Mrs Grant, on the phone. She made an appointment to visit me in my own home. I made sure the flat was gleaming as I was eager to impress her. She arrived punctually and I nervously offered her tea. After explaining how much I had enjoyed looking after my sister's children, I had convinced her that I was quite capable of looking after her three little girls.

A few days later I received a phone call from Mrs Grant asking me when I would be able to start. I was so proud of myself for achieving my first ambition – getting a job I really wanted. Mrs Grant sent my fare for the two-hour bus journey. I excitedly spent the next few days packing. Mum Donaldson shared my enthusiasm and was pleased I had found a good job with a decent family. She said I had showed a great deal of courage in the face of disappointment and praised me for not giving up.

Mrs Grant met me at the local bus station in Arbroath and we chatted during the ten-minute journey to their beautiful farm. She told me all about the farm staff and the cattle that grazed on their land. When we arrived, I was shocked at the size of her property. I had expected something small but, in fact, the farmhouse stood on a thousand acres of land.

I had no fear of animals and went to inspect all the creatures that lived on the farm. My heart pulsed with excitement as I entered the milking parlour and admired the rows and rows of well-fed cows. That is where I met Mr Grant, a big, healthy-looking, bespectacled man with sun-kissed hair. In contrast, Mrs Grant was petite and, like her husband, attractive. They were a well-matched couple.

Mrs Grant didn't expect me to work on the first day. She said I should just settle in and familiarise myself with my new surroundings. I went indoors to meet the two younger girls, aged two and three. The six-year-old girl arrived home later in the day, after school.

My room, which was large and beautifully decorated, was at the top of the enormous house. I unpacked my bits and pieces, delighting in the fact that there was more than enough space for everything. I had a little jewellery box with a ballerina on it, which I had bought for myself a few weeks before. Mum Donaldson had given me some real gold earrings that belonged to her and I felt they needed a suitable dwelling place. The box took pride of place on the mantelpiece above the fireplace.

I couldn't believe how lucky I was. There was even a

television in my room. A thick, colourful patchwork quilt was draped over my single bed. I had my own toilet next to my room but shared a bathroom with the children.

I joined the Grants for supper at five o'clock, which was to be the daily routine. I came to learn that the whole household worked on a firm, unwavering timetable. Everything was very well organised. My first meal with them gave me the opportunity to see the Grants as a family for the first time. The three little girls were well-mannered, cheerful little things and were clearly accustomed to having nannies. They didn't view me in the novel sense that I viewed them. It was a new experience for me and I bubbled with enthusiasm. To the friendly Grants, I was the new girl in the family.

My daily routine consisted of waking six-year-old Lynn and getting her ready for school at seven in the morning. She had a different breakfast every day and was beautifully turned out for her journey to school. A bus would collect her at the bottom of the drive and I saw her safely on board.

I would then return to the house and see to the two small girls. I fed, washed and dressed them in preparation for toddling about the sitting room with their toys while I did the ironing. I would read them stories and take them to different areas of the farm to stroke the animals.

One day Ally, the cowman, asked me if I would help him to separate some Hereford cows from the Friesian cows. I was glad to. I had to jump into the pen and open the gate on his command. I had been there several months by this time and was very confident with the animals. As I opened the gate, however, I lost my grip and toppled face down into cow muck. I rose to find it stuck to my hair and embedded in my ears. Everyone though it was wildly amusing but I couldn't appreciate the funny side until I cleaned every last bit of manure off my body.

That same day Mr Grant had an important visitor coming to the farm. I entered the scullery covered in cow muck only to come face to face with the visitors who thought I was the Grants' daughter.

Mr Grant was very concerned about the mess I was in but couldn't control his chuckles. He gave me some special soap to wash myself with and explained that cattle carry certain unfriendly germs. The soap would leave me well sterilised and out of danger of infection.

Ally and the rest of the farm staff were in fits of laughter. I reappeared gleaming, relieved to be free of the pungent odour. I had scoured my skin until it turned pink, which made me look as if I had been on a sunshine holiday instead of on a little trip in the cowpen.

A few days later the bull escaped from the barn and appeared at the kitchen window while we were enjoying our lunch. He caused havoc on the farm, dodging all the staff as we frantically tried to catch him.

Later in the afternoon I was hanging out our clean laundry when I heard Mr Grant bellow for me to run for my life. The bull came charging at the clean laundry on the line and I have never been so frightened. My heart was in my mouth and it took me a good while to recover. I cowered indoors and peered through a window as the bull stampeded over Mrs Grant's flowerbeds before heading down the drive. Twenty minutes later, the staff appeared with a rather sulky bull being led by a rope around his neck. His adventure was over and he had surrendered peacefully but not before causing chaos on the well-kept property.

I had most evenings off as Mr and Mrs Grant truly enjoyed spending time with their children. When they had guests for dinner, I would help Mrs Grant to prepare the meal. I always looked forward to these special occasions as the Grants made sure plenty of food was put aside for me.

I loved my free weekends and would return to Mum Donaldson's for overnight visits. Our relationship had become a very easy, friendly one. Mum was proud that I had a good job and a bank account, and was very well settled.

One Saturday, a girl I had become friendly with in the village invited me to the local town club. I wasn't able to drink, being under-age, but was quite content to sip orange juice and meet lots of new people. During the course of the evening, a chap called Roy introduced himself. He told me I was an attractive young lady and that he wanted to date me. I had never been asked out on a date before. The invitation sent exciting little shivers through me. I accepted.

He explained that he worked on the oil rigs, three weeks on and two off. He said he would phone or write to me. He wanted to arrange to see me during his next break and would inform me of his working schedule. *I was thrilled.*

I couldn't wait to tell Mrs Grant. I caught sight of myself in a mirror and noticed that my eyes were sparkling and my skin glowed. There was something different about me. It was the difference between being a young girl and a young woman. I was growing up. My figure had slimmed in some places and blossomed in others. That cherub look that children carry had disappeared. The change had been so sudden that I thought it must have happened in my sleep.

I started buying more sophisticated make-up. I let my hair grow to my shoulders and fall in a natural parting in the middle. Mrs Grant, who was always elegant, gave me good advice about looking well turned out.

Roy phoned me several times during the week and I also received pleasant letters from him, telling me about his job and what the weather was like. I wrote back, telling him of my adventures on the farm and of the fun I had with the Grant family. When the time arrived for Roy to return to Aberdeen, I was overwhelmed with eager anticipation. Mrs Grant gave me the complete weekend off and Roy arranged to collect me from the farm at 7.30 on Friday night.

I rushed to bathe and prepare the children for bed. All my chores were completed on time because Mrs Grant chipped in. This was my first real date. I wanted to look perfect and feel confident. I wanted it to be the most wonderful evening of my life.

I carefully applied my make-up and spread lotion over my freshly bathed body. I conjured up different images of what the evening might be like. I pictured us laughing and chatting over dinner and walking in the moonlight through the town centre. Finally, the hour arrived and so did Roy, right on time.

I had taken a great deal of care in preparing for this moment. I had been so excited about the event that I had visited Sheena and Mum Donaldson the previous weekend and told them all about Roy. They had helped me to choose a new outfit from a mail order catalogue that belonged to Sheena. I didn't earn enough money to buy new clothes but, by ordering from a catalogue, I was able to pay the bill over a period of a few weeks. Sheena gave me a bottle of perfume called Sea Jade to mark my special event. I sprayed myself with the scent before greeting Roy at the door. He had a little orange MGB Midget sports car with a black convertible top, which he kept up because there was a chill in the air.

He told me I looked beautiful. I wore a new burgundy cowl-neck jumper which fell loosely around my collar-bone. This was matched with dusky, bibbed dungarees, which were very trendy in those days. On my feet were a pair of new wedges, also very trendy. My earrings were burgundy studs with a matching burgundy bead necklace. My handbag matched my shoes perfectly and I thought I looked terrific. I was confident and ready to go.

Roy wore black trousers and a checked shirt for our informal evening. He was 24 and very tall with thick, dark brown hair. Smooth eyebrows and thick lashes framed his dreamy hazel eyes. We looked the perfect couple as we set off for the town centre.

We went to an Italian restaurant and both ordered spa-ghetti bolognese. Roy drank a beer and I had an orange juice. We sat for hours talking about his work. He fasci-nated me. He was like a James Bond character telling me of the dangers he faced when he dived into the North Sea to work under the rigs. I was very impressed but, looking back now, I realise how easily all young girls are influ-enced by experienced, sophisticated men. I pictured him in his wet suit and air tanks and a funny shudder shot up my spine. I felt as if butterflies had made a home in my stomach.

I glanced at my watch and was horrified to see how the time had flown. I was on curfew and had to be back home by 11 p.m. We had an hour left and drove directly to the farm where we sat chatting for some time in the car. He said he had thoroughly enjoyed my company and my sense of humour. He quoted some lines from *Romeo and Juliet* but I did not recognise them. He saw this in my face and explained the story of Shakespeare's play.

We laughed about my ignorance of Shakespeare and I suddenly found myself in his arms – quite a feat, I assure you, in a tiny MG. My stomach did somersaults and the strangest feeling rocked my body. Our eyes met and our lips touched. For the first time in my life, I was filled with innocent passion. I felt that I had fallen in love. In fact, I had, for after that evening, just the mention of his name caused everything inside my body to flip.

We drew apart and looked deep into each other's eyes as I recovered from the dizzying experience of my first kiss. I didn't want the moment to end. We arranged to see each other soon.

I skipped excitedly into the hallway after waving goodbye. Mr and Mrs Grant were waiting up and were anxious to hear all about my first date. I told them about the meal and Roy's exciting job. I left out the details of the passionate kiss. They were delighted for me. I excused myself so that I could race to the privacy of my own room and pore over the evening's events in my mind. I was thoroughly convinced that I was madly in love with Roy. It was pointless to prepare for sleep as adrenalin was ripping through my body. I sat there with fire burning in my heart.

I turned the television on to find that a film had just started called *I Want to Live*, starring Susan Hayward. It was a gripping story about a woman accused of killing a man, who constantly pleaded her innocence. She was the mother of a small child and the separation from her little one tore her apart. She was sentenced to death and I wept buckets.

I became so involved with the film that I totally forgot about Roy. I just kept thinking that Susan's character was innocent. She took her child's teddy bear to the death chamber. She wanted to wear her best clothes so that she could die with dignity. It was so sad. The film finished and, still feeling energetic, I tidied my chest of drawers, threw my tear-stained hankies into the washing basket and admonished myself for getting so upset over a film. I fetched a glass of orange juice, a couple of biscuits and a newspaper. I dozed off as I thumbed through the pages and woke later next morning but stayed in bed for a while as it was my day off.

At 11.30 I went for a walk around the farm but could think of nothing else but Roy. He was to collect me at 1 p.m. I started getting ready at noon and wore a ribbed top with jeans as we were only going for a drive. My hair was done beautifully and my make-up carefully applied. He was, once again, on time.

We went for a long drive and stopped for a pub lunch, but I was refused entry because of my age. Roy was shocked and tried in vain to persuade the landlord to allow us to have lunch. People stared at me and my cheeks flushed with embarrassment.

I asked Roy if he knew of Broughty Ferry in Dundee. I told him I had a favourite rock on the waterfront and wanted to show it to him. That is where we headed. Near to the waterfront was a small playing area filled with happy children. Roy said he wanted to sit for a few minutes and watch them play. He said that childhood is the best part of life. I became frightened and wondered if he had discovered something about my past, so I changed the subject and suggested we visit my rock. He wanted to know why the rock was so important to me, so I told him that it was where I would sit and listen to life. I wanted him to listen to the sea and all that surrounded it.

He said that most young ladies would retreat to their bedrooms when they wanted to ponder on life. I was the first girl he had ever known who would choose the outdoors instead.

It was obvious that he didn't sense the magic or understand what I gained by sitting there. I asked if he had ever watched tropical fish glide peacefully in the waters of a tank? That was how I felt when I sat on my rock watching the tide and ripples in constant, changing motion. He had no idea what I was talking about.

Roy was a good conversationalist but not a deep one. He changed the subject and told me about an upcoming annual dinner that he would like me to attend. It was a special function for people who worked on the rig and would mean going away for the whole weekend because the ball was in Aberdeen, some 80 miles away.

I said I would be delighted but had to make sure it was OK with the Grants. He then said he had to go because he had some business to attend to and had to be there shortly. I couldn't understand why he had bothered to see me for such a short period of time and asked if I could go with him. He said I couldn't but that he would collect me later that evening.

As soon as I got home, I immediately asked the Grants if I could attend the function, which was to be held in three weeks' time. They agreed to allow me to go. I really looked forward to the outing. It would be my very first ball. My first formal event.

I lazed around for the rest of the day and made sure I was ready for Roy that evening. He was a stickler for punctuality and I was surprised when he didn't appear at 7.30 on the dot.

By 9.30 he still hadn't arrived and I was frantic. I had no number on which to contact him and wondered if he had been in an accident. All sorts of horrible things passed through my mind. By midnight I had managed to fall asleep, assuming that he had probably got held up with his business arrangement.

I still hadn't heard from him by 2 p.m. the next day, so I caught a train to Dundee, got off near Broughty Ferry and made my way to Jack's house. I hadn't seen him for months, although I had spoken to him on the phone and kept him informed about my life at the Grants'.

Before I had a chance to close the gate behind me, Jack's front door opened. He gave me a big hug. I told him I was very settled and was truly sorry I hadn't visited in so long. I said it was my day off. He put his hand on my shoulder and said, 'Was yesterday your day off, too?'

I looked at him in amazement and then realised he had seen me on my rock. I felt embarrassed that I hadn't called on him.

I explained that I had been with a friend and didn't want him to know about Jack. Our special relationship belonged to us and no one else. He understood.

He asked about my arrangements for the rest of the day and I said I had hoped to spend it with him. We bought the bare necessities for a picnic, prepared sandwiches, fruit and flasks of tea, and drove to a grassy area near the beach and sat there in the mild weather enjoying our lunch. I told him I was short on news and had already told him what was going on in my life during our phone conversations. Jack wanted to hear it all again. He said it was much better talking to me in person as my expressions said so much more.

He asked me to tell him all about my friend Roy. When I had finished, he asked whether I had met any of Roy's family or friends. I said that it was too early yet. He suggested I tread carefully and be wary. It was the first time Jack had given me advice that I was reluctant to accept. I wondered why he had said this.

Jack said there was so much to learn in life and that sometimes young girls don't see things clearly. He said I shouldn't take everything at face value and that I would learn this as time went on. He spoke to me as if I was his own daughter.

I tried to change the topic but Jack wouldn't have it. He was surprised that I had brought Roy to the rock. He felt I had invaded my own privacy by taking someone there. I realised that he was absolutely right. I wondered if I had spoiled the magic of the rock. I didn't want to talk about it any longer and wanted to hear what was going on in his life.

Sadly, he had still had no word from his daughters. I suggested that he should try to contact them and offered to do it on his behalf because he was so heartbroken without them. I said I couldn't replace his daughters for ever; he owed it to himself to find his girls. I knew Jack's love for me was a replacement for the love he couldn't show to his own children. I felt so sad for him. There was I, at sixteen, giving wise old Jack advice. I said that life was cruel, as we both knew through our own experiences. Somehow we compensated each other for the pain we had separately endured. I only hoped I would be able to repay Jack for the love, kindness and wisdom he had shared with me.

Although I hadn't seen Jack for months, it was if we had never parted whenever we were in each other's company. He was full of stories about dangerous seas, tangled nets and the fiery tempers and arguments of the fishermen. I wondered if he found it stressful at times, but it was part of his life and he wouldn't choose another career if he could.

I asked if he would make me his famous smoked kippers for supper. He said, of course, but without butter. We both laughed because Jack never forgot that I liked my kippers without butter. Once we were back in the warmth of Jack's house, he started preparing the kippers while I fed the fire. The smell of his cooking was very inviting. The TV talked to itself; no one paid it the slightest bit of attention. The flames of the fire roared high. I'll always remember the loving atmosphere of the house that Jack lived in.

We sat by the fire, feasting on kippers and fresh brown bread. In all the time I had known Jack he had never asked if I knew how to play chess. Now, he offered to teach me and, to his astonishment, I announced that I already knew. When I used to run away and squat with university students, they had taught me to play chess. We would play into the early hours of the morning. I had never known Jack owned a chess set, let alone played.

As soon as we had cleared the dishes, we sat down to a game: the fisherman versus the reformed runaway. Jack said he marvelled at the new, growing me. To think, a few short years ago, I was a petrified runaway on the brink of suicide and now I had a job, responsibilities, a boyfriend and a promising future.

He said I was full of surprises. He regarded chess as an intellectual's game, not a runaway's. I set the board and the battle of minds began. We concentrated so hard that we could almost hear the inner gears of our brains ticking away like well-oiled clocks. Ages passed and Jack wiped the floor with me. I conceded that, in his household, he was the chess master.

Jack excused himself and disappeared for a few minutes. I called upstairs to make sure he was all right. He returned with a shoe box and brought out lots of family photos. I complained that I had wanted to challenge him to a title match rather than trip down memory lane.

I liked the pictures of Jack as a young boy. Through the series, I could clearly see him growing into a young man.

There were many pictures of him competing in chess competitions and I knew then that there was no chance of beating him. I realised how little I knew about him. He told me about his parents and childhood, which made me realise where Jack had inherited his kindness. He spoke very highly of his parents.

He said the day I lost Dad Donaldson reminded him of the day he lost his mother. He had been about the same age as me. He said: 'Now, Anne, you may understand better why I took a personal interest in your life. I was very fortunate to have the sort of life you did not.'

He was glad that he had had a chance to return to the world all the good things he had been provided with. I looked at him, my heart flowing over with love. Little did I know, nor did Jack, that this would be the last I would see of him for many years to come.

It was late and I had missed my train back to the Grants. Jack gave me a lift to the farm and, after learning that Roy had not phoned nor called round, I retreated to my room in a most disappointed frame of mind. I didn't want to think about Roy and couldn't forget the warning Jack had given me. I fell asleep in the armchair in my bedroom and woke at 5.30 in the morning with a very stiff neck. I had a quick shower before the rest of the household began to rise.

I had realised that Roy had been my last thought at night and my first thought in the morning. As I stood in the shower, my thoughts turned to the possibility of Roy being involved in an accident. I was furious with myself for not getting a number where he could be reached. I thought of phoning the oil rig, hoping they would have some information because of the possibility that he might have been called back to work.

I couldn't find a number in the telephone directory so I just had to sit tight and wait for him to contact me. I tried to push the thought out of my mind that this might be another let-down in my life. I had to have faith in him.

Every time the phone rang that day, I hoped Mrs Grant would say it was for me. It never was. I found it difficult to concentrate on anything and hoped that the day would end quickly so that I could have some time to myself. By 10.30 that evening, I still hadn't heard a thing from Roy. I ruled out an accident as I was sure I would have been informed somehow. Because of what Jack had said, I came to the conclusion that Roy had gone off me or was hiding something.

I didn't know what to do with myself. I tidied my room and ironed a stack of crumpled clothes. I wanted to go for a walk but it was too dark so I went to bed and read *A Tale of Two Cities*. After the third chapter, I threw the book on the floor, not even remembering what I had read. I thought that just when life had seemed to be going well for me, I had spoiled it by falling for Roy.

The week passed very slowly. Each day seemed to get longer. By the following weekend I still hadn't heard a thing from him. I decided that Roy had lost interest and, for some reason, I thought that our relationship was cursed because I had taken him to my rock. I spent the weekend at Mum Donaldson's. I told them Roy had disappeared and I hadn't heard from him in a week. Sheena was playing Connie Francis records and the song 'No One Ever Sends Me

Roses' came on. It made me feel very depressed. Despite that, my weekend at the Donaldsons' was most enjoyable apart from the low points when I thought about Roy.

On Saturday I took my niece Wendy to the circus and decided to have a good time. I concentrated on staying very active to keep Roy out of my mind. The circus was great fun. I laughed and ate popcorn and candy floss with little Wendy. Then something happened that sparked my confidence. A dashing circus employee started paying particular attention to us.

After a while, I realised that he was flirting with me. It made me feel really good. I felt as if I was still attractive and it gave me a well-needed lift. He asked me for a date but I said no because I had an uncanny feeling that Roy would return.

I felt restless once I had returned to Mum Donaldson's and Sheena teased me by saying, 'Wee Anne is in love.' I denied this and stormed out of the room. Sheena didn't mean any harm. I just over-reacted because I was feeling sensitive. I headed back to Mrs Grant's the following morning and decided that I would give my room another unnecessary cleaning. No one was at home so I changed into the old clothes I wore for housework. Then I noticed a letter in the kitchen, addressed to me. It was from Roy, the first correspondence in a week. I hesitated, worried that it might be a parting note.

It was the complete opposite. It was a very personal love letter explaining that he had had to return to the rig unexpectedly and was working practically 24 hours a day. When he didn't work, he slept. He claimed it was the first chance he had had to put pen to paper since he last saw me.

I found it hard to believe. Something didn't seem right. I wondered why he hadn't phoned as that would have been very quick and easy. I took my letter back to my room and reread it several times.

This time I read what was between the lines and began doubting what he was saying. Things just didn't add up and I was just about to hide the letter beneath my jumpers in the wardrobe when I looked at the postmark. It read Dundee, not Aberdeen. I knew then that Roy was not on the oil rig. My suspicions were aroused even more and I was determined to find out the truth. I tormented myself with questions that only he could answer. I didn't like the idea of being involved with a deceitful person and realised how little I knew about him.

I greeted the Grants when they arrived home and thanked them for leaving the letter where I could find it. I told them all was well as I didn't want my personal affairs to interfere with my work situation.

I decided that two could play the same game and that I would not let on to Roy that I had noticed the postmark. I looked forward to the oil rig ball as it would give me an opportunity to meet some of his friends and find out a bit more about him.

The weeks that followed were filled with the same clockwork routine, which I enjoyed. Nearly three weeks had passed since I last saw Roy. I had received several more letters from him, only this time bearing an Aberdeen postmark. I looked at the time mark on the letters from Aberdeen. They had been placed in the second post. The one from Dundee bore a first postmark, which meant it was put in the box the night before.

As a first romance, it had got off to a very bad start. Roy was due off the rigs the following weekend. He rang on the Thursday evening to say he would collect me on Friday night and head straight to Aberdeen. My weekend bag was already packed.

I was very proud of my very first ball dress. I had used my savings to invest in a long halter-neck dress with a matching wrap. I had bought black evening shoes and a matching handbag. A pretty necklace and earrings completed the outfit. The dress didn't fit in my overnight bag and would have to be hung in the car. Mrs Grant had given me extra money in my wage packet to ensure that I had a splendid outfit and spare cash while I was away from home.

I wondered whether Roy would arrive or not. I began panicking because of the way he had stood me up when we last arranged to meet. At 9.30 p.m. sharp I heard the engine of his sports car. Mrs Grant wished me all the best and said she hoped I would have a lovely weekend.

When I got into the car, Roy began to tell me how sorry he was for the worry he had caused me. He said this sometimes happened. I didn't tell him I had noticed the different postmarks. He was full of questions about what I had been doing with myself in his absence. I didn't go into much detail, claiming that the children took up all my time. I asked if he would like to meet my family on our return from Aberdeen. He seemed delighted at the prospect. Half an hour before arriving at the hotel, I suddenly wondered about our sleeping arrangements and asked if he had booked separate rooms. He had booked us under Mr and Mrs in a double room. I told him I preferred a room of my own and was appalled that he took it upon himself to think I would share a bed with him. He assured me there would be two separate beds in the room and said that the hotel was fully booked because of the oil convention.

When we arrived we were escorted to our accommodation. Everything was lovely, right down to the bathroom. Sure enough, there were two beds in the room. I told him I didn't mind as long as he afforded me privacy to shower and dress alone. He wasn't happy with this arrangement and I realised that he hadn't taken me there to show me a good time but for his own lustful needs. This put a damper on the whole weekend. I barely knew him and was insulted that he assumed I would sleep with him. I wasn't ready for such a commitment. He said I shouldn't have accepted his invitation. I replied that I had no idea I was being invited on a dirty weekend. He wasn't pleased with this but had to accept it.

By nine that evening, we found ourselves in the cocktail bar. I wore a peach blouse, navy mini-skirt and fashionable wedged shoes. My hair and make-up were carefully in place.

I finally met some of his friends, who had all brought their wives. I decided I would keep my ears and eyes open and carefully read their reactions when they met me. We joined a group from the same rig as Roy. We all said our 'How do you dos'. I took to one very charming lady, named Izzy Clarkson, and her husband Jim. Her husband was a diver with Roy. She said I must be one of the youngest women at the convention. I told her about myself and how long I known Roy. I said I thought he was nice and hid my real thoughts from her.

Roy joined his friends at the bar and the women were left to chat among themselves. By 11.15 couples started going to their rooms so Roy and I arranged to meet his friends at breakfast. I asked Roy to give me ten minutes to wash and prepare myself for bed before coming to the room, which didn't please him one bit. He came in and started to undress in front of me. He removed his shirt and I was surprised at his very hairy, muscular arms and torso. The sight made me blush but then my sense of humour got the better of me. I said I thought I had come with a man, not a gorilla. I asked him to put the light out while he finished undressing. He was surprised at my shyness. He had no idea about nasty Steve and that I had never had a relationship with a man. He slipped into his bed and I was disappointed that he did not give me a goodnight kiss. I supposed it was for the best as it could have led to other things.

I could hear Roy snoring, which made me feel relaxed, and I drifted off to sleep. I don't know how much time had passed before I was wakened by hands touching my shoulders. I sat up in bed and Roy said it was all right and not to be frightened. I tried to shove him away and told him to leave me alone. He said I was frigid. I didn't know the meaning of the word and demanded that he explain himself. I put the lights on and told him I wasn't there for sex. I had come because I wanted to be with him and meet his friends. It was a new experience for me to stay in a hotel and I regarded it as a great adventure. Sadly, Roy was not in the mood to reason. I asked him to let nature take its course and not force himself on me as I wasn't ready for any of that.

He tried to blackmail me emotionally and said that if I

cared about him I would let him show it physically. I said if he touched me, I would pack my bag and hitch-hike back home, then he would have a lot of explaining to do to his friends in the morning.

I couldn't sleep well after that. I had breakfast with Izzy and stuck to her like glue for the rest of the weekend. The men stayed together while we went shopping.

When we returned at 2 p.m., we went straight to the bar where I drank several shandies of lager and lemonade. I suppose you could say I was tipsy by the time Roy returned. Izzy took the blame for that but I had quite a job sobering up for the ball later that evening. I had a shower and nap and the effects of the lager had worn off by the time I woke.

I was quite looking forward to the ball and had a good two and a half hours to prepare myself. I could feel the strain between Roy and me when he was in the room and I wondered, at this point, if I was purely infatuated or really in love. The letter posted in Dundee had made me see him differently and my feelings for him weren't as strong as they had been in the beginning.

I pushed the negative thoughts to one side and concentrated on preparing for the ball, as I wanted to look my best. I was a neat size 10 and looked petite at five feet four inches tall. Once my hair and make-up were finished, I put on my evening outfit, which absolutely stunned Roy.

When I saw him in his dinner jacket and bow tie, I thought I had never seen a more handsome man in my life. I was proud to be on his arm. We made our way to the ballroom. Everything was perfect: the lighting, flowers on the tables, candles and food. It was the first time I had ever been in such a formal situation.

Izzy was there to greet me and took me under her wing. She told me to follow her when we were ready to be seated at the tables. I had never seen so much cutlery at single settings, and I was surprised that there were three glasses per setting, all of different sizes. There were separate knives and forks for everything. Izzy told me just to copy her. I studied every movement she made and took her lead.

I was out of my depth with the conversation at the table and didn't say much but simply listened. It took a good two hours to get through the meal, dessert and coffee. I was so full from the meal and bored by the shop talk that I felt too drained to dance.

People started leaving the table to mingle with others, go to the bar or dance. Music played in the background. Izzy complimented me on my beautiful dress and said Roy must be very proud of me. I began to ask her about sex. I asked if it happened naturally when you were in love with some-one. I explained I thought I was in love but wasn't ready to get involved with sex. She said that it was natural to be reluctant and it would happen when the time was right. I knew it wasn't the time or place for me. She gave me a hug and said not to worry or rush things.

A man approached me, introduced himself as Bill, and asked me to dance. I accepted. I was glad a slow ballad was playing as I wasn't in the mood to dance to rock and roll. I caught a glimpse of Roy darting disapproving looks my way. He was waiting at the table when I was escorted back to my seat. He didn't say much. As the evening wore on, people became seized with the party spirit. Men discarded their jackets and ties and people relaxed as the party became less formal.

At 3 a.m. I started wilting fast and was ready for bed. I told Roy I was going up and he said he would join me later. I thought it strange. I thought he would at least escort me to the room but he did not. I bade goodnight to Izzy and agreed to meet her at breakfast. Just as I was about to leave, I overheard a woman say to Roy that she had been waiting ages for the dance he had promised her. I decided to stay. Roy realised I was still there and told me to make up my mind whether I was going to bed or not. I just turned on my heel and joined Izzy. Roy returned to the bar with his friends and I kept an eagle eye on the provocative woman. She stood next to Roy and flirted with him. She was laughing and joking with him with the greatest of ease. I called Roy over and asked who the woman was. He embarrassed me by asking if I was his keeper. I decided it was time for me to go to the room.

He came up two hours later and I didn't ask any questions. I had started seeing him through different eyes and thought he was a lout. I glared at him and told him never to humiliate me like that again. I felt he was most ungentlemanly. I said he had brought me there just to get me into bed and I resented it. He said I was like all other sixteen-year-old girls. He ranted and raved while I packed my bags. I couldn't wait to get away from him and return to the Grants.

My dream weekend had turned out to be a dreadful mistake. I had innocently thought we were going there to be in each other's company. I was so naïve. I said I was going to breakfast but went to Izzy's room instead. She gave me her home phone number and invited me to visit and perhaps babysit her children when I wanted to earn extra money. I didn't let her know that I had been arguing with Roy. I went back to the room and asked Roy if we could leave straight away. We didn't say a word to each other on the entire journey back. When we arrived at the farm, I reached for my bags and simply said goodbye. Roy looked mortified.

I went straight to my room where I stayed for most of the day. I needed to catch up on my sleep so that I would be as bright as a button for the children the following morning. I told the Grants the weekend was lovely and the hotel beautiful. Mrs Grant guessed something was wrong, of course, because, in all my details, I made no mention of Roy.

I didn't hear from him or see him for a further three weeks. This didn't bother me at all, which made me feel I couldn't really be in love. All my defence systems went up, creating a wall between myself and Roy. After three weeks, I received a call from Roy's friend Izzy Clarkson. She asked if I would like to babysit for her. I was more than delighted. She asked if I had heard from Roy and I said we had had a difference and I didn't expect to hear from him again. She said I mustn't worry and was bound to hear from him again. No sooner had I replaced the telephone than a florist's van arrived. There was a bouquet of flowers for me. I was amazed because I had never received flowers in my life.

It was a splendid assortment of carnations, daisies, orchids and lilies. The attached note was from Roy, asking me to forgive his behaviour and hoping that the flowers would show how sorry he was. I was pleased to receive the flowers but was in two minds whether to put them in water or throw them in the bin. I decided to keep them. Mr Grant laughed and asked if I had a secret admirer. It wasn't often that flowers were delivered to his farm.

Mrs Grant provided a vase and I placed the huge display in my room. I played the situation down but I saw the knowing twinkle in Mrs Grant's eyes which said that she knew something wasn't exactly right.

As I bathed the children, I heard the phone ring. It was for me. I said I was busy and the caller should leave a message as I didn't want to leave the children unattended in the bath. I knew it was Roy. I got the children ready for bed and took them to kiss their parents goodnight before chasing them up the stairs.

Mr Grant said Roy had phoned but didn't leave a number. I wondered why he was so secretive. How could he send flowers and then phone but not leave a number? I decided Jack had been right in saying I knew too little about Roy. I didn't have the answers to my own questions. Roy did. I didn't want to wait for his call and decided to pop over to Izzy Clarkson's to meet her children whom I was to babysit.

I phoned her and she said she looked forward to seeing me and would have the kettle on. I was there within an hour and she made me feel most welcome. We spoke about the ball. I told her what happened between Roy and me and she looked as if she already knew. She said things would sort themselves out. I was still young but, even at that age, I knew something was not right. I had been completely open with her and, instinctively, I knew she hadn't returned that genuine honesty.

We drank tea and I played with the children. Her husband was on the rig. I told her I had received flowers from Roy and she said it wouldn't be long before he was in touch. I changed the subject and told her I had to be heading back home. Just as I was leaving, it dawned on me that her husband and Roy had known each other for years. I asked her if she knew where Roy lived. She said if I didn't know then it wasn't her place to tell me. I thought that rather odd.

Four days later, Roy phoned. He wanted to collect me that evening and said that he had something for me. I didn't say much on the phone but agreed to see him. I didn't make any special effort getting ready for our date.

He arrived and we drove out into the countryside where he pulled the car over and handed me a box. Inside was a beautiful diamond and sapphire ring. He said he felt he had been unkind and unfair to me and had realised that he was madly in love. He said he was frightened of his feelings and this was reflected in his bad behaviour. He placed the ring on my finger and asked me to marry him. I instantly felt guilty and ashamed of my horrible thoughts I had harboured about him. I couldn't believe I had been so wrong about him.

I wanted time to think about the proposal as I was very young and, in reality, hardly knew him. This was now my opportunity to ask Roy where he could be contacted. If we were to be engaged I felt it necessary to meet his family and thought he should meet mine. He thoroughly agreed and said he would meet my family on his next visit from the rig, but I insisted that he should meet them before that.

My head was spinning. When I got home to the Grants that evening, I immediately showed them the beautiful ring but I said I hadn't made up my mind yet as to whether I should marry Roy. They were delighted for me.

Two days later, we went to tea at Mum Donaldson's. I showed Sheena and Mum the ring but explained that I hadn't given Roy an answer. Mum Donaldson took to Roy and thought he was very charming. Sheena, on the other hand, thought there was something not quite right about him.

We left after a couple of hours and I thought it a perfect time to ask him for his phone number and address. He gave me a number, which, again, made me feel I had misjudged him. I vowed I wouldn't let my imagination run away with me again, and put the number straight into my diary so that I wouldn't lose it.

As we approached home, Roy said he didn't live far from the Grant farm. I asked him to drive past his house if it was so near but he said he had a lot to do and I would see it in due course.

There were a few days left before he was to return to the rig. I told him that evening that I accepted his proposal of marriage and I wanted to spend the next few days with Mum Donaldson, discussing it. I went to Mum Donaldson's the next day and broke the news that I had accepted Roy's proposal. They were delighted and Sheena said I could wear the white wedding dress that she wore when she married. The gesture meant a lot to me. At that moment I felt I was among real family. I stayed the weekend and we spoke of nothing else but weddings.

The few weeks that followed were blissful. Then, one weekend when Roy was meant to be on the rigs, I decided to visit Mum Donaldson again and to stop off in the centre of Dundee on the way. As I walked down a street, I saw Roy standing at a bus stop. I paused long enough to see him give a woman and three small children a kiss before putting them on a bus. I couldn't believe my eyes. Here was a man I had recently become engaged to kissing another woman when he was meant to be on an oil rig. I was shocked.

I didn't want him to know I was there so I hid in order to take in the whole scene. After the woman and children were on the bus, Roy headed in the opposite direction. Rather than going to Mum Donaldson's, I headed straight for Izzy's. I wanted to know the truth about Roy and knew she had the answers.

I didn't know if she would be home but took the chance. I didn't think it would be wise to phone first as it might have put her on her guard. One hour later I was at her door. My heart quickened and my mouth went dry. I didn't know what to expect when I confronted her. As she opened the door, I put on a calm face. I felt like a magician, a master of illusion. Izzy was surprised to see me and invited me in for a cup of coffee.

I made small talk, which carried on for a while but only made it more difficult to broach the topic. I finally asked what she really knew about Roy and she claimed she didn't know much more than I. She seemed shocked when I told her I had seen Roy in Dundee town centre. She paused for some time and stared at me. I told her she didn't have to lie any more as I suspected that he was married. Her eyes were locked on to the engagement ring on my finger. When I told her I was engaged to Roy, she went ashen. She blurted out that she had known all along Roy was married but that he was trying to find a new life. I told her he had certainly lost one with me because I had no intention of being involved with a married man. I also pointed out that he and his wife had looked like a perfectly happy couple to me. Izzy apologised for misleading me but I wasn't in the mood for apologies. I was in the mood for the truth.

She begged me not to let Roy know she had confirmed that he was married. I gave her my word on this, and kept it. She offered me more coffee but I declined and said I had to go to Mum Donaldson's to tell her what I knew. I didn't want my entire family to be made fools of.

Izzy advised me not to say anything to my family until I had spoken to Roy first. I had his phone number and thought it was time to use it. Izzy looked at the number and told me it wasn't the same one she had.

I dialled it, only to find that it was a dead number. I tried repeatedly, only to hear the same disconnected tone. There was a sad look on Izzy's face, for she could see he had made a complete fool of me. He had obviously given me the number just to humour me. Izzy insisted that I stay for another coffee. I was furious and thought it might be a good idea to cool down before leaving.

Then Izzy told me about Roy's wife. She was a good mother and totally besotted with her wayward husband. I wasn't surprised to learn that there had been other women before me, but this was the first time he had bought a girl a ring and asked her to marry him.

I was dumbstruck. I could feel a lump form in my throat as I asked Izzy what she would do in my position. She said she would finish with him and hoped that I would too. I felt there was no alternative. I had heard enough and wanted to leave. Before I left, Izzy gave me Roy's real phone number.

I headed straight to Mum Donaldson's but didn't tell her what had happened. I just sat brooding, instead. Despite my claims that I was tired, she noticed something was wrong. As the minutes turned to hours, I became more angry than upset. I was raging inside over Roy's deceit and thought it best to sit quietly for the rest of the day. As soon as Sheena arrived, later that afternoon, she sensed the atmosphere straight away.

Mum and Sheena assumed I had had an argument with Roy because my emotional state went from bad to worse. I was too humiliated to tell them what I had found out. Then I snapped myself out of the doldrums and the rest of the evening went beautifully – that is until Sheena started playing love songs on her record player. I became very moody, flew into a temper and snapped at her to turn the music off. Then I stormed off to the bathroom and threw the ring down the toilet. I pulled the chain and watched with glee as it disappeared into the sewer system. I turned and saw Mum and Sheena staring at me in disbelief.

I simply said I didn't want to discuss the matter and never wanted to hear Roy's name again. I silently gathered my belongings and left to visit my brother John.

John's wife Julia was surprised to see me arrive unannounced. In an effort to explain my distressed look, I blurted out that I had had a terrible day. She gently guided me in and poured me a strong rum and coke. She enquired after Roy and I told her I never wanted to hear his name again. She noticed the ring was not on my finger. I told her it was swimming with the rats somewhere under the streets of Dundee. Then a girlfriend of Julia's arrived and I heard her say, mockingly, that I had had a tiff with Roy. I was insulted. I had been on the point of telling Julia all about Roy. She obviously didn't think my distress was important.

I sat for an hour listening to the girls gossip then got bored and headed back to Mum Donaldson's. The following day, when I returned to Mrs Grant's, I kept a low profile. I couldn't bear any questions about Roy. Around 6 p.m. that evening, he phoned. I found it difficult to act normally but I was determined to not scare him off as I wanted a proper confrontation.

I gritted my teeth and kept my temper when he told me he was on the rig. I knew he was really a short ride away in Dundee with his wife and children, which just added insult to injury. I was young, but certainly not stupid. He said he would be home in a couple of weeks and looked forward to seeing me. I said I looked forward to seeing him as well and, believe me, I meant it!

Immediately after putting the phone down, I dialled the number Izzy had given me. I was not surprised to hear his voice answer the phone. I said nothing and quietly replaced the receiver in its cradle. As I did so, I thought how much I hated him.

I phoned Izzy and found out Roy's rig schedule, then I worked out how he was able to juggle me and his wife around. I felt like a blind idiot when I realised how much he had lied to us both. As a first experience of love, it was lousy.

I wanted revenge and decided to string him along and humiliate him so I allowed him to collect me and take me out for meals and assorted dates. He entertained me to my heart's content for a further three months. I wanted him to be deeply and irreversibly hooked on me and I used all my power to charm him. It seemed to work and he did really seem to fall for me.

He arranged to join Mum Donaldson, Sheena and me for a family game of cards. He wanted to be with me as often as possible. He must have had to cut in on his wife's time to be with me but he wasn't to know I was aware of that. I sat watching him laughing, joking and enjoying himself with my family. It made me feel sick but I didn't let on. I was determined to keep the charade going until the moment was right to hurt him as much as he had hurt me.

My brother John arrived and I introduced them. It was John's first meeting with Roy. They got along beautifully. John invited Roy to a party that was to be held in a fortnight. Roy accepted happily. It was a New Year's Eve party and I thought it would be fun to watch Roy squirm out of his commitment at the last moment. My family were so pleased I was with Roy, believing him to be a decent, honest man. I wondered how they would react when they discovered the truth.

We continued to have a good time into the early evening. Mum served tea and sandwiches. After he had eaten, he suddenly looked at his watch and said, 'Oh no, isn't it funny how time flies when you are having fun. I'm terribly sorry but I'm late to meet a friend.' My family believed him but I knew he was racing back to his wife. Roy never even offered me a lift back to Mrs Grant's. I suppose he thought his dinner at home must be burning.

I planted a kiss on his cheek. He took me to one side and asked why I didn't give him a proper kiss. I told him I thought I had a cold coming on and didn't want him to catch it. I disliked him so much that I hated even having to hold his hand, let alone kiss him.

I returned to the front room, picked up my cards and rejoined the game. My brother commented that Roy was very nice. At that moment, I felt bad about the game I was playing with Roy. I suddenly felt as deceitful as he was and it filled me with guilt. I realised I was deceiving the Donaldsons as well as Roy. The thought made me uncomfortable. I went to the phone half an hour later and dialled Roy's number. As I expected, a woman answered. I put the receiver down without saying a word.

I told Mum I had better catch the next train back to Mrs Grant. As I headed for the station, it occurred to me that, during the past three months, Roy hadn't even noticed I wasn't wearing my engagement ring. It made me dislike him even more.

I went straight to my room when I arrived at Mrs Grant's and fell into bed thoroughly exhausted. I was determined to humiliate Roy thoroughly, and I wanted to do it in front of my family and friends. He had deceived all of them as well as me. I would make sure he went to my brother's party and wouldn't let him squirm out of it. That is where I planned to confront him. I lay on my bed and wrote Roy a letter which I planned to hand to him on the night of the party.

I spent Christmas with Mum Donaldson. It was a very happy occasion and not nearly as strained as the previous year when we had just lost Dad. Needless to say, Roy claimed that he had to work on the rig. Obviously, he was at home where he belonged, with his wife and children.

Then the moment I had been waiting for arrived. I agreed to meet Roy at my brother's. I watched the door right up to the moment he entered, thinking the whole time that I would be shattered if he didn't arrive. He walked in at 9.30 p.m. and, from that moment on, the hours ticked by quickly for me. I was actually enjoying myself. As midnight drew close, everyone gathered to sing 'Auld Lang Syne'.

At the stroke of midnight, Roy turned to kiss me and wish me a happy new year. I smirked at him and said my new year would be far happier than his. He looked at me strangely. I pulled out the letter I had written weeks before and handed it to him in front of my brother, who looked on curiously. I told Roy that his belated Christmas present was inside the envelope. I watched his face pale as he read the letter. He looked up slowly as I told my brother and family that I had discovered Roy was a married man with three children. I owed it to them to let them know.

Roy denied it at once. I then took his telephone number out of my pocket and suggested that we dial it and ask for his wife.

I turned away and left my brother's house but Roy was right behind me and, snapping at Roy's heels, was my brother John. I stopped in the middle of a park. Roy caught up with me and my brother arrived moments later.

My brother didn't say a word but watched as I had my say. I bellowed at Roy that he was a cheating rat who had used me. Then I suggested that John should return to his guests because it was obvious that I was able to deal with the situation. John left.

Roy tried to explain but it fell on deaf ears. I told him to get out of my life. He still tried to insist that he was not married. I couldn't believe he had the effrontery to stand there and continue lying.

Finally, he left and I was surprised to find myself weeping uncontrollably. I was finally experiencing the pain that I had buried over the past three months. I pulled myself together and returned to my brother's house. To my horror, there was Roy, telling my brother that, truly, he was not married. I couldn't believe my ears, nor could my brother. I felt at that moment that I would never trust another man for as long as I lived. Roy again tried to reason with me until my brother stepped in and told him to get out of the house and never show his face again. I stayed the night at my brother's house and woke up determined to pick up the pieces and start my life over again.

I had been invited to a party that evening and was determined to enjoy myself. I phoned Izzy to tell her what had happened the night before. Izzy was not surprised. She wanted to know how Roy had taken it. She was disgusted to learn that he denied having a wife and children. I then telephoned Roy's house and found myself speaking to his wife. I told her the whole saga. She laughed. I said that, had I been in her shoes, I wouldn't find any of this amusing.

She then informed me that she and Roy had formalised their divorce six months earlier. I was dumbfounded. She added that Roy still lived with her and was not a one-woman man. She was well aware that I existed.

I was terribly embarrassed about my outrageous behaviour and also furious with Izzy for misleading me. I stormed straight over to her house and told her everything in detail. She insisted she knew nothing about a divorce and said Roy must have kept it very quiet.

One week later, I received a letter from Roy. He said I was wrong to think badly of him but couldn't blame me because he had been so secretive and had not told me he had children and was divorced but still living with his ex-wife. He partially blamed himself.

He said he felt we would have been very good for each other. He wanted to leave things open so that I could contact him and perhaps sort it all out. I mulled it over for a long time and concluded that he hadn't been honest with me and it might be a pattern for the rest of his life. I also remembered that both Izzy and his wife had told me he had always had mistresses throughout his marriage and I realised that his adultery had caused his marriage to break down. I felt it best to leave things as they were and not get involved with him again. I did not reply to his letter and I never heard from or saw him again.

I wanted to make a new start in every way and decided to apply to join the Royal Navy. I handed in my notice to Mrs Grant. She wanted me to stay but understood that I was getting older and had more to experience in life. It was natural to start thinking of a career and higher earnings.

I failed my medical for the Navy and stayed with Mum

Donaldson for a few months. I was nearing my seventeenth birthday and decided to head for London. I found myself back in the same boat as before. The only way I could get to London and have accommodation and an income, albeit small, was to take on another nannying position. I celebrated my birthday by taking a train to London to start a new job I had successfully applied for.

27

KARL AND KANDY – ADVICE AGED 16

Many students will be leaving school this year but, if things have gone to plan, as I hope they have, this is something you won't have to do. You will be living with marvellous guardians, as well as Daddy, who are all determined to give you a good education and they will have been encouraging you all along. There should be no need for you to leave school to earn a living at this point.

By this age I would assume that you will probably have encountered emotional traumas over girlfriends or boyfriends. If you have not done so by now, it is on the cards around this age. When you fall in love and it doesn't work out, it feels like the end of the world but, believe me, it is not. It is safe to say that, at some point in their lives every human being will fall in love and experience some form of heartbreak. Life goes on and love will always turn up again: often it gets better and better.

In the face of heartbreak, you must just carry on. There is another feeling, called infatuation, which feels like love but isn't as long-lasting. There is also lust, the purely physical desire for a certain girl or boy. At times, this also feels like love or infatuation but you will soon see the difference because lust wears off more quickly than any other emotion. It is just a physical need.

I am advising you as a mother and also as someone who has experienced a lot of emotional disappointment. I am not a psychologist who can analyse all these things. I am your mother, who simply understands that, at some point, you will encounter what I have just spoken about. I can only assure you that the wounds heal. Sometimes you will even look back and thank your lucky stars that certain relationships are actually over.

Each year of your life will be different and, as I have said before, each cloud has a silver lining. No matter how hard a situation seems at the time, it will get better. Believe me, I know. I've been there more than once. Always remember that, no matter what happens, if you have the strength, you will always come out on top eventually. I was lucky enough to have Jack to turn to every now and then. On the whole, my life was a struggle because I didn't have a person like Jack at all times to guide me. I didn't have someone around the whole time who loved and cared enough about me the way I love and care about you.

You know by now who Jack was. I valued him very much. It saddened me to keep him a secret when, in actual fact, he should have been congratulated for picking up the broken pieces of my life. I have to thank Jack for sharing a great many things with me that I now share with you.

Even as I write this, despite my illness, I feel Jack is still nearby, helping me along. Some things never die.

28

MUMMY – AGED 17 – 21

Mr Sitwell, my new employer, was at London's King Cross station to meet me. Naïvely, I had assumed that my new family would be as nice as the Grants. I had been given a description of Mr Sitwell and had no difficulty finding him in the crowded station. He was wearing a bowler hat and a pinstripe suit. He spoke just like the Queen.

On the drive to his posh four-storey house in Ladbroke Grove, he told me about his wife and children. All darlings, I understood. There were two boys, aged five and six, and a fourteen-month-old baby girl. As soon as I arrived, Mrs Sitwell introduced herself. She seemed to have a dozen plums in her mouth. I was given a tour of the house. By the time I reached the fourth floor, I'd decided to give up smoking, a vice I had recently taken up.

The children's room, my room and the bathroom I would share with the little ones were all on the fourth floor. I could tell from the moment I stepped in the house that it wasn't for me. Mrs Sitwell had a very condescending, forceful manner, and the two little boys nearly drove me to a nervous breakdown within an hour of my arrival.

I knew I was in trouble with the baby as well. There was a very large, heavy, Victorian chest of drawers in her nursery. She had pulled out the bottom drawer and systematically emptied it by slinging items all over the room. This baby looked like a mini-version of a world heavyweight boxing champ. She actually had bulging muscles on her little biceps.

Mrs Sitwell asked me to make her a cup of tea before unpacking my belongings. This annoyed me as I had thought I was to be a nanny, not a lady in waiting. As the day wore on, I began to find out about the household rules and regulations. I was informed that I had to wear a nanny's uniform. When I took the baby for a walk, I would easily recognise other nannies in the neighbourhood by our matching slave outfits.

I had no intention of being identified in this fashion. I thought it a good idea to use the uniform while indoors, because it saved wear and tear on my own clothes, but there was no way I was stepping outdoors in such an unsightly outfit.

The Sitwells had a garden that would have put Hyde Park to shame but Mrs Sitwell insisted that baby needed the fresh air of a park, not her own backyard. I prepared the baby in order to take her to Holland Park and then nearly died when I saw her pram. It looked like the Batmobile. In actual fact, the pram was much larger than I was and nearly my height. Upon manoeuvring this enormous vehicle through the gates of the park, it became obvious who were the nannies and who were the natural mothers.

I went rolling in as if I was about to save Gotham City. The poor souls sat on benches with their backs straight and their chests out. They recognised the Batmobile and realised I was the Sitwells' new nanny. They scrutinised my jeans, anorak and desert boots and then scoffed. With equal distaste, I scrutinised their brown coats, hats and striped uniforms, these lovely ensembles being completed by thick tights and nurse's shoes.

I lit a cigarette and one nanny nearly fainted. She snorted that it was outrageous to smoke around the baby. She did not seem to realise that we were in the centre of a massive open-air park and not confined in a closet. I didn't want to be a part of that group. Over the next six weeks, I took great pleasure in scandalising them with my un-nanny-like behaviour. I marvelled at the stark difference between working in a Londoner's private residence and a Scottish one.

It was a first-hand experience of the English class system and its never-ending eccentricities. They were a law unto themselves. I appreciated and admired their code of conduct, which clearly stated that they were proud to be British, and lived in a world all their own. I actually felt endeared towards the majority of the people I met and was pleased to get an insight into their world, but my admiration did not extend to the Sitwells, who had trouble defining the difference between human beings and slaves.

Within the first couple of weeks, I had become a cook, cleaner, handywoman, lady in waiting and personal servant to the Sitwells . . . apart from nanny to the children. I had no intention of hanging on to that multi-talented position much longer. I didn't go to sleep at night; I collapsed with exhaustion.

I dreaded the moment I woke up every morning. In the kitchen I would be greeted by a woman I called Fag-Ash-Lil. She was the hired house cleaner. That was a joke, of course, because she spent the whole morning in the kitchen drinking tea and chain-smoking. I always ended up doing the chores she inevitably left uncompleted. After cutting through the thick fog of cigarette smoke to prepare the Sitwells' breakfast, I would dress the children and clean up the monstrous mess they had made on the fourth floor, which always made me feel I was nanny to a family of poltergeists. Then Mrs Sitwell would call me down from the fourth floor just to send me back up to the fourth floor to fetch something.

In the afternoon, Mr Sitwell would arrive home; hurl his bowler hat on to the hat stand and place the umbrella that was always by his side, even in sunshine, in its appointed place. This was the cue for Mrs Sitwell to instruct me to prepare his supper. After supper I would serve them coffee. Then I would be asked to serve them brandies in the library hours after I should have been in bed.

Mrs Sitwell ran me so hard that I barely had any time off for myself. I was lucky to sneak out on a Sunday afternoon once a fortnight. I did her cooking, cleaning and ironing and looked after all her children to the point where I might as well have been married to Mr Sitwell instead. If I hung around much longer, she would probably have asked me to carry out her matrimonial obligations as well. It wouldn't have surprised me.

I gave her my notice and ran, not walked, on the day I left. I had already answered an ad, and been accepted, for another nannying position.

I was to work for a corporal named Sid Walters in Wiltshire. He had two children, Tom aged two and Jane aged four. Sadly, he and his wife Noreen were going through a divorce.

I had my own room. Sid was at work all day so I had complete control of the house. Sometimes he was on 24-hour duty and I felt as if it was my very own home. I absolutely loved it there. My duties were cleaning, washing, cooking, ironing and taking the children to nursery school. It was a lot of work but I was my own boss and it made all the difference. I became very attached to the children, especially Tom. Jane was at school all day so I spent much more time with Tom. I would take him to a small river near the house where I would teach him to catch frogs which we looked at and then released again unharmed. We would sit for hours enjoying nature. Sometimes we had picnics. Little Tom was very loving and sensitive. He clung to me in such a way that I felt I could never part from him. I felt sorry for the children because of their parents' divorce. I was very aware of their special needs. Tom's character and personality were still developing whereas Jane's seemed already to have formed. In the years that followed, I became very attached to Tom and am still as fond of him today as I was then.

As the months progressed, Sid spent more and more time away on exercises. I was left to my own devices. I became a little mother hen to both children and was very houseproud. I was so content and happy that, for some reason, I didn't contact anyone back home in Scotland. I didn't want anything to spoil my paradise. I got great satisfaction from seeing the children go out smartly dressed. Because I was so young I was determined to gain respect by showing I was responsible enough not to need someone looking over my shoulder.

When Sid returned home, sometimes after weeks away,

it was a great event for the children. I looked forward to his return as I felt proud that I had managed so well. I would prepare special dinners and lay the table beautifully. Then, after six months, it struck me that Sid and I had something in common. His marriage had crumbled but he wouldn't allow the army to remove the two children from his care. I, on the other hand, had been removed from the natural care of my mother. He was prepared to fight tooth and claw and risk losing his army career to keep his babies. I was prepared to make sure that the children never lost such a caring parent. In that, we shared a common bond.

As time wore on, it became very difficult to share the same house without sharing our feelings. I then realised that I cared very deeply for Sid. Unknown to me at the time, he, too, was drawn to me. I was nearing my eighteenth birthday and Sid was 27.

Sid had never found the time to date other women since his wife left. I found that strange at first, then thought it might have been because of the two children. Only at a later date did I learn that he had fallen in love with me.

Just before my eighteenth birthday, I moved out of my room to share his. The children did not realise for ages that their daddy and I had become lovers. We would always make sure we woke up before the children so that they wouldn't catch us in bed together.

My eighteenth birthday was not a special event, not like it is for most people, yet it was a milestone for me because I was so very happy and in love.

As time progressed, problems started arising over Sid's wife's access to the children. I didn't know which side to take. In retrospect, I realise that it's best to mind one's own business in such matters. I learned that Sid had caught his wife in bed with his best friend. He was determined to prove her an unfit mother and hurt her for what she had done. I felt that the children were being used as a weapon, a common occurrence in custody battles.

Sid asked me to appear in court on his behalf, to give evidence that the children were well-balanced and content in his care. I was torn apart. I wanted to stand by the man I loved but, at the same time, my heart went out to the children's mother, Noreen.

The very first time I met Noreen was on an arranged visit. Sid finally allowed her to come over a year after she had left. He insisted that he was present during the visit. During the year that she had been apart from the children, she had done everything in her power to ensure they didn't forget her. She sent birthday, Easter and Christmas cards but the children never received them. Army quarters didn't have phones back then, making it impossible for her to speak to the children. I knew all this and sympathised deeply with her. I did not approve of Sid denying the children their right to see their mother. When I said this he would remind me of the horrible thing that had happened to him, but I felt that the children were also suffering for it and I thought it was very unfair. I told him that, no matter what happens between a couple, the children shouldn't be used as a weapon of retribution. In my mind, that was what he was doing. I was young and immature in some respects. I had let my heart rule my head and become deeply involved with Sid and I felt guilty that I was slowly taking Noreen's place.

When the day arrived for Noreen's visit I was shocked.

She was not as I had imagined. She had long dark hair growing down past her shoulders and big brown eyes. She looked just like Jane. Noreen was tall, with a size 12 figure, and very attractive. When I opened the door to her, I was nervous as I didn't know what to expect or how the visit should be conducted.

I invited her in and explained straight away that I was the nanny. I didn't get the impression that she believed me. She resented my presence in her home, with her children and her husband. During the year of her absence, there had been great changes in the house. I had refurnished it to my taste and, at Sid's persuasion, all traces of Noreen were gone. I easily read the look on her face. She was knocked sideways.

I went into another room with the children so that Sid and Noreen could talk in private. They raised their voices now and again and I knew they were throwing accusations at each other. I began to feel embarrassed by the situation I had found myself in. I walked into the room and asked them to keep their voices down as the children were finding it upsetting. It was selfish of them to ignore the fact that their quarrel would affect the youngsters. Her look told me to mind my own business but I ignored it. I felt that she was a visitor in my home. I asked them to come to an amicable decision that would be beneficial for the children. I told Sid, right there on the spot, that I was disappointed by his behaviour. He knew I spoke from experience because of my own childhood.

Both Noreen and Sid stared at me with gaping mouths. I told them I knew only too well what they were doing to their children.

Then I took the children in to Noreen. All the torment and anguish she had suffered during the past year showed. The children were distant at first, especially Tom. The children clung to me and it was clear to see how much that hurt Noreen.

The strain in the house was too much for me. Noreen was taking the children out for the afternoon and Sid left me to sort out the arrangements as to when they should be returned. I felt sorry for her. I found myself telling her that her own children had to be back indoors by 6 p.m.

I watched them walk up the street and wondered how I would feel if I were Noreen. The thought made the hairs on my arms stand on end. I could hear Sid calling me. I sat with him but felt very withdrawn. I told him I felt the way he was behaving towards Noreen was disgusting. I suggested he forget the past and show some forgiveness, if only for the sake of the children. I told Sid that there were two sides to every coin and something must have made Noreen stray. She couldn't be entirely to blame. Sid looked at me as if I were a stranger. I reminded him that outsiders can sometimes see things more clearly than those close to a situation.

I couldn't help being outspoken. If he thought anything of me, then he would listen to what I had to say and take some notice. I wasn't an expert on such matters but I felt that Sid was being unreasonable. He had married and had his children out of love and he should keep that in mind.

We watched television for the rest of the day. The difficult atmosphere faded a bit and we didn't talk about Noreen or the children for most of the day. Then, out of the blue, he asked what I would do if I were in his shoes. I replied with a question. I asked if he was fighting for the custody of his children out of love and concern or purely for vindictive reasons. He said he was doing both. I felt it was pointless to discuss it any further as our views differed so much.

The children returned with Noreen and I made tea for everyone. Sid left us alone to chat. I wanted to get to know her better and thought it would help me to understand the situation more clearly. I hoped she could tell me why things had deteriorated so badly. I told her I wanted to know about her custody battle and that I did not approve of Sid's behaviour. She wasn't forthcoming at first. She was still trying to take it all in and decide whether to trust me. I said that, no matter what she did, she was still the mother of her children. I didn't want her to feel I was a substitute. I told her I would keep her informed of the children's progress, with or without Sid's consent. I said we could keep it to ourselves. She didn't seem either grateful or disappointed at the suggestion. She said she would write to me. I told her that, when Sid was away, I would get in touch with her and she could visit the children provided he did not know about it. I would talk the children into keeping it secret. I knew I risked falling out with Sid if he should find out but I felt the children came first and they shouldn't be made to suffer for the actions of adults. There was too much heartbreak and confusion already.

I didn't feel Noreen was a threat to me as far as my relationship with Sid went. She had already guessed I was more than a nanny. At bathtime Jane was quick to tell me that her mum had asked her a lot of questions about me. It altered my opinion of Noreen. I had been lecturing Sid about confusing his children by keeping them away from their mother, only for Noreen to confuse them with grown-up questions. I began to realise that I might have misjudged her.

After the children were bathed and put to bed, I sat in the dimmed sitting room. It was very cosy. I snuggled up to Sid and we listened to an album. A song called 'Bridge Over Troubled Water' came on. I looked into Sid's eyes and saw bitterness and anger. I chuckled and said, 'Penny for your thoughts.' He laughed at my Scottish attempt at imitating a London accent and then started to cry.

He said that for a man's wife to have an affair with another man is one thing, but to have an affair with his best friend was even more degrading and humiliating. He wasn't prepared to forgive her and put it behind him as if it had never happened. I felt my heart thud. I knew what he was about to stay. He told me Noreen had asked for a reconciliation and that the divorce proceedings should be stopped. I couldn't believe my ears. I told him to do what he felt was right for himself and the children. I wouldn't stand in his way. He said I was a very caring person and, in some respects, extremely sensible.

I felt he should follow his heart. If he really loved Noreen, there was nothing to stop him from trying one more time. He assured me he had no intention of having her back. He said that once trust is betrayed it is difficult to rebuild. The betrayal would always be at the back of his mind. He wasn't prepared to take the chance of it happening again. I felt foolish at my attempt to help Noreen when, behind my back, she was trying to reconcile things with Sid. I decided I wouldn't fight to keep Sid but just sit on the fence and watch what happened. I didn't want to nag him back into the arms of his wife. I would keep a low profile and bite my tongue rather then voice my feelings. It's called swallowing one's pride.

As we climbed into bed together that evening, I couldn't bring myself to snuggle into Sid's arms as I had done in the past. For the first time since we started sharing a bed, I lay apart from him.

I waited until his breathing grew heavy, signifying that he had fallen asleep, and crept out of bed. I went downstairs to root through a box I had seen in a cupboard. I had seen Sid clean out the cupboard but never touch the box. I wondered about its contents.

In the box I found photo albums. I made some coffee and slowly studied the pictures. I could see that Sid and Noreen had once been a very happy couple. I was amazed to see how that happiness had turned into hate. I pored over the photos for a good three hours. I felt it was pointless to try to sleep as my mind was too active. I wondered why Sid had joined the army at the age of 25. It was a very late age to start a career in the forces. I decided to wait for Noreen's next visit and pump her for information. I had a feeling that something had happened that forced Sid to leave civilian life for a career in the army, although I should mention now that I never did get to the root of it.

I was just closing the cupboard door, after returning the box to its rightful place, when Sid appeared. Panic overcame me because I knew I had tampered with something that was personal to him. I told him I couldn't sleep and realised that he didn't know I had been looking in the box. He asked me to join him for a coffee. Before I could answer, he pulled me to him and begged me not to leave him. He said he would sort things out very quickly so that we could have a settled life together. I held on to him for dear life. Although I had told him to follow his heart and had meant it at the time, in reality, I didn't want him to choose Noreen rather than me.

Somehow, my confidence had left me for a moment and I felt Noreen had an edge on me. Having once shared a good life with Sid in the past gave her an advantage. I began thinking of Jack. I wondered what he would think of me now if he knew I was involved in this messy situation. Someone was bound to be hurt. He wouldn't be proud of me. I could always rely on Jack's good, old-fashioned advice. I wished I could run to my rock at that very moment and let the sea deliver the answers I desperately needed. As Sid loosened his embrace, I returned to reality. There was no Jack, rock or sea in Wiltshire. Just me. I wondered if I had made a mistake by getting involved with Sid and his messy divorce.

It was nearly dawn and, outside, the birds began to whistle and chirp. I ran to open the dining-room windows and whispered to Sid to listen to the birds. It was a better sound than adults bickering. Sid looked at me strangely and I realised that he didn't really know or understand me.

In the year that followed, I allowed one sneak visit by Noreen. Sid found out about it through the children but, much to my surprise, did not get upset. The year was filled with letters from lawyers and arguments between Sid and Noreen. Thankfully, it did not affect my relationship with Sid. Our love continued to blossom.

Noreen was awarded access to the children once a fortnight but Sid got custody. Sadly, she could not visit every fortnight as she didn't live near enough and had difficult working hours.

My nineteenth birthday had passed and Sid was divorced soon afterwards. We had never discussed marriage so, when he actually proposed to me, I was dumbfounded. I couldn't imagine myself married, with a ready-made family, but I soon warmed to the idea. After all, that was the life I was leading anyway and a marriage certificate would make it official, a seal on our love.

I felt the Donaldsons would have a lot to say about it and would do everything in their power to stop me marrying a man ten years my senior who had children from a previous marriage. I decided it was time to phone Mum Donaldson and explain the situation. This would be the first contact I had had with anyone from Scotland in two years.

I shook as I dialled Mum Donaldson's number. She answered and was startled to hear me. I apologised for not contacting her in so long. I said I had needed time to go in my own direction and was now in a position to tell her about my life. I announced my marriage plans for the fourth of December 1976 and said I wanted the whole family to be present. To my disappointment, none of them attended my wedding. There was only Sid, myself and a few close friends. My entire family boycotted my wedding as an act of protest and disapproval. I decided to take Sid and the children to Scotland and I asked Mum Donaldson not to form any opinions about him until then.

Sid and I decided to go up that very Christmas. On Boxing Day we drove to Dundee with the children. I knew that once we arrived Mum Donaldson would warm to the children and Sid. Mum Donaldson gave us a warm welcome and invited us to stay for the whole of our four-day visit. This was a turning point in my life. I was married and settled and everyone approved of Sid and the children once they got to know them.

I didn't visit anyone else over the four days because I wanted the family to get to know each other well. Mum Donaldson, Sheena and I got along very well and continued to do so after I returned to England. We stayed in close touch, which pleased me very much.

During the drive back to England, I realised that I should have paid Jack a visit as well. I felt selfish knowing that the only time I ran to him was when I had problems and it bothered me that I hadn't gone to him to share my joy.

When we arrived back in Wiltshire, everyone was shattered after the journey. It was nice to be home. Sid thought Mum Donaldson was very nice and I agreed with him. She seemed to have changed.

The year that followed found us desperately trying to have a baby. We were the perfect couple, with practically everything, the only thing missing was a child of our own. Sid thought it was strange that I had never become pregnant in all the time we were together as we never took any precautions. He really wanted me to have a baby, so I went to a doctor for various tests to see why I hadn't conceived. I discovered that my Fallopian tubes had never developed properly and that it was impossible for me to conceive unless I had an operation. After that news, it upset me to see pregnant women. The more I saw them, the more I was determined to do anything to have Sid's child.

A date was fixed for me to have an operation to implant plastic Fallopian tubes. Back then, I was only the second woman in Britain to have this operation. My useless tubes would be removed and replaced by man-made ones.

I was admitted to Odstock Hospital in Wiltshire where the operation was performed by Mr Feld and his team. Only time would tell if the tubes would serve their purpose. I remember phoning Mum Donaldson from the hospital and was shocked when she said to me that if nature intended me to have children, I wouldn't need the help of doctors. I thought it was an insensitive remark.

I couldn't wait for visiting hours, to see Sid. When he arrived I was in quite a state. He could see I had been crying. When I told him what my mother had said, he told me to forget it. He said some lucky women can't understand what it is like for those who can't have children. He went to the sister's office and returned with an enormous parcel. I struggled to pull myself up in the bed so that I could unwrap the gift. It was a fur coat. (This was in the days when it was acceptable to wear such things.) I flung my arms around Sid and couldn't thank him enough. I asked where he had got such a wonderful gift. He didn't answer but looked filled with pride that he had made me so happy. He said it was my early Christmas present and that he couldn't resist buying it for me. That's what he was like. Whenever he went away with the forces, he would always return with special gifts for the children and myself. So much thought went into everything he gave us. I was nearing the end of my term in hospital and was so looking forward to seeing Tom and Jane. They had missed me as much as I missed them. The months that followed were blissful.

When I was twenty, I finally became pregnant but then miscarried within the first three months. That was to be repeated two more times up to the age of 21. It was heart-breaking and I was losing hope of ever having a baby. I slipped into depressions which lasted months at a time. All I could think about was what Mum Donaldson had said to me about not being able to have babies. I'm sure one of the most horrible things that can happen to a woman is the inability to conceive. It makes one's life seem so empty. At times I felt inadequate, as if I wasn't a complete woman. I worried that Sid might start seeing me in this light. He wanted a baby as much as I did. But he was lucky; at least he had two of his own already. Although his children were now very much like my own, they really still belonged to Noreen and Sid.

I wanted to be able to share the miracle of reproduction with Sid. I wanted to produce a baby, an act of love, with the man with whom I intended to spend the rest of my life.

My sadness was temporarily pushed to one side when Sid came home with the news that he was to be posted to Germany. We were given six months' notice so that we could do whatever was necessary to prepare for our future abroad. I was quite looking forward to the change. I had never lived in another country and it appealed to me for I was born with adventure in my soul.

Noreen was shattered by the news as it meant she would see very little of her children. I arranged to ship the items we would be keeping and sold what remained. Whatever didn't sell went to charity and friends. I thought we should pay Mum Donaldson another visit before heading off. We planned to spend a month in Scotland. Jane and Tom would attend school in Dundee during the four weeks leading up to our departure. There I was, entering a new phase of life as a happily married woman with two step-children and none of my own.

The children were left in Mum Donaldson's care while Sid and I prepared to hand our house back to the army. Once everything was ready, we headed for Scotland to join the children. The only thing we still waited for was our flight passes.

I spent most of my time indoors with Mum Donaldson. One afternoon, I told Sid I was going to pay Isobelle a visit as I wouldn't have the opportunity again for some time to come. I had thought about Jack and decided to pop in on him on the way to Isobelle's. I hadn't seen him for five years. When I arrived at Jack's, I realised he wouldn't be in if he had kept to his old routine, so I headed towards the pier. I walked along the waterfront and stood there for some time. I thought about the past and how I had been prepared to jump off the very rock I was standing on such a long time ago.

All of a sudden a man's voice behind me said, 'I remember a little girl who stood on that rock many years ago.' I said, 'I was that girl,' and turned to look at the owner of the familiar voice. Jack threw his arms around me and held on tightly. I couldn't apologise enough for not visiting in so long. He wasn't angry with me. He was simply delighted I was there.

He said I had turned into a fine woman. He couldn't get over how mature I looked. I was no longer a lost thirteen-year-old. I was a grown woman. We headed to Jack's house and I wasn't surprised to find that nothing had changed. As soon as he opened the front door, the first thing I noticed was the familiar, clean smell. Memories flooded back as soon as I entered the sitting room. I thought of the days and hours I had spent there, talking about my problems. There I was again, but for the first time, I was trouble-free.

We talked for hours on end and I completely forgot about the time. I was very excited about my new life abroad. Jack was delighted that I had landed on my feet. He was pleased that I was happy and leading a stable, balanced life. He looked at me and said he wondered if I would find a rock in Germany. I said I hoped I would never need to find one again. I slipped off to have a final look at the room I had stayed in so many times. It was spotless and arranged just the way I had left it so many years before. I felt rather sad. I had promised as a child that Jack would always be my secret and, when I did eventually leave his house, I knew I was right to have kept him all to myself.

During the days that followed my excitement about going to Germany began to fade. I was concerned for Jack and had a feeling I would never see him again. When I had said my farewells, I was tormented with the thought that they might be the final ones. I decided I would visit him once more before going to Germany but I never made it. Our tickets had arrived from the ministry and we had to leave at five in the morning to catch our flight. I never managed to see Isobelle either, but that didn't bother me as much as missing the opportunity to see Jack one last time.

We arrived at RAF Brise Norton in the evening in order

to deal with our luggage and other routine formalities. Once we were comfortable on the plane, bolts of excitement rushed through me. I began to look forward to a new life.

After our arrival in Germany, we were taken by an NCO to our new house on the army base. I didn't like the look of it from the outside because all the windows were so small and I didn't expect it to be as nice as it actually was. Inside, it was spacious and well-decorated and it was well stocked with all the bare necessities of life, including furniture. I longed for our crates of belongings to arrive so that I could turn it into a proper home.

The NCO told us where we could dine that evening and offered to give us a guided tour of the base the next morning. I looked forward to shopping in the Naafi, an army store that only residents on the base could use. Cigarettes, coffee, tea and alcohol could be purchased tax-free.

I decided I would enjoy living in Germany as everything seemed so clean. The women took great pride in their homes and they all seemed to be gifted with green fingers. I settled in quickly. Tom and Jane began attending a school located within the army base. I was left with plenty of time to work on our new home. A few weeks later we bought a car and I decided now was as good a time as any to learn to drive.

After seven one-hour lessons, I passed my test. My instructor told me I was a natural behind the wheel. Sid thought I should drive the car around the base for a while, to gain confidence, before going on the road.

I was able to converse in German within six months. I noticed that many army wives spent a lot of time having coffee with each other while their husbands were away. I never really fitted into that lifestyle and preferred to go on great adventures by car with the children.

I was about to celebrate my twenty-second birthday. It would be my first birthday abroad.

29

KARL AND KANDY – ADVICE AGED 17–21

You two have now reached the age when you can apply for a driving licence. If you have the opportunity to do so, I am sure you will take up driving with a vengeance. All young people want to drive and own their own cars! You are probably going to dances or pubs by now. Be careful about alcohol consumption. Alcohol alters people's personalities; they can become argumentative and nasty accidents can happen through drink. Sadly, this is one of the things you only understand through experience. If you find yourself in a situation where drunken people are being aggressive, it is wiser to walk away. Don't interfere or get drawn in. People do shocking things under the influence of alcohol.

Don't ever get into a car with a driver who has been drinking. Try to discourage any friends you may be out with from driving when they are under the influence of drink. Alcohol affects the speed of people's reflexes and, sadly, many adults and children are killed each year by drunken drivers.

It is hard for me to imagine what you two may be doing now or what decisions you will have made in your lives. By now, you will have formed your own characters and likes and dislikes. You know the sort of people you like to be with and you will have developed your own tastes in everything, from food and clothes to morals and beliefs.

I can only hope that, in some way, the account of my life and the advice I have given you has been of some use. If your education has gone as planned, I hope you have achieved all that you had hoped to. The only thing I would ask is that you have the intelligence and determination to work towards your dreams and that you try not to settle into marriage and parenthood too early. There will be opportunities to widen your horizons, travel, learn other languages and so on. My only regret is not being able to see you do all these things and then, eventually, marry and have a family.

Maybe someday you will share your treasure chest with your own families. Perhaps you will say to your children, 'This is your Granny, a person you would have been proud to have known and can know through what she left us.'

My love for my own babies motivated me to create the treasure chest. When you have children of your own, you will be surprised at what you would do for them. I remember you promising that no matter how upsetting the account of my life might be at times, you would always remember the days we spent together as nothing other than filled with love and endless fun.

This will be my last letter of advice to you, although the story of my life continues up to the age of 35. This letter is dated one minute before midnight, 3 July 1993.

After the age of 21, there isn't an awful lot I can do to guide you. You should have well-established personalities by now, and, as adults, you will have taken control of your lives.

All my love to you, Karl, the son I was so lucky to have, and to you, my angel Kandy, the daughter I was so lucky to have. I'm so grateful for the time, albeit short, that I shared with you two. God bless. I love you dearly. I guess you know that by now.

With you always in spirit, and with you always the love I left behind. Mum xxxxxx

30

MUMMY – AGED 22–28

My twenty-second birthday was a real treat. The day started with the most fantastic gift I had ever received to date, a light blue Volkswagen Beetle. I wasn't keen on the colour so the car had a two-tone beige and brown respray. I loved my little car.

The evening was spent celebrating my birthday with our new friends. We went to a small pub across from our house, called the Heidi Kotton. They served fabulous food. It was such a romantic evening. I looked at Sid and realised how much I admired, respected and loved him. He was an excellent husband and a good, caring father to his children. He loved cooking and would always prepare the Sunday roast if he wasn't away on exercise. We had a lot of good times in the kitchen.

In my eyes, I had come a long way since I was a child. It seemed strange to be sitting with my husband and step-children. Sid explained that it wasn't strange at all – it was normal life.

The years with Sid sailed by. They were among the most blissful years of my life. Then I began to have difficulties with Jane, which became so bad that the problem started interfering with our marriage. As much as I tried to make life work with her, things went from bad to worse. By the time she was eleven, she had betrayed my trust to the point where I found it difficult to stay under the same roof with her. Children can be very powerful and manipulative. I believe that their abilities are often underestimated. I reached the point where I couldn't bear to breathe the same air as Jane, and I took it out on Sid.

I refused to communicate with him unless he sorted his daughter out but I should have realised that no one was capable of doing that, not even her own father. I had a row with Sid and reached the point where I refused to sleep in the same bed with him until something was done about Jane's behaviour. That was a terrible mistake. I had created an immeasurable distance between Sid and me. We grew so far apart that we couldn't find our way back into each other's lives again. I felt so sorry for Sid. I had worshipped the ground he walked on. He had never done anything to hurt any of his children or me. I made the mistake of giving him an ultimatum over believing his own wayward child or believing in me. I wouldn't accept any compromise. I knew I could never trust Jane and trust was the most important thing to me. Finally, it cost me my marriage. I split up with Sid still loving him as much, if not more, than I always had. It was the most difficult decision I ever made in my life. In March 1982, I left Sid never to return as his wife. I was 25 years old. In letters that will be given to you later in life, you will learn about the children Mummy left behind.

I returned home to Scotland. Home is usually the first place that people run to when things go wrong, but things weren't the same. I didn't find the comfort and support I was looking for. Everyone said: 'I told you so. I told you not to take on so much responsibility. You shouldn't have taken on children that weren't yours.' Even Isobelle echoed these feelings, which I really resented, considering that she had half a dozen children that weren't hers.

I didn't visit Jack. I didn't want to return to him when things were going wrong. I was ashamed and felt like a failure. The last time Jack saw me I had had a wonderful and a promising future. I didn't want him to know that things hadn't worked out. I made a decision not to contact him again until my life was in order.

After spending six months trying to pick up the pieces, I became restless and decided that a complete change of scenery might be the perfect tonic. I went to Holland for a month and fell in love with it. I was attracted to the many canals and the bold sense of freedom the locals seemed to enjoy. It was near enough to Germany to visit the family and friends I had left behind. My holiday helped me to reach the decision to live abroad permanently. I returned to Dundee, sold all my furniture and belongings and moved back to Germany, not to live with Sid but to be where I had spent the best years of my life to date.

I began my new life as a free woman who would soon enjoy single status again. It's good to have friends on whom you can rely. I stayed with a couple of chums until I found a job and flat of my own. I was so enthusiastic that I went somewhat overboard and took on three jobs at once. I had to prove I could fend for myself and I wanted to do it as soon as possible. I worked from 10 a.m. to 4 a.m., a good eighteen hours a day. I worked in catering during the day, as a supervisor in a steel mill during the afternoon and in the evening as a barmaid.

When I began work in the 'Wirtshaus' (German for pub) I began to meet lots of colourful characters. Then, one evening, I was invited to a party, which I really looked forward to as I was tiring of all work and no play. I was ready to make new friends.

At the party, I noticed a man staring at me for the best part of the evening. He finally asked me to dance and said I had the cheekiest face and most beautiful eyes he had ever seen. I was flattered as the process of divorce can leave a woman feeling quite unattractive. I told him what had brought me to Germany and why I wanted to live there. I made sure he understood I had adventure in my soul. He told me I was either a glutton for punishment or a workaholic for holding down so many jobs.

I learned a bit about him and found him very interesting. His name was Nobby and he was an English staff sergeant. The stirring of emotion that occurs when one is attracted to a member of the opposite sex reawakened in me. I had almost forgotten what it was like. I was still a bit wary of men because of my previous experiences but thought that if I didn't give someone a chance, I could end up spending the rest of my days alone.

Nobby asked if he could look me up one day but I never expected it to happen so soon. He showed up at my workplace the following morning. I didn't know whether I was pleased or embarrassed when I saw him standing there. He wanted to take me out after work but I told him I had to rush off to my next job. I had a quick coffee with him and really enjoyed his company. I left him my phone number and truly hoped to see him again.

I got more time off work so that I could develop a relationship with Nobby. We picnicked, swam, and danced the next three months away. Then, just when our relationship was deepening, I was shattered to discover that he had been posted to Münster, another city that was hours away from where I lived. Nobby vowed to keep in touch and we promised to see each other at weekends.

He came to see me every other weekend. After five weeks, I made my first trip to Münster. I stayed in a lovely little hotel and had bags of fun going to restaurants and living it up with Nobby. He knew how to make a lady happy. I hadn't slept with him at this point in our relationship and I liked him even more because he wasn't just after my body. I was to make this trip over and over again. I soon began to make lots of new friends in Münster and eventually packed up and moved there. Secretly, in my heart, I did it just to be near Nobby.

Nobby made arrangements for me to stay with a friend of his until I found a new job and my own accommodation. I had saved up a fair amount of money and knew I would find a new place to live in no time. Then, just as I settled down in my new life, Nobby was posted to the Falklands. He was to spend six months there. I couldn't handle it at all.

I became so distraught that I broke off our relationship just as he was about to depart. I had to get my life into order and I didn't want the heartbreak of being in love with a person who might not be returning. I wouldn't have been able to cope if Nobby had become a casualty of the war. I was still too fragile to deal with something like that. Breaking up with him was a form of self-protection. I refused to write to him and wouldn't accept any letters he sent.

During the six months that Nobby was away, I began to drink too much. The combination of moving and then finding myself alone once more was just too much to bear. I couldn't stop thinking about the ironic pattern that always formed my life. Just when everything seemed wonderful, something always happened to ruin it. I found comfort in endless bottles of booze.

My routine disintegrated to the point where I started each day with a bottle of strong lager. I was waking, swollen-faced, at odd hours. Regardless of what time I woke up, my first drink of the day had to have alcohol in it. I let myself go. I still kept myself clean but always dressed sloppily and didn't bother putting on make-up. It didn't matter to me if my jeans or T-shirts were creased; as long as they had been washed, I'd sling them on.

I found a little pub that I practically lived in from opening hour to closing. On many occasions I couldn't even remember how I got home or to whom I had spoken the evening before. I didn't care what happened from one day to the next. My life became a drunken haze. My only comfort and my worst enemy was a bottle.

The little pub I spent so many hours in had a landlady called Nana who would tell me over and over again that drink doesn't solve anyone's problems. She noticed my rapid disintegration and that I never ate. She made a point of ensuring I had at least a sandwich a day. Nana asked me on many occasions to share my problems but the more I drank, the deeper I buried them. I grieved over not being able to be with Sid and my family and thought I would become more depressed if I talked about it.

I longed for a normal life but everything always seemed to go wrong. I was afraid of living in a sober world as I couldn't deal with the pain that went with it. Nana pushed me to leave drink alone but I didn't want to. I had become an alcoholic. Then Nana told me she had friends in a small village who needed a young lady to work for them in their tiny, family pub. I had to consider the offer as my savings had finally run out. I went for an interview at the pretty little country pub. There was a florist just opposite and everything was so beautiful that I wanted to be part of it. The tranquillity of the surrounding fields and towering trees attracted me. A happy couple, named Bernard and Elle Schneider, who had three children, ran the pub. They couldn't pay much but found somewhere for me to stay. I felt it was the best opportunity I would ever get to clean up my life and give up drink. I took the job.

I lived in one room which had a television set. The landlady was a sweet woman who washed and ironed my clothes for me. I stopped drinking instantly and enjoyed the warmth and love offered by the Schneiders. Within three months I was back to making new friends and looking attractive and healthy again.

My best female friend was a girl called Anna. She helped me develop a new social life. We went to parties and dances together. One evening, I met a man called Stan who was to become my second husband.

In the beginning, Stan was just a buddy. He would go to lots of parties with Anna and me and our friends. He was married with three children. I met and socialised with his wife and family on numerous occasions. His wife appeared to be a nice, home-loving lady and she invited our crowd over for Sunday lunch a couple of times a month. Stan was very fond of his children but had very little to say about his wife.

Several months later, Stan's wife seemed to become

hostile towards his friends. I couldn't understand why and Stan wouldn't talk about it. I decided to stay out of the way and have as little as possible to do with them. I didn't want to be around anyone with marriage difficulties.

I now had complete control of my life again and was pleased that my equilibrium had returned. I became wildly ambitious and wanted a career. I took a day off work to go job hunting, but I didn't have a clue as to what I wanted to do so I went for a walk through the local town centre for inspiration. I was attracted to a large car dealership and made sure I was beautifully dressed when I approached a salesman and asked him for the address of his head office. I explained that I was job hunting. An interview was arranged and, within a few days, I found myself employed by Ford as a saleswoman. I walked to the interview and left two hours later with a new Ford Fiesta, various brochures and the necessary paperwork for closing deals on cars.

I worked strictly on commission and was self-employed. The idea appealed to me. I viewed it as a major challenge as I had never sold a thing in my life before. If I was to survive, I had to sell lots of cars. All I had going for me was the fact that I was bilingual and had a lot of determination and faith in my own abilities. Even more importantly, I had the gift of the gab, the one talent great salespeople need.

The first thing I learned was that the car sales business was a rat race. Given a chance, other dealers would poach my customers. I spent days quietly watching the best salesmen at work while I picked up their best tricks and tactics. Two weeks later I sold my first car. Once I had done that, there was no looking back. I started on 6 per cent commission, so that I made between £400 and £800 on each car I sold. Within six months, I was raking in up to £6,000 commission every four weeks.

Throughout all this, Stan remained a regular friend. He revealed that his wife thought we were having an affair. I had known something was wrong because she was always so tense when she saw me. I assured her nothing was going on with Stan but she didn't believe me. I started receiving hang-up calls at work. I couldn't ignore this and didn't want it to interfere with my work.

Stan told me his marriage was disintegrating. I felt sorry for them. She had decided I was the other woman and I resented that. It reminded me of when I was a small child and was accused of doing things I didn't do. As an adult, I wasn't prepared to take it lying down.

Stan was great fun. He was very handsome and well built and attracted a lot of female attention. I wanted to keep him at arms' length but, some time later, I ended up in his arms instead. I think he pursued me because we were, first and foremost, friends and he needed comfort because his marriage was crumbling.

One day, I was standing by a car with several other sales reps when his eldest daughter, aged sixteen, appeared and called me every nasty thing you can think of. It was humiliating. I packed up for the day, drove straight to the barracks where Stan worked and told him I wasn't amused by his daughter's actions. I thought Stan's wife had put the young girl up to it. We met later in the day and drove to his house to meet his wife. She didn't want to discuss it. Stan lost his temper and I objected strongly to being classed as a home-breaker. I told her that if she continued to accuse me, I might end up doing something that she would regret.

I drove home in a furious state. Later, however, I analysed my feelings and realised that I felt very fond of Stan, although I still wanted to keep him at bay. He had to go to Canada for six weeks and I was grateful for this as it would get his wife off my back. I needed time to think about my feelings towards Stan.

I threw myself into my work and socialised with my good friend Marion. I found myself talking about Stan for hours on end. He sent me a letter from Canada saying that he had heard his wife had hurt me. I phoned him and told him that no such thing had happened but I did explain that I would lodge a complaint against his wife if she continued interfering in my life and harassing me at work. I was concerned about my peace of mind and about keeping my reputation at work, where I was greatly respected.

On the day Stan returned from Canada, he came straight to me rather than going home. He shocked me by announcing that he had realised during his absence that he was in love with me. I told him to think about the consequences if we got together. We discussed it all very carefully and, after he left, I imagined what a future with Stan would be like. I didn't welcome the idea of the complicated problems that lay ahead but I liked the idea of being with him.

Next day he told me that he had turned over in his sleep during the night and cuddled his wife with the words, 'I love you, Anne.' That was another nail in the coffin of his marriage. I was furious because it would further convince his wife that I was responsible for the break-up of their marriage. We hadn't even kissed at that point.

The following night, Stan appeared on my doorstep and that was when his marriage ended once and for all. He told me that, while I had been accused of being the other woman, he was, in fact, having an affair with his wife's best friend, who lived next door. He had confessed all of this to his wife and had left the other woman for good.

Stan and I began a relationship that very night. All the trouble that followed caused my car sales to suffer and I was harassed at work so I joined another car firm in Münster. Stan was still in barracks but had moved out of his marital home.

We saw each other every day and Stan eventually gained permission to move out of the barracks and in with me. We were madly in love. Stan was so wonderful in so many ways. The first nine months were blissful. We were so happy to be together that we weathered the trials and tribulations of his divorce with ease.

Stan's parents travelled over from London to meet me. I got along well with his father but his mother resented me. She claimed that she was pleased that Stan was happy but her words hid her true feelings.

Stan had to go to Canada once again and I accepted an invitation from his parents to stay with them for a week in London. During my holiday, I barely stepped out of their home. Eventually, I was dying to get out of the house and went to the airport to meet a friend. Stan phoned during my absence and his mother made me feel guilty that I wasn't there for his call. I began to dislike her.

Stan's father apologised for his wife's behaviour. She cooked breakfast for me the following morning and explained that she had felt sorry for her son when he phoned because he was desperate to speak to me.

When Stan returned to Germany, I told him I didn't care much for his mother. He explained that she had always been a bit disagreeable. He had arranged to visit London for three weeks but I didn't look forward to seeing his mother again. I begged Stan not to stay with his parents. He promised me that he would keep everything under control. During the first week of our holiday, I fell and broke my arm which put me in a rotten mood.

Then Stan's mother invited his ex-wife and children over while we were there. We were shocked. Over lunch, his mother suggested that I should return to Germany as my arm was broken and that Stan should stay behind and visit his former wife. I was livid. Stan packed our cases and we left, although we first popped into his brother's to explain why we were leaving. We tried to continue a normal life back in Germany but I had started to have second thoughts about spending the rest of my life with Stan and having to put up with his interfering mother.

I loved Stan very much, but after a while, I noticed a change in his mood and temperament. He became very jealous and possessive. Most of my colleagues were men and his attitude interfered with my work. I couldn't understand it because I had been working with men since I met Stan and it had never bothered him before. If anyone paid me a compliment, be it man or woman, Stan's face would become twisted with disapproval. It got worse when he had had a few drinks. I never gave him a reason to mistrust me.

I lived for him and my job and always made a point of being there for Stan. Jealousy simply overtook him and then, one night, he snapped. A man paid me a compliment on the beautiful coat I was wearing that evening and when we got home Stan tore it to pieces.

He wasn't the man I had fallen in love with. He took his jealous temper out on the flat and broke many things I had worked hard for. I couldn't understand what was going on in his head. He had given up so much for me, only to develop a personality I couldn't live with. I thought, if that was love, I would rather live without it. He knew I was growing distant and would go to great lengths to make up for his temper. He promised to keep it under control. In so many ways we were really meant for each other but his jealousy eventually soured the love I had for him.

Finally, he struck me while in a jealous fit. I forgave him but it soon became a routine. A doctor told me that Stan was insanely jealous and that it could become very dangerous. When I fell in love with Stan, I thought we would be together for ever. It wasn't to be.

After three years of fire and love, we split up. He left the services and returned to London. I stayed in Germany. I was devastated by having to part from Stan. It is hard to leave someone you love dearly. For the second time in my life, I found myself making that decision. I missed him but couldn't live with him. I ended up drinking once again to soothe my pain. I received many letters from Stan following our separation. I never dated anyone else and believed, from what Stan wrote in his letters, that he wasn't either. We spoke many times on the phone. He told me he had changed and would never do anything to hurt me again. I decided to move to England to see if things would work out. I moved to Southampton so that I wouldn't be too near nor yet too far. I drove to London to surprise Stan and popped in on his brother first.

I explained what was going on and that Stan knew I was moving back to England. I waited outside Stan's flat while his brother broke the news that I had arrived. I was excited about seeing Stan again. He was overwhelmed with joy. We embraced one another with such desperation that we knew our love and desire for each other were still burning strong. He had missed me as much as I had missed him. I stayed with him that evening and returned to Southampton the following day. Stan had numerous things to sort out and we spoke on the phone every day. We thought it best to take things slowly and visit each other at weekends. I collected Stan and he stayed for our first weekend in Southampton. He was impressed that I had turned my flat into a home so quickly. We didn't go out during the entire weekend. We had so much to discuss and were happy to remain indoors, entwined in each other's arms.

Stan kept saying that he had many things to sort out but he never went into details. I became suspicious when I drove him back to London and noticed a woman's blouse lying on the sofa. I knew it hadn't been there when I had collected him two days before.

Then Stan phoned but seemed very distant. I had the feeling that someone was present. I had keys to his apartment and decided to pay him a visit, unannounced, as I expected to find another woman there. As I neared his flat,

I could hear a female voice. I entered and saw a woman with her blouse open and her breasts exposed. A tremendous row ensued.

I discovered that Stan and Agnes had been together for a very long time. I was devastated. I had moved from Germany to be with him again and he hadn't had the decency to tell me about her. I was very bitter about having given up so much for him. The pathetic thing was that I still loved and wanted him despite the deception.

Agnes stood her ground and firmly announced that she wasn't giving Stan up. Stan did not say to Agnes that he loved or wanted me and only me.

My head spun in turmoil. I felt as if I had been stabbed through the heart. I became temporarily deranged. I was so racked with emotional pain that I blurted out if she wanted him, she was going to have to take me as well. I grabbed a carving knife and violently cut my wrists. I must have passed out immediately for I woke up in hospital following a four-hour operation. I had seriously damaged my wrists.

I discharged myself a few days later and Stan drove me back to Southampton. We discussed our future and agreed to get married and make a fresh start. He told me to give him two weeks to sort everything out. Two weeks later he collected me to start a new life with him in London.

When Agnes arrived on our doorstep, demanding to know if she had any place in Stan's life, he announced that he was marrying me in fifteen days' time. The only people to attend our wedding were his sister and brother-in-law.

We married on 15 April. Three months later, on 27 July, I left him. We never recaptured what we once had and I knew it was pointless to continue with the marriage. I never sought a reconciliation and saw him only four times over the following six years. Nine months later, when I was 28, I met Eddy, your father.

31

MUMMY – AGED 28–35

I met your father, Edward Kirby, in 1986. He offered to help me one day when my car broke down. One thing led to another and we found ourselves dating.

I never did marry your father. As you will have learned from my letters and tapes, I had been down that road before and I shied away from repeating what had been mistakes in the past. We call it once bitten, twice shy. We cared about each other and, at the time, that was quite enough.

We really enjoyed living with each other for two good years before I suspected I was pregnant. I couldn't wait for the doctor to confirm it. There were 'at home' pregnancy tests on the market, but I was afraid of getting a negative reading and then wondering or hoping the home test was faulty. It took a bit longer to follow the proper medical route but the best feeling in the world was when the doctor said, 'Congratulations!' It was the best news I had received in years. You, Karl, were very much wanted and I had been hoping to become pregnant for years. I couldn't believe how lucky I was. I had hoped for a son and got everything I dreamed of.

I left the surgery bubbling over with excitement. I almost forgot to pop round to Eddy's place of work to give him the good news. Before I had gone to the doctor's, I had told Eddy that if I turned up with a bottle of champagne, he would know that he was going to be a father. When Eddy saw me crossing the road with the bottle of bubbly, he was so excited that he walked out in front of a moving truck. The driver hit his brakes so violently that I dropped the bottle.

The shaken driver told Eddy off for being careless but, when we explained the situation, he offered his congratulations and presented us with another bottle of champagne ten minutes later. He lightheartedly told Eddy to be more careful or else he wouldn't live long enough to be a dad.

Within a few months I had developed some bizarre eating habits. Eddy would sit at the table and go pale when he looked at the things Mummy put on her plate. I must say to you, Karl, that if you like beetroot, it is because Mummy ate four jars a day, every day. I called you the beetroot baby. I was afraid you would be born the same colour as a beetroot.

I didn't work while pregnant. I just lived a life of leisure tending to my flowers in the garden. I loved cooking. Eddy always had a lovely meal and delicious dessert waiting for him when he got home. Most of my day was spent dreaming about you, son, while preparing your nursery and being a housewife, although not a married one.

When I had an ultra-scan at five months into the pregnancy, they confirmed that you were a boy. I knew now that I could decorate the nursery in blue. However, I kept the fact that you were a boy a secret from Eddy. I wanted to see how long it would take him to guess that he was going to have a son. Well, he never did. Colours didn't seem to mean a thing to him. I shopped every day for baby things. To my surprise, Eddy arrived home with a Moses basket one month before you were born. As you already know, he is six feet two inches tall and rather burly. He looked like a gentle giant holding the beautiful, frilly gift.

On 17 June 1988, at six, in the morning, I woke up because the bed felt wet. I looked at Eddy in shock and stuck my elbow in his ribs. Dozily, he gave me a bewildered look and I realised that my waters had broken and it was time for our baby to be born. I panicked. Eddy was cool.

I thought I had prepared myself for motherhood but I wasn't ready for the real event. We had practised the proper drill in preparation for this moment but now I forgot everything. All I could think of was that I wanted a cup of tea. As if that would solve everything! I refused to go to the hospital without the tea. People can become most unreasonable at a time like this. I was doing anything to delay the moment of birth. Poor Eddy drove three miles looking for an open shop where he could buy milk. He returned, made the tea and I refused to drink it. I announced that there was no time for that now; I was about to have a baby! Thank heavens that obvious fact had finally dawned on me or you, Karl, would have been born on the kitchen floor.

When we arrived at Whipps Cross Hospital near Leytonstone, we were taken straight to the maternity ward where I had to go through the procedure of being booked in. I thought I should be doing more important things, like giving birth, rather than filling forms. It suddenly occurred to me that I felt marvellous. Everyone had warned me that having babies is messy, painful and horrible. I didn't have a single ache and thought your birth would be a breeze. As the day wore on, I was still lying in bed wondering what was going to happen next. It didn't seem normal that I was sitting there, pain-free, while all the other women in the maternity ward were screaming their heads off. I thought that maybe you had dozed off or changed your mind about being born that day. Some babies do, you know.

Eddy was impatient and also somewhat bored. I kept saying, 'Hang on, don't go anywhere. It's going to happen.' Fourteen hours later visiting time was over. Eddy was told he had to go because I wasn't in labour. According to hospital rules, there was no need for him to be there.

The following morning, 24 hours after I had arrived at the hospital, the consultants discussed the possibility of putting me on a drip to encourage you to be born. So, on 18 June, at 4.30 p.m., the drip went into my arm to induce labour. Twenty minutes later the unconcerned, pain-free smile was wiped off my face. I started having contractions and labour pains. I was soon outscreaming all the other girls in the ward. I was pathetic. I realised that your birth was not going to be as easy as I had thought only a few hours earlier. At one point, I was in such agony that I thought it couldn't get any worse. Well, I was mistaken. I hoped it was near the time for you to be born and began wondering if anyone had actually dropped dead from the sheer pain of it all.

I kept watching the clock. The time went very very slowly. I swore I would never have a baby again. It was not fun.

Approximately ten hours later the midwife came into my room and told me that I was very brave to insist on a natural birth. I wasn't brave; I was stupid. I swore that if I lived through your birth, I wouldn't make that mistake again. She examined me quietly while I called her all sorts of names. She had heard it all before from other women suffering the pains of birth and wasn't at all put out. She informed me that I was five centimetres dilated. This, she explained, meant that the channel for giving birth was getting ready for the baby's exit. I grinned for the first time in hours but it didn't last long because of the contractions. Twelve hours later I was still waiting and I marvelled at the fact that I was still alive. The midwife suddenly decided that we needed a doctor. Panic set in. I feared that something was going wrong but I calmed down when I heard your heartbeat on a monitor at the side of the bed. You didn't seem to be in distress – well, not as much distress as I was in.

When the doctor examined me, he said you were posterior, which meant that you were not in the right position to be born. He said he would give me another hour to see if you would alter position on your own. Well; Karl, you couldn't be bothered. You were staying put. You were quite happy in that position and, as a matter of fact, you didn't even feel like being born yet. If only you knew the problems you caused me that day. Furthermore, you didn't change much. This was a pattern that you stuck to for the next five years.

The doctor returned. I knew by the look on his face what he was going to say. The situation was now dangerous, so we had to take you out by Caesarean section. I was rushed to the theatre to bring you into the world in a most unnatural fashion.

A Caesarean is an incision that is made in an expectant mum's tummy so that the baby can be lifted out, as opposed to using the natural exit. I was not amused. I had spent all those hours in agony so that we could have a natural birth, only to end up on an operating table. (I have, by the way, now forgiven you, Karl, for your stubbornness.)

I was anaesthetised and you were born. I missed the magic moment. Eddy, although not in the operating theatre itself, was the first to see you, apart from the doctors. I was the last to see you, which I resented considering I had carried you for nine months and had gone through all that agony. Even the cleaners had a good look at you before I did. Twenty-four hours passed before I saw you because I was too dozy from all the anaesthetic. I suppose I deserved a good rest anyway.

Karl, the moment the nurse brought you into my room, she placed you in my arms. You were a tiny little bundle wrapped in a regulation white blanket. Only your little head was visible. I thought you were the most beautiful thing I had ever seen. You had a little turned-up nose and a head like a perfect round football, which is the result of being born by Caesarean. Natural births result in heads being squashed into an egg-shape. Suddenly, I didn't regret the Caesarean at all.

My eyes filled with tears as I automatically felt a warmth pass between us. I felt the bond at once. I was so happy to have you in my arms at last. You, my dear, slept through the magic moment. I still had the memories of you inside me, swimming about and kicking, but there was nothing like having your little face pressed against mine and feeling the bursts of hot air that came out of your little nose. You were my baby. I was determined that nothing would ever cause us to part. I'm sure, by now, you know why.

During my pregnancy, it had already been decided that I would breast-feed you. You wouldn't leave me alone from six in the morning to eight at night. You drove me crazy, always wanting to feed. I don't know what possessed me to want to be such a natural mother. It wasn't what I thought it would be. I don't know if you will remember but you had to have a dummy so that Mummy could have a break from feeding you.

Don't ask me how I did it but I kept it up for six months. Then I sent Eddy out and told him not to come back without the complete feeding works: bottles, disinfectants, powdered milk, everything. I had had enough of being a natural mother. I'll never forget it. It was a Sunday morning. The chance of finding a chemist open was very remote – as remote as you wanting to be born on time in the first place. It took Eddy four hours to find it all. You were not wildly popular with him by the time he came back. He was cursing and you were screaming because I had banned you from my breasts.

Luckily, you took to your new feed like a duck to water. You didn't care as long as you were fed. It made me wonder why I had bothered doing it the natural way in the first place.

As the months wore on, I started seeing a change in your features. You were becoming a proper little person, or so I thought. I was later to learn that the change is continual. I could appreciate this all the more because, as opposed to being demanding, you were enlightening. You became aware of sounds, shapes and colours. You started becoming mobile, rolling around on the floor and touching and exploring anything you could wrap your little fingers round. The house suddenly became a danger zone. Ornaments I once adored became deadly weapons in your hands. They say children can make or break a marriage. I was glad I didn't have a marriage to break because you were doing a fine job of testing poor Eddy's wits by destroying everything in your path.

I felt sorry for Eddy. All he saw when he came home was the havoc you wreaked. I saw all the best things, the fascinating moments when you made new discoveries. Every time you broke something, I could see it wasn't wasted, for you had learned something as well.

It got to the stage where, when Eddy came home, the first words out of his mouth were: 'What did he break today?' You could do no wrong in my eyes. It was at this point that I realised, sadly, that working men really miss out on a lot and how lucky women are to share these precious moments with their babies – the growing moments.

This pattern continued for some time until you learned the difference between right and wrong, which you adapted to rather well. I saw the moments of awareness in you. I was as fascinated with your progress as you were, and I saw it all.

It was nearing your first birthday, which sent me crazy with excitement. I decided against a party and settled for a family get-together. In other words, an excuse for the grown-ups to have a party while you slept. I did say to you, although you were not old enough to understand, that I would give you a party on your second birthday.

Oh, and by the way, someone rather special arrived in time for your first birthday. Your little sister, Kandy, who was born the month before.

On my very first night of passion after your birth, Karl, I became pregnant. Kandy was not actually planned, although very welcome. I was dreadfully confused and Daddy was over the moon. So, my darlings, you can understand why I needed a grown-up party on Karl's first birthday. Thank you both for sleeping soundly that evening and accommodating your poor old mum.

Meantime, I had my hands full. I had lost my own identity because I was bogged down with babies. I couldn't work. I didn't have a social life and had difficulty in finding a babysitter who could cope with two young babies. It's not easy to look after toddlers and babies under the age of one. Most mothers worry that no one else will look after their children the way they can. When children are over the age of four and know the difference between right and wrong, it is less worrying for mothers to rely on child-minders.

To me as a mother, you children always came first and everything else was second. Sadly, it led to Eddy and me drifting apart. It wasn't his fault, nor mine. It was just our situation. He was, and still is, a lovely person. I must say this, Karl, Eddy was a very good provider and we never wanted for anything. It actually brought him joy to look after us in a responsible fashion.

Karl, you were two years old and Kandy was one when Eddy and I finally parted, despite our efforts to make things work. Eddy had provided me with two marvellous children and we still liked each other but we weren't in love any more.

This is something you may learn later in life. It is possible to feel deeply for each other but find it impossible to live together. That was the case with Eddy and me. I am glad to know for certain that you two already know, and will be able to remember, that Eddy and I remained firm friends as he visited us often over the years and sometimes looked after you both during Mummy's illness.

I remember the day when I made the decision that I would be better off living alone than living with the wrong person. I turned and looked at you, Karl, playing on the floor. I bent down, picked you up under one arm and tucked Kandy into the other and left the house, never to return. I took only my babies with me.

We stayed at a girlfriend's for a few days. She looked after you both while I went house hunting. One week later, we moved into our new home. Once we were settled in, Eddy came round and made sure we had everything we needed.

I loved the house when we first moved in but, within a few weeks, bizarre things started happening. Complete strangers showed up at all hours of the day and night, asking for the former residents. As a single mum with two babies, I got a bit scared. I thought it would be better to find another house. The landlord was very understanding and was willing to let me break my lease. After we found a new house, he even let us stay on for a further two weeks while Mummy decorated our next home.

The house I chose was, initially, a shambles but I knew

that, with a bit of original thought and a lot of determination, I could turn it into a beautiful home in no time. We had to do without certain luxuries because it turned out to be a bit more expensive than I thought to run a home on my own. We skimped on clothes and things like that but we certainly ate well.

Karl, you had to get into everything. While we were decorating our new home, you decided to spill a five-litre drum of white paint all over our carpet. All I could think of was how to replace it. We had no money and the carpet belonged to the new landlord. I managed to get the worst of the paint off after spending a fortune on turpentine. The carpet was ruined but I managed to hide that fact from the landlord for the duration of our stay. By the time we left, I had managed to save enough money to replace it.

I made up a fresh bucket of wallpaper paste and you decided to go paddling. To my horror I found you standing with both feet submerged in the glue. You thought it was water. I don't know what was harder – decorating or cleaning up after you.

I reached the point where I was walking around the house like a ten-eyed neurotic. You weren't destructive; you just couldn't resist exploring something new.

Thankfully, Kandy, you were still too young to get up to much mischief. You were still at the stage when you found sucking a bottle the most enchanting pastime. You were happy to laze in your cot until you matured a bit and began to view it as a baby prison.

We didn't have much in the way of material goods when we moved house but we were rich in love. We had each other and that was enough for us. Slowly, but surely, the house started looking good. Within four months, it was organised.

Then, one day, a well-meaning neighbour asked Mummy to pick a number because she was having a flutter on the horses. My number came up and I was shocked when she knocked at my door and handed me £575. I thought it was Christmas and my birthday all rolled into one. What a windfall when we had so little! I was so excited by the unexpected money that, by the following morning, I had spent it all. Like most women with a little bit of spare cash in their purse, I decided it was time for a shopping spree. For half a year I had yearned for a set of porcelain plant pots to put in our enormous hallway. It was to be the final touch to the house.

Karl, you smashed them almost immediately. Thinking back, it was an absolute disaster even bringing them into the house. My windfall was not very well spent. However, I know all mums have disasters with their children and, as I'm sure you have gathered by now, I wasn't excused that privilege.

I spent 24 hours a day with you both for many months. Then I bumped into an old girlfriend who invited me to join her locally for a drink. I regarded the invitation as an absolute luxury. It hadn't dawned on me in ages that I could go out once in a while, especially as you two had become more manageable.

It was like learning to ride a bicycle again. As the day neared, I became very excited. I had organised a sitter. I knew exactly what I would wear. A black trouser outfit, topped by a chino jacket.

I did my hair and make-up perfectly. I felt like a million

pounds. We had arranged to meet at 7.30 in a pub and then play it by ear as to what we would do with the rest of the evening. I walked along hoping and praying she would be there waiting for me. I was nervous about going out as I hadn't done it in such a long time. Fortunately, she was there.

I remember catching sight of a man in a corner as I sat down. He had thick, beautiful, whitish hair. I thought he was very attractive and had a smashing smile. I couldn't concentrate on what my friend was saying because I was so distracted by the good-looking man. I was aware of a magnetic attraction and felt an urge to speak to him but I didn't have the courage to approach him. My brain deserted me and I couldn't find any excuse to strike up a conversation.

I left without having spoken to him and then spent days regretting it. I couldn't stop thinking about him. I hoped he was local and spent a lot of time daydreaming that I would bump into him.

Then, to my horror, only two weeks later, I received the devastating news that Isobelle had died. I had to leave instantly for Scotland. I organised someone to look after you. I ran to a travel agent and bought my ticket. Then I threw a few things in a suitcase and realised I didn't have enough cash for a taxi. I searched high and low for my chequebook and cash card but, in my state of shock and confusion, I must have mislaid them. I was probably staring straight at them and didn't know it. I panicked with the fear of missing my flight.

I phoned a friend to ask her for a lift but it was impossible because of her obligations at home so she phoned a friend of hers and told him about the mess I was in and he offered to take me although he didn't know me from Adam. Well, talk about fate. The kind-hearted stranger who arrived to give me a lift was the very same man I had spent weeks daydreaming about.

Considering the circumstances, flirtation was the last thing on my mind. He introduced himself as Charlie and, at the same time, said that he remembered my face. He had seen me in a pub some weeks before. He offered his condolences and said it was a pity we had met under such bad circumstances. Bitterly, I told him not to worry as I barely knew my mother, but, inside, I felt as if my heart was disintegrating.

The conversation stopped before it even started. We drove to the airport in silence. Neither of us knew what to say to each other. I was crying my eyes out and he seemed somewhat embarrassed. Charlie offered me tea before I boarded my flight. He was a good listener, charming and interesting, and he had an abundance of human kindness. In that short space of time, I felt that he genuinely cared about me. It's a weird thought to have about an absolute stranger.

My flight was announced. As I headed for the departure lounge, he impulsively took my hand and pressed his calling card into my palm. I looked at the card as I headed for the plane and heard him call out to use the phone number if I needed anything. I just looked at him and walked off. He caught up with me and said that if I had any problems in Scotland, he would fly or drive up to collect me. He then said that he knew I was without my chequebook or credit card and handed me some cash so that I wouldn't be without it in Scotland.

For reasons which you can now piece together, Isobelle's funeral was a bitter event for me. People gave their condolences to her two sons. No one recognised me, her daughter.

I went to find Jack and discovered that he had passed away a few years before. The post mortem couldn't conclude what he had died of. His neighbours said it was from a broken heart.

I was back home two days later. I had accepted a lift from another mourner who happened to live in London. Two weeks passed and I did not contact Charlie. I don't think he even knew I was back from Scotland. I was still upset about my mother and found that she was constantly in my thoughts. Then, suddenly, I decided to go for a stroll with you two.

As we entered our local park, we bumped smack into Charlie. He was as shocked to see me as I was to see him. He was surprised that I was back in London and had not phoned him. I asked him to forgive me but said that I needed to collect my thoughts.

I invited him to dinner at our home that evening and he said he would be delighted to join us. It is always said that every cloud has a silver lining and I was beginning to believe it until I heard what Charlie had to say that evening.

He told me that he was trapped in a loveless marriage. My dreams where shattered but at least I did not feel betrayed. I hadn't known him long enough for that. At least he was honest.

What can you do when someone clearly wants you but they are committed to someone else? I decided that evening that I didn't want any involvement with him. I would have liked to keep him as a friend but that doesn't happen in real life. Charlie wanted more than that and he told me so. It was Catch 22. I knew it was wrong to get involved with a married man and tried hard to keep things on a platonic level with no physical or strong emotional involvement.

He had been visiting us for four weeks and it was becoming impossible for him. He brought in the food shopping and covered all our bills. I felt I was losing control of the situation and was starting to become his property, although no physical contact had been made. Had he not been married, I would have felt happy to be his lover, wife or anything, but he was married and I didn't want to be the 'other woman'.

Half a year later, I did become the other woman. I became his lover; his mistress as it were. My life soon became complete hell when people realised that Charlie and I were having an affair. I was called every condemning name imaginable but I was in too deep. There was nothing I could do. I loved him. Charlie separated from his wife who later filed for divorce. All those people who said those dreadful things about me and who pointed fingers had never even met me. I was just the other woman and at the centre of a small town's big gossip.

What people didn't know was that, for the first time in my life, I was truly happy. Charlie, who became your daddy, was also experiencing the same thing.

Eddy and Charlie became friends. You two know who your natural father is as you see him now and again, but everyone involved accepted that Charlie would become your daddy. We were so well suited. All we both wanted was to be left in peace and to continue our lives together. . .

Karl, you were two years old and Kandy was one. We had been house hunting. Charlie (Daddy to you), surprised us by announcing that we were all going to move to a house we adored. In the excitement of planning our new life, I began to feel off-colour and very weak. At first I thought I was just coming down with a bug and decided that there was nothing to worry about.

And, my darlings, you know the rest . . .